10/14

We Are the Ones We Have Been Waiting For

We Are the Ones We Have Been Waiting For

The Promise of Civic Renewal in America

PETER LEVINE

OXFORD
UNIVERSITY PRESS

OXFORD

UNIVERSITY PRESS

Oxford University Press is a department of the University of Oxford.
It furthers the University's objective of excellence in research,
scholarship, and education by publishing worldwide.

Oxford   New York

Auckland   Cape Town   Dar es Salaam   Hong Kong   Karachi
Kuala Lumpur   Madrid   Melbourne   Mexico City   Nairobi
New Delhi   Shanghai   Taipei   Toronto

With offices in

Argentina   Austria   Brazil   Chile   Czech Republic   France   Greece
Guatemala   Hungary   Italy   Japan   Poland   Portugal   Singapore
South Korea   Switzerland   Thailand   Turkey   Ukraine   Vietnam

Oxford is a registered trade mark of Oxford University Press
in the UK and certain other countries.

Published in the United States of America by
Oxford University Press
198 Madison Avenue, New York, NY 10016

Library of Congress Cataloging-in-Publication Data
Levine, Peter, 1967–
We are the ones we have been waiting for : the promise of civic renewal
in America / Peter Levine.
pages cm
ISBN 978-0-19-993942-8 (hardback)
1. Political participation—United States. 2. Civil society—United States.
3. Local government—United States. I. Title.
JK1764.L48   2013
307.1′4—dc23   2013005193

1 3 5 7 9 8 6 4 2

Printed in the United States of America
on acid-free paper

Contents

We Are the Ones We Have Been Waiting For

I

Overview

THE PUBLIC AND OUR PROBLEMS

GOOD CITIZENS DELIBERATE. By talking and listening to people who are different from themselves, they enlarge their understanding, make themselves accountable to their fellow citizens, and build a degree of consensus.

But deliberation is not enough. People who merely listen and talk usually lack sufficient knowledge and experience to add much insight to their conversations, and talk alone rarely improves the world. Deliberation is most valuable when it is connected to work—when citizens bring their experience of making things into their discussions, and when they take ideas and values from deliberation back into their work. Work is especially valuable when it is collaborative: when people make things of public value together. They are typically motivated to do so because they seek civic relationships with their fellow citizens, relationships marked by a degree of loyalty, trust, and hope. In turn, working and talking with fellow citizens builds and strengthens civic relationships, which are scarce but renewable sources of energy and power.

A combination of deliberation, collaboration, and civic relationships is the core of citizenship. If we had much more of this kind of civic engagement, we could address our nation's most serious problems. Indeed, more and better civic engagement is a necessary condition of success; none of the available ideologies or bodies of expertise offers satisfactory solutions, which must emerge instead from a continuous cycle of talking, working, and building relationships. Unfortunately, genuine civic engagement is in decline, neglected or deliberately suppressed by major institutions and ideologies and by the prevailing culture. Our motivation to engage has not weakened, but we have lost institutionalized structures that recruit, educate, and permit us to engage effectively.

Nevertheless, we live in a period of civic innovation, when at least one million Americans, against the odds, are working on sophisticated, demanding, and locally effective forms of civic engagement. These Americans see the need for citizenship and are building impressive practices and models. Their work remains scattered and local because it is contrary to mainstream national policy. Civic engagement cannot achieve sufficient scale and power without reforms in our most powerful institutions. The way to achieve such reforms is to organize the one million most active citizens into a self-conscious movement for civic renewal.

That is the argument of this book. In this introduction, I begin not with civic engagement but with the tangible problems that afflict us as a nation. I want to suggest that these problems are intractable without civic engagement but are beginning to yield where citizenship is strongest.

Certainly, we Americans are in a bad mood about our nation and our public life. Unemployment, bankruptcies, bailouts, and other repercussions of the great recession are surely on our minds, but our pessimistic mood started well before that. Between 1998 and early 2002, a majority of Americans said they were satisfied with the way things were going. At all other times since 1993, most Americans have been dissatisfied.[1]

Perhaps this is because we face an accumulation of profound problems. They have been called "wicked problems" because better policies alone could not fix them (although our bad policies surely make matters worse).[2] Our problems interlock, so that each one can be seen as a symptom of another. They are entangled with cultural norms and personal behavior as well as conflicting rights and limited resources. Any of the purported solutions could do more damage than good. How to define and diagnose our problems is fundamentally controversial, inseparable from our diverse religious and philosophical commitments. Advancing some Americans' interests and values would set others back. For citizens who identify with particular interests and ideologies, watching opponents express themselves in public can be deeply frustrating. For those who feel little stake in national debates, the bitter controversies are alienating. Because our problems are complex, entangled, and divisive, the status quo is favored in ways that special interests can exploit to block even the most straightforward reforms.

I do not claim that our condition is worse than it usually is. On the contrary, we are richer, safer, and more respectful of rights than we were half a century ago—and far more so than when Abraham Lincoln took the oath of office. A consistent theme in American politics is the Jeremiad, a lament that we have suddenly lost our way and face imminent destruction. Just six years after the Pilgrims had landed in Massachusetts, one of their leading pastors was already accusing them of having forgotten their principles.[3] After four more centuries of such Jeremiads, we should doubt that our current problems are unprecedented. The end is not nigh.

But I do claim that the obligation to address our problems falls on *us*—American citizens—more profoundly than in the past. Our political institutions are inadequate to address our accumulated problems, and the prevailing ideologies offer no plausible solutions.

Consider, for example, that we have put 2.2 million of our own people in prison, far more than any other nation in the history of the world.[4] (China is second with 1.5 million incarcerated citizens, although its population is three times as large.) That is vastly expensive: the corrections system alone costs $68 billion annually, not counting the expense of law enforcement, courts, and the lost work of those imprisoned.[5] It also represents millions of tragedies for all those convicts *and* their victims. Yet imprisoning millions of Americans does not make us safe. Our homicide rate remains at least three times as high as the rate in any other wealthy nation in the world.

Perhaps one cause of the incarceration problem is the failure of our schools. After all, one in ten young men without a high school diploma is in jail or juvenile detention. We spend more per child on K–12 education than almost any other country in the developed world, yet one-third of our young people drop out before they complete high school.[6] Considering that almost all stable and well-paying jobs today require *more than* a high school diploma, the dropout crisis is a human disaster, quite apart from its link to crime and incarceration.

We also spend far more on health care per citizen than any other country in the world, yet unlike other wealthy nations, we provide no health insurance at all for many of our people. Roughly 45,000 Americans die prematurely each year for lack of medical insurance.[7] Even if the Affordable Care Act of 2010 meets expectations, we will still have the most expensive system in the world, with some of the worst health outcomes for poorer people.

At the time of writing, we have recently survived one of the worst economic decades in our nation's history, with no net creation of jobs between 1999 and 2009. Modern economies are cyclical, and it is possible that from the perspective of 2020, the past decade will appear a mere dip. But it is significant that no party or movement has a plausible plan for how to prevent such a period from recurring. And other economic disasters are unfolding more slowly. Detroit's population is less than half what it was in 1950, the exodus compelled by the permanent closing of factories and the withdrawal of capital from the region. Again, no one has a plan commensurate to this problem, which interlocks with the others mentioned so far. Detroit's high school dropout rate is 75 percent; Michigan incarcerates five times as many people as it did in 1973 and spends 20 percent of its state's general fund revenue on

prisons. We could add that Detroit's traditional industry contributes significantly to global warming, which is another serious "wicked problem."[8] Detroit
is just one example among many in the Rust Belt that stretches from Baltimore to Milwaukee. Even though Congress is often described as ideologically
polarized and dominated by political extremes, national politicians actually
show little appetite for debating such matters as deindustrialization, mass imprisonment, or serious responses to climate change. The scope of debate is in
fact very narrow.

Plainly, our institutions do not work. Their failure is not just wasteful; it is
deadly. They are not just broken; they are corrupt—making some people rich
and comfortable while failing the rest of us.

Libertarian-leaning conservatives diagnose the problem as the corruption of
the public sector. The federal government, they say, was created for sharply
limited purposes (the enumerated powers of the Constitution) and has since
been corrupted by elites to serve their own illegitimate ends at the expense of
individual freedom. One can debate whether the functions of the modern federal government are appropriate and beneficial. But it is not the case that the
federal government has expanded in scope or power domestically. Between
1947 and 2012, federal revenues have fluctuated in a narrow band between 17
percent and 21 percent of gross domestic product (GDP), with no consistent
trend over time and no expectation that they will rise above 21 percent in the
future.[9] What has changed is the nature of federal regulation and activism. Forty
years ago, the national government was involved in welfare and school integration, it drafted many young men to fight in an unpopular war, and it regulated
the financial markets, which were basically public stock and bond exchanges. It
has *retreated* in all those important—and potentially invasive—areas.

Good-government liberals argue that the root of our problems is corruption, the illegitimate use of private money to influence campaigns and government. I am sympathetic to that argument, having worked for two years for the
reform lobby Common Cause and written a book largely about campaign
reform.[10] But I think the focus must be broader because corruption—in the
sense of the perversion of the purposes of institutions—is much more pervasive. Consider, for example, that financial markets are supposed to allocate
resources to the most productive purposes, but the cost of the financial sector
grew from 1.5 percent of the economy in the 1800s to 8 percent in 2009—a
sure sign (along with Wall Street bonuses and other blatant evidence) that
this sector is seizing value for itself and not allocating it productively.[11] Another sign: in 1970, 5 percent of male Harvard graduates worked in the financial sector. In 2007, 58 percent of male Harvard seniors said they were headed

for jobs in that industry.[12] We need Wall Street, and we need some smart people to work there. But when an outright majority of the graduates of America's most famous university choose to devote their talents to finance, Wall Street is absorbing far too much of our assets, offering excessive rewards, and distorting other institutions, including the university itself.

It is certainly worth considering the possibility that better laws might fix our institutions. For example, a steep tax on carbon would cause people to burn less of it. The money raised from the tax could make every American eligible for Medicare. Reforming criminal sentencing laws would cut the prison population. These and many other plausible ideas have been proposed for addressing our problems.

But we lack the political will to do anything difficult. Consider the struggle to get even a modest health reform bill through Congress in 2009–10, which seems to have exhausted the nation's capacity and appetite for significant legislation. Besides, we do not necessarily know the answers. In the past, many promising proposals—radical, liberal, and conservative—have failed because they did not work as expected in the real world. Especially when institutions are broken and corrupt, we cannot count on wise laws to be implemented well.

Finally, we cannot rely on laws to make people and institutions work better. Some of our school systems have plenty of money, yet they still produce high proportions of dropouts. We could change our criminal penalties, but that wouldn't stop individuals from committing violent crimes and victimizing others. We can provide better health insurance by law, but if not enough doctors provide primary care to low-income residents, the insurance won't help.

To make schools, neighborhoods, hospitals, police departments, and public institutions in general work better, we must get inside them and change people's hearts and minds—not just reform the rules or provide more money. But outsiders have a poor record of changing other people's hearts and minds (although sometimes a bit of external advice or inspiration can be helpful). So my thesis is that people must change the norms and structures of *their own* communities through deliberate civic action—something that they are capable of doing quite well.

An example that I know from direct, personal experience is the public school system of Washington, DC. Educational outcomes in DC are very poor: less than half of public school students graduate on time. Spending per student is quite high (approaching $13,000 per year), but the actual services delivered at the school level are worth much less than that. In 2008, only

$5,355 per pupil was spent on teachers, classroom equipment, and other forms of "instruction." The rest of the money seems to be lost somewhere between the taxpayer and the classroom.

Many of the city's schools are chaotic and sporadically violent. News reports frequently reveal startling examples of bureaucratic failure: warehouses full of new textbooks that are never distributed to students, and payroll systems that cannot keep track of employees. There are excellent teachers—much more skillful and dedicated than I would be—but the system as a whole is dysfunctional.

The context outside the schools is certainly difficult and could be blamed for some of the failures of the system. Thirteen of every 1,000 babies born in the District die in infancy, twice the rate for the United States as a whole. More than one-third of the city's children are obese. The death rate for teenagers is more than twice that of the United States as a whole, and the violent crime rate is more than three times as high.[13] As usual, each problem can be seen as a symptom of a different one.

There is also a question of motivations, which can lead us to different diagnoses. An opening point is to ask why a student should align his or her efforts with what the schools expect. The *Washington Post*'s Lonnae O'Neal Parker wrote a fine series about a young man who graduated from Washington's Coolidge High School—barely, years late, after scraping through the required courses. He was smart, he had supportive parents, but he rarely attended class or completed assignments, and he aimed for Ds.

> Jonathan walks toward the cafeteria doors. A question follows him: If you want to make your mother proud, if you know you can do the work, if you swear to everybody you see that you want to graduate, why don't you go to class?
>
> Jonathan stares silently for a few moments.
>
> "I don't know," he says quietly. "I really don't know."[14]

A similar question would have had a straightforward answer half a century ago. In 1950, more than half of 19-year-olds in the District had not graduated from high school—the same rate as today. But the city then housed 35,000 industrial workers, including more than 1,000 each of machinists, typesetters, and automobile mechanics. Washington was never an industrial city (compared, for example, to nearby Baltimore, where 30,000 men used to work in the Sparrow Point steel mill alone), but the federal government offered thousands of positions, like stenographer and office boy, that were the local equivalent of factory work.[15] Young people could obtain these jobs without college diplomas—sometimes without graduating from high school.

Most adults held working-class jobs. They collaborated in teams composed of people from similar backgrounds, with middle-class authority figures keeping a distant eye on them. This was an orderly world, with a reasonable social contract: you did what was required, and you received a secure paycheck. Work life was a continuation of classroom life, with foremen and office managers replacing teachers and principals. Skills were concrete and could be learned on the job. A large, anonymous, urban high school, like Coolidge, served the purposes for which it had been designed. Youth culture within the school reinforced a sense of solidarity, compliance, and limited deference to distant authority that would continue in the workplace. It was easy for young people to envision concretely the benefits they would obtain from completing school. Crime and academic failure occurred, but they were marginal, not prominent.

Today, only about 7 percent of the city's jobs are traditionally blue collar (including maintenance, moving, and repair jobs), whereas more than half are "management, business, science, and arts occupations."[16] Despite the presence of the federal government in Washington, this ratio is not unusual: management and professional jobs outnumber construction, extraction, maintenance, and repair jobs by three to one in the United States as a whole.[17]

If you obtain credentials and skills for the business and professional world, you have wide opportunities. Sex, skin color, and age are less profound obstacles than they once were. But it is a long way from today's Coolidge High School to the professional world; the curriculum is too easy to prepare students for college, and there are few role models in the community. It is unrealistic that most teenagers will be self-disciplined enough to delay gratification and get themselves through a school like Coolidge. Even if they do, the benefits will be hard to see. If most other students basically doubt the social contract and do not want to participate, it is difficult for any individual student to comply.[18]

College-educated parents in a city like Washington have adjusted by spending unprecedented sums on their own children's education (including private schools and after-school activities)[19] and by applying what Annette Lareau calls a strategy of "concerted cultivation" to raise their children.[20] They devote almost every waking minute of the day to giving their offspring educational experiences. Even ordinary conversations are opportunities to develop kids' cognitive and language skills. Working-class parents are in no position to provide this kind of investment and, for valid moral reasons, prefer a different strategy, what Lareau calls "the accomplishment of natural growth." They want to spare their children from the rigors of the adult world but expect them to organize their own games and entertainment. The poor and working-class children in Lareau's book are in many ways more admirable than the middle-class children. But the middle class is preparing its offspring to succeed in a white-collar world without any help from the local public schools, while working-class youth are set up to fail. Although the segregated nation's capital was very far from utopia in 1950, a prevailing social contract then made parenting styles, teaching styles, neighborhoods' norms, school structures, and employment markets work together to produce adequate results.

The breakdown of that whole system is the kind of "wicked problem" that America faces today. Could better public policies change cause schools to succeed in a place like Washington? During the first decade of the twenty-first century, the city underwent two major reform experiments. First, one-third of the city's public school students began to attend publicly funded schools that are independent of the central bureaucracy and governed by charters. Most of the charter schools are small and have specialized themes or missions. To move one-third of the student population from a centralized system to new, highly diverse, small, independent charter schools represents a fundamental reform. And the results seem positive: students in DC charter schools do perform somewhat better than those in regular schools.[21] But that statistic does not account for all differences among the students and their families before they entered school, nor is the gap impressively large. Other research on charter schools finds mixed results. They may be part of the solution; they are no panacea.[22]

The second reform experiment was a cleanup of the bureaucracy that still oversees two-thirds of the city's public school students. Schools Chancellor Michelle Rhee was photographed on the cover of *Time* magazine holding a broom, a metaphor for her efforts to sweep out waste and corruption. She argued that the *teacher* matters most to a student's success. Every classroom should be led by a competent and motivated teacher who is supported by efficient systems for distributing textbooks, cutting paychecks, and so on. The most skillful teachers should be deployed in schools where they are needed most, those where test scores are lowest. The least effective teachers should be fired. The chancellor's priorities were to remove poor teachers, assign strong ones to troubled schools, and reduce bureaucratic waste. She was not interested in civic engagement, democratic participation, parental voice, or other strategies I will recommend here. In fact, she said openly that "cooperation, collaboration and consensus-building are way overrated."[23]

Research lends her strategy some support: the best teachers have a lasting, positive impact on their students.[24] But leaders cannot cause better teachers to appear in the classrooms where they are needed most—and persuade them to remain there, year after year—simply through better management. Urban teaching will remain a frustrating job if the social context is difficult, the motivations of students and parents are misaligned with the goals of the schools, and even high school graduates face poor job prospects. I have personally known teachers who were reassigned to more difficult DC schools and who immediately left for the suburbs instead.

In order for Rhee's top-down, housecleaning strategy to work, she would need to maintain political support. She had a patron in Mayor Adrian Fenty. But Fenty was defeated after one term in office, in a Democratic primary in which the teacher's union spent $1 million against him and voters who were teachers—or relatives or sympathizers of teachers—clearly played a large role.[25] Just 12 percent of the city's voting-age population turned out on primary day to reelect the mayor.[26] Rhee blamed her own failure to "communicate . . . the great things that are happening" to voters.[27] She seemed to acknowledge that leaders must pay attention to the democratic political process, because voters ultimately rule. She did not say, however, that democracy is a good thing. In fact, a low-turnout primary election in which private money has substantial influence does not seem like an excellent way to assess and change public policies. If civic engagement means voting and spending money on campaigns, then one could sympathize with a leader who thinks that collaboration is "overrated."

But assume that the chancellor's strategy worked better than the alternatives could. In other words, assume that by firing bad teachers and streamlining administrative procedures in the teeth of self-interested opposition, she improved students' test scores and graduation rates. If the teachers' impact was limited to the classroom and the school day, it could not be profound enough to overcome crises in the broader society, from obesity and violence to a lack of jobs. If the teachers *were* able to change parenting styles and other aspects of their students' home environments, we should ask whether this change was desirable. A working-class culture would have been modified to match the norms and expectations of Georgetown and Cleveland Park. In the case of Washington, DC, a specifically African American, urban culture of long-standing would be modified to resemble more closely the white precincts of the city. There are good reasons to admire that culture and to resist outsiders' right to change it. As usual, our social problems are entangled with culture and connected to our deep moral commitments, about which we have no consensus.

The previous mayor, Anthony Williams, had introduced different ways for citizens of the District to discuss and shape policy. In particular, his Citizens Summits (large, representative, deliberative meetings) had generated strategies to "support [the] growth and development of all youth." In addition to holding summits and other forms of deliberative democracy to engage citizens in planning, a city could build daily opportunities for citizens, civic groups, churches, businesses, youth, and others to collaborate with schools on the actual work of education. After all, Robert Putnam finds that "states where citizens meet, join, vote, and trust in unusual measure boast consistently higher educational performance than states where citizens are less engaged with civic and community life." Such engagement, he finds, is "by far" a bigger correlate of educational outcomes than is spending on education, teachers' salaries, class size, or demographics.[28] Engaging citizens would have been an alternative to both top-down administrative reform (Michelle Rhee's strategy) and radical decentralization in the form of charter schools. But civic engagement has not yet been tried in the District of Columbia.

My thesis is that citizens must address our most serious problems, exemplified by the situation of children in Washington, DC. There is no alternative to more and better work by the residents of a whole community.

That is not an unusual conclusion. For example, after listing some of our grievous national problems, *New York Times* columnist Thomas Friedman concludes, "The standard answer is that we need better leaders. The real answer is that we need better citizens."[29]

This position tends to provoke pessimism. We know what it means to get better leaders—we can at least hope for that—and we know how they would improve the world: by changing laws and policies. But how are we supposed to produce better citizens? The problem seems insoluble.

In fact, a whole network of groups and individuals has already sprung up to produce better citizens and to solve serious problems through civic engagement. The process of urban revitalization and school reform in Bridgeport, Connecticut, offers just one, rather typical example. Bridgeport, an old port and manufacturing city of 139,000 people, was a basket case in the 1980s. It was hard hit by the loss of manufacturing jobs, crime, and the flight of middle-class residents to the suburbs. The city literally filed for bankruptcy in 1991. The schools were so troubled that 274 teachers were arrested during a strike in 1978.[30]

Bridgeport is now doing much better, to the point that its school system was one of five finalists for the national Broad Prize for Urban Education in both 2006 and 2007. A major reason for Bridgeport's renaissance is active citizenship.

In 1996, a local nonprofit group called the Bridgeport Public Education Fund (BPEF) contacted organizers who specialized in convening diverse citizens to discuss issues, without promoting an ideology or a particular diagnosis.[31] No one knows how many forums and discussions took place in Bridgeport, or how many citizens participated, because the 40 official "Community Conversations" were widely imitated in the city. But it is clear that at least hundreds of citizens participated, many individuals moved from one public conversation to another, and some developed advanced skills for organizing and facilitating such conversations. A community summit convened in 2006—fully ten years after the initial discussions—drew 500 people. The local League of Women Voters estimates that a minimum of 25 local residents, quite diverse demographically, are now highly skilled moderators and conveners of public discussions.[32] The mayor, the superintendent, the city council, and the board of education had agreed in advance to support the plan that participants developed. The business community also signed on. The president of the Bridgeport Regional Business Council said, "Our business community has learned to be very patient with change here, because they know that community involvement is one of our cultural traits now and we've got to have it. [It] is the preferred route because the end product is normally better. The more inclusive it is, the more supportable it is."[33]

So far, I have described talk, but the civic engagement process in Bridgeport involves work as well. Each school has an empowered leadership team that includes parents along with professional educators. The professionals take guidance from public meetings back into their daily work. People who are employed by other institutions, such as businesses and religious congregations, also look to the public discussions for direction. Meanwhile, citizens are inspired to work as volunteers. The school district has a large supply of adult mentors, many of them participants in forums and discussions. In turn, their hands-on service provides information and insights that enrich community conversations and improve decisions.

Bridgeport's citizens have shown that they are capable of making tough choices: for instance, shifting limited resources from teen after-school programs to programs for younger children. Collaboration has become routine for businesses, nonprofits, and government agencies. Everyone feels that they share responsibility; problems are not left to the school system and its officials. The school superintendent says, "I've never seen anything like this. The community stakeholders at the table were adamant about this. They said, 'We're up front with you. The school district can't do it by itself. We own it too.'"[34]

This is a local example, typical of hundreds that could be cited. Other cases are threaded through this book. They are not uniform. Bridgeport's process was highly deliberative and began with private nonprofit organizations. In Hampton, Virginia (discussed in chapter 6), a nonpartisan city-manager-style government built a system for engaging citizens in service and deliberation. In San Antonio (also discussed in chapter 6), a much more confrontational social movement, rooted in the city's traditionally oppressed Hispanic communities, ultimately added deliberative and collaborative practices that resembled those in Bridgeport. The organizers won more than $1 billion in funding and enough political clout to choose mayors. Universities, schools, and news organizations, as well as cities, have been venues of civic renewal.

These efforts have been called "public work" to emphasize that participants do not just volunteer their time in the evenings, nor do they merely discuss issues. They actually create, build, and teach, often as part of their paid jobs.[35] These projects have also been called "citizen-centered" to emphasize that they are fundamentally about people in their capacities as members of a community. The starting point is a group of citizens rather than a problem or a formal system.[36] This does not mean that organizers must recruit citizens by inviting them to amorphous and interminable discussions. Often, effective recruiters emphasize specific issues and potential solutions. But the goal in citizen-centered politics is to strengthen citizens' capacities for deliberating, defining, and addressing problems together.

Yet another possible title would be "open-ended politics." The origin of "politics" is the Greek word for citizen, *polites*. When politics is open-ended, citizens decide what to do as they work together. Their goals are not predetermined. I will emphasize the open-ended nature of this kind of work because I think its main alternatives are ideological or interest-group movements whose goals are set in advance.

None of these phrases is catchy. In fact, we know from national surveys that no appropriate terminology really excites people or conveys the core values that I defend in this book. Offered the opportunity to comment on the phrases "democracy," "politics," "service," "civics," "citizenship," "activism," "social entrepreneurship," and "community organizing," representative Americans either gave lukewarm responses or indicated that they were not thinking about open-ended, citizen-centered, public work.[37] For example, many liked the phrase "community organizing," but thought that it meant raising money for charity. It seems that no phrase is more popular or resonant than the others. We have the opportunity to choose the most accurate terminology and then build support for it. I write in this book about "civic engagement," with the understanding that it means deliberation (talking and listening in reasonably diverse groups about public issues), collaborative work, and the strengthening of civic relationships.

Civic engagement, so defined, is essential for addressing really serious, large-scale problems. That means that you and I can contribute to solving grievous problems by engaging civically. But it is not enough for individuals to want or try to participate as good citizens. Major institutions are set up to ignore and even frustrate civic engagement. The kinds of practices that I advocate in this book are poorly funded, invisible in federal and state law, understudied by academics, neglected in education, and ignored in news and popular culture. Thus our task is not only to engage as citizens but also to work together to reform rules, incentives, and ways of thinking so that civic engagement becomes much more common and influential. I will use the phrase "civic renewal" to mean efforts to expand and enhance civic engagement.

In order to make a persuasive case for civic renewal, I must demonstrate that it can address the kinds of wicked, intractable, interlocked problems with which I began this chapter. That is not a simple case to make, since most of the efforts are small and beset by local challenges. Only a much larger and more robust civic renewal movement could really change the objective circumstances in America. But I will offer suggestive evidence of impact here.

An example of a serious social problem is unemployment, acute during and after a recession, but chronic in our poorest communities. My colleagues and I have found that when more residents were engaged in civic work, unemployment rose less in counties, cities, and states during and after the recession of 2008. After accounting for the major economic factors thought to influence unemployment (demographics, dependence on the oil and gas industries, housing-price inflation, and residential mobility), civic engagement emerged as a stronger predictor of communities' resilience against unemployment. The two most important elements of civic engagement were the density of associations in each community that engaged local citizens as members or clients, and the degree to which residents reported having friendships and relationships with other people nearby.[38]

Previous studies suggest possible explanations. Maybe participating in civic affairs teaches skills that are also useful in the job market, encourages people to trust one another so that they are more likely to undertake business partnerships, strengthens citizens' affection and loyalty to their communities so that they choose to spend and invest locally, or creates a strong set of independent organizations that hold governments accountable and improve their performance.[39]

All these explanations are plausible and consistent with my theoretical framework. But I think Sean Safford offers the most persuasive explanation by means of his close look at Youngstown, Ohio, and Allentown, Pennsylvania. These two old manufacturing cities were economically and demographically similar when the crises of global competition and automation hit American manufacturing in the 1970s.[40] Youngstown entered a downward spiral and now has a median household income of $25,000 and a median home value of $50,000. Meanwhile, Allentown has turned into a successful postindustrial economic center with a median household income almost twice that in Youngstown, homes worth almost three times more, just one-fourth as many murders per capita, and a substantially higher life expectancy.[41]

Safford traces the starkly different outcomes to the civic infrastructure of the two communities. In their heyday as manufacturing cities, both had economic networks dominated by the interlocking boards of their local businesses. And both had social networks composed of private clubs. But only Allentown really had a separate, robust civic network. Safford defines "civic organizations [as] those for which the primary goal is to improve the community in some way."[42] In Allentown, the universities' boards and the Boy Scouts were among the most prominent civic groups. Youngstown also had civic organizations but not a network of overlapping civic boards. When the economic crisis killed Youngstown's businesses and left the local elite competing for scarce financial resources, they had no place to gather, plan, and collaborate. But in Allentown, local leaders talked and cooperated in their overlapping civic organizations.

Their discussions launched specific new initiatives, like the Ben Franklin Technology Partnership, which has incubated high-tech businesses. They also developed new overall strategies. The business elite, organized as a civic cadre through the Lehigh Valley Partnership, converged on a similar development strategy as the grassroots activist groups, organized as the Community Action Coalition. Meanwhile, Lehigh University reoriented itself as a civic hub that connected to both activists and businesses.[43]

Allentown has not drawn much more external investment than Youngstown but has used its indigenous capital much more effectively, with less damaging competition.[44] Importantly, it was not the number of associations or the rate of associational membership that mattered. Rather, organizations were configured into a network that encouraged deliberation and collaboration in Allentown but not in Youngstown.[45] In national data, we find a correlation between the number of civic organizations per capita and a community's economic success, but Safford's closer look suggests that the density of organizations is probably just a rough proxy for the strength of the local network that permits discussion, collaboration, and relationship building.

In a magisterial study of Chicago neighborhoods, Robert Sampson finds that a strong organizational infrastructure boosts a community's capacity for collective civic action, which has substantial benefits for the neighborhood's safety and health. Sampson observes, "It is the totality of the institutional infrastructure that seems to matter in promoting civic health and extending to unexpected economic vitality, whether in the form of rebuilding New Orleans or in rehabilitating vacant houses in economically depressed neighborhoods in cities around the country."[46]

The benefits are not solely economic. As I noted earlier, Allentown has much better social outcomes than Youngstown, including lower crime rates and longer lives. A different stream of research also finds that people are much healthier and happier—in the original Aristotelian sense of happiness as flourishing—if they can say that "their own daily activities [are] useful to and valued by society" and if they have a "sense of belonging to, and comfort and support from, a community." In turn, strengthening civil society at the community level increases the odds that people will flourish in these ways.[47] YouthBuild USA is a program that enlists marginalized young people and gives them opportunities to serve and lead. One graduate of the program told my colleagues, "Doing those kinds of things changes something inside of you, you develop a whole new kind of happiness inside of you—that you don't feel like smoking weed, buying $150 dollar sneakers—it's the kind of happiness that only you can get by doing good deeds and helping others."[48]

A different kind of social problem is the incarceration crisis.[49] Incarceration involves highly controversial public policy, and nowhere has civic engagement led to dramatic or lasting reforms of the criminal justice system. In fact, the huge number of prison sentences can be understood as the *result* of citizen action. Draconian sentencing laws often begin with referenda or with legislative votes that respond to popular pressure. The phrases "populist punitiveness" and "penal populism" are used to describe an international phenomenon: politicians seeking approval by posing as tough on crime and denouncing lawyers and other elites who would coddle or protect criminals.[50]

But accumulated evidence suggests that when citizens deliberate, they arrive at merciful or nuanced decisions. For instance, when judges disagree with jury verdicts, it is generally because they think the jury was too lenient.[51] Capital punishment is a popular policy in the United States, yet juries reach capital verdicts in very few cases.[52] When a random sample of British citizens deliberated about criminal justice policy, they shifted markedly against the proposition that incarceration reduces crime and became much more protective of defendants' rights.[53]

Unfortunately, public deliberation is now rare within the criminal justice system. The severe and inflexible penalties required by referenda strongly encourage plea bargaining, which is one reason that the proportion of felony cases that go to trial has dropped from one in 12 during the 1970s to just one in 40 recently.[54] Ninety-seven percent of criminal convictions in the federal system and 94 percent in the state systems result from plea bargains and not trials.[55] The people (using the ballot box) have chosen to remove the people (convened as jurors) from criminal law.

Why would they do that? In 1964, three-quarters of Americans said they generally trusted the government and 53.4 percent said they generally trusted other people. By 2010, trust in government was down to 30.4 percent, and trust in other people had fallen to 34.6 percent, both having lost ground steadily over the decades.[56] Distrust of people of color, especially young African American men, is particularly acute and directly relevant to the incarceration problem. (In fact, "distrust" is much too soft a word for public attitudes toward young black people.) If we trusted the government but not our fellow citizens, we might be willing to let judges set sentences. If we trusted our fellow Americans but not the government, we would be less eager to incarcerate citizens and more protective of the jury system. Trusting neither, we are tempted to require the state to put people in jail without trials.

A minimum sentencing law is a simple, understandable rule imposed on a complex system. It is a classic example of the prevailing view of accountability as external and driven by numbers, rather than deliberative and determined by arguments. (See chapter 4.) It transforms criminal cases from transparent public events, full of explicit moral rhetoric and judgment, into bargaining sessions managed behind the scenes by lawyers.[57] That is a recipe for even lower trust, which encourages even more draconian sentencing laws. The resulting crisis of incarceration is largely invisible because citizens do not serve on juries or even read about jury trials. Even though criminal justice is officially public business and transparent (in the sense that one has a right to obtain court records), it rarely impinges on public consciousness.

In Oklahoma in the 1990s, the League of Women Voters saw the state's incarceration rate—the third-highest in the nation—as a serious public problem. They also recognized that politicians were afraid of any reforms that could be depicted as weak on crime. So they organized a series of meetings across the state that involved nearly 1,000 citizens who held diverse views.

Many participants expressed anger about the costs of incarceration and favored prevention and rehabilitation. Politicians and reporters attended these meetings and witnessed the prevailing mood, which changed their estimate of what would be popular. The League then recruited participants to advocate a bill that would reduce certain felonies to misdemeanors while devolving some authority over sentencing to "community boards with citizen representation." The bill passed by wide margins. It reflected deliberative public opinion, and it created a mechanism for the kind of sustained public engagement in criminal justice that might restore public trust.[58]

The sentencing reform legislation was later repealed after lobbying by law enforcement officials. The state chose instead to reduce costs by expanding private, for-profit prisons.[59] In 2008, companies that run such prisons spent almost $69,000 on Oklahoma state political campaigns and received almost $77 million in state funding; the state even imported prisoners from Arizona.[60]

This chapter of the Oklahoma story is a reminder—as if one were needed—that engaged citizens face formidable enemies and need political reform to prevail. The relationship between institutional reform and civic engagement is a central theme in chapters 5 and 6. But even though the legislature retreated on incarceration, community sentencing boards still handle nonviolent cases in most Oklahoma counties. The state's Department of Corrections argues that these boards save money and reduce incarceration.[61]

Oklahoma's community boards resemble other widespread initiatives in which the justice system engages lay citizens. Problem-solving courts, for example, specialize in particular issues, such as drugs or domestic violence. They reject the traditional measure of success in a judicial system (speedily rendering appropriate verdicts in cases) and instead try to address an underlying problem, whether drug abuse, violence, or urban blight. Effective problem solving requires partnerships both within the government and across the community. Thus these courts "aggressively reach out to neighborhoods to educate community groups and find new ways for citizens to get involved in the judicial process."[62] The cast of characters traditionally involved in a court broadens to include social workers, community organizers, and planners, and their relationships shift. In Portland, Oregon, the president of an advocacy group called the Black United Front naturally refers to a local problem-solving court as "we." He does not officially work for the court, but he helps set its agenda. Judges, for their part, frequently speak in community settings and even serve on nonprofits' boards.[63]

In youth courts, panels of teenagers are empowered to sentence their peers for minor offences. In restorative justice programs, violators negotiate agreements with representatives of their community to repair the harms their actions have caused.[64] Modern restorative justice was first proposed by outsiders to the legal system (Mennonite activists and others), but it has grown thanks to the support of prosecutors and corrections officials, who see substantial financial savings and much higher satisfaction among victims and other residents.[65] Like youth courts, restorative justice has shown promising effects on recidivism. These reforms also engage citizens in deliberations within the legal system.

By expanding such opportunities, we may be able to change the national conversation about crime and punishment.[66] Restorative justice tends to satisfy both victims and offenders.[67] Jurors who successfully reach verdicts in conventional trials hold more favorable views of political institutions (including the jury trial itself), trust their fellow citizens more, and are more likely to vote in regular elections compared to citizens who are not randomly selected for jury service or whose trials end without verdicts.[68] That finding suggests that by making traditional juries (or modern alternatives such as restorative justice programs) more common and more prominent in the public discourse, we could raise public trust in courts and reduce the demand for draconian sentencing. In chapter 6 and throughout this book, I advocate other ways to engage citizens in governance beyond courts. If alienation from institutions and from our fellow citizens is a root cause of the incarceration epidemic, these strategies offer the best hope for a solution.

These cases suggest that civic engagement offers answers to large-scale, serious, wicked social problems. I still owe an argument that we can expand and enhance civic engagement. To do that would require not only shifts in priorities and resources (described later) but also a change in our public philosophy.

In general, we treat the people who will be affected by social policies as "at-risk," as victims, as baskets of problems or potential problems. Those labels apply especially to the young and the old, poor Americans, and minorities. Civic engagement acknowledges inequalities and injustices, but it treats all people as assets, capable of addressing their own problems and contributing to the whole community. We should welcome and expect them to contribute not only because doing so has good effects, but also because respecting them is a fundamental moral obligation.

In general, we see education as the job of teachers, professors, and administrators, whose clients are students. Education is a specialized task to be measured by experts. Success then boils down to passing tests. But education should be a community-wide function, the process by which a whole community chooses and transmits to the next generation appropriate values, traditions, skills, practices, and cultural norms. Civic engagement at its best crosses the lines between schools or colleges and communities and reflects a more inclusive definition of "education."

In general, our politics is government centered. Liberals want the government to accept new tasks, such as health insurance; conservatives believe that problems would be mitigated if the state were shrunk. Governments are important, but they are not the only institutions that matter. Furthermore, a state-centered view of politics leaves citizens little to do but inform themselves and vote. In citizen-centered politics, however, people form relationships with peers, express their interests and listen to others, and then use a range of strategies, some having little to do with the state.

In general, our democracy is threatened by the mobility of capital. A community cannot govern itself if it relies for jobs on private companies that are able to move their operations and investments at will. Capital mobility is a threat to progressive policies, such as corporate taxation and unionization, and also to conservative policies regarding social issues. But an array of economically powerful not-for-profit institutions—colleges and universities, co-ops and land trusts, community development corporations and social enterprises—are anchored in communities and accountable to local citizens because their fates are permanently tied together. These are no longer marginal elements of our economy: for example, America's 4,600 community development corporations finance and build 86,000 housing units annually.[69]

In general, our politics is manipulative. Experts—politicians, pundits, consultants, marketers, leaders of advocacy groups, and the like—study us, poll us, focus-group us, and assign us to gerrymandered electoral districts; they slice-and-dice us; and then they send us tailored messages designed to encourage us—or to scare us—into acting just how they want. This is true of liberal politicians as well as conservative ones. It is true of public interest lobbies as well as business lobbies. It is true of big nonprofits as well as political parties.

It is also true of many civic groups. For example, my organization, CIRCLE (The Center for Information & Research on Civic Learning & Engagement) has been part of the movement to increase youth voter turnout. Techniques for that purpose are becoming increasingly sophisticated. In the 1990s, you might just mail people flyers reminding them to register. Then organizations began to test various messages with focus groups before they printed their flyers. Now they do true experiments, randomly selecting some addresses to receive one flyer instead of another and keep track of the response rates. (The messages that people like best in focus groups often perform worst in the field.) This is just an example of growing efficiency in public-interest, nonpartisan politics. CIRCLE has embraced it because resources are scarce and the environment is competitive. We believe that engaging young people is valuable, and resources should be used in the most efficient possible way. We collected research-based "best practices" in an influential 2006 guide, and many of those techniques were used by the 2008 Obama presidential campaign to mobilize an unprecedented share of under-30 voters.[70]

These techniques work. Yet overall, Americans know they are being manipulated, and they resent it. They want to be able to decide for themselves what is important, what should be done, and then act in common to address their problems. They are interested in what other people think; they want to get out of what students call their "bubbles." They want an open-ended, citizen-centered politics in which the outcomes are not predetermined by professionals. We should not try to manipulate our students or neighbors into adopting opinions or solutions that we think are right. We should give them opportunities to deliberate and reflect and then act in ways that seem best to them. In a time of increasingly sophisticated manipulative politics, these opportunities are precious.

2

How to Think About Politics

VALUES, FACTS, AND STRATEGIES

WHEN I SPEAK to groups of civic activists and educators, I often read the following quotation: "Never doubt that a small group of thoughtful, committed citizens can change the world. Indeed, it's the only thing that ever has." I ask people to raise their hands if they recognize the quotation and who wrote it. Sometimes every hand goes up, and everyone seems able to cite Margaret Mead, the great American anthropologist, as the author. I have jokingly asked audiences to keep their hands up if they have printed these words and hung them on their office walls. Quite a few hands remain raised.

In fact, this quotation is only attributed to Margaret Mead. It cannot be found in her printed works and may be apocryphal.[1] But it is certainly popular among Americans who see their goals as "civic." Google found it on more than four million websites in 2012.

I think I understand the motivations behind these two sentences. Margaret Mead—or whoever composed this quotation—was exhorting us to work together and make the world better. That is a worthy objective.

But these propositions are literally false. Not only small groups of thoughtful citizens "change the world." So do technological inventions, institutional inertia, markets, clashes of social classes and ethnic or religious groups, governments, armies, violence, terror, and sheer accidents.

For instance, a huge flood changed New Orleans profoundly in 2005. Hurricane Katrina changed New Orleans for the *worse* (at least in the short term), and that brings up a separate problem with Margaret Mead's quotation. Changing the world is morally ambiguous—change can be good or bad. The World War I veterans who gathered around Mussolini and Hitler were "small group[s] of . . . committed citizens," and they made the world a lot worse. I deleted the word "thoughtful" in describing them, but they did think a lot about social issues and strategies. They just thought in a bad way.

Mead also implies that small groups of thoughtful and committed citizens always succeed. She begins: "Never doubt . . ." But it is easy to list groups of deeply thoughtful and fully committed citizens who have failed—some at the cost of their lives, and some with hardly a ripple. A cynic might counter: "Never doubt the capacity of large groups of ignorant and selfish people to squelch good ideas and make the world worse."

I do not mean to disparage Margaret Mead (or the real author of these sentences), but rather to emphasize that we need a serious investigation of three questions:

1. When can "a small group of thoughtful, committed citizens" change the world?
2. How can they be most effective?
3. What are good means and good ends for these groups?

One would think that these three questions would be essential to the whole enterprise of research and education. To be sure, they are not the *only* questions that matter to us as human beings. We should also consider what private individuals may and should do. For instance: "Is it acceptable for me to lie?" "Is an abortion permissible?" "What will happen if I buy this product?" "Would this be a beautiful object for me to create?"

We should think, too, about large social forces and mass behavior (not to mention the natural world, the past, and purely abstract truths like those of mathematics). But the scale of human affairs that lies between a lone individual's decisions and entire societies seems especially important. This is the domain of groups that one can choose to join or to leave, that one can tangibly influence through one's own choices and actions, and that can (in turn) influence the larger world. "Civil society" is the name for that scale of human action where the minuscule powers of an individual obtain enough leverage to count but are not lost entirely in the mass. It is the world of "we," but not such a huge or abstract "we" that "I" no longer matters. It is politics at the human scale.

When we discuss macropolitics, our grammar is typically passive or impersonal. We use phrases like, "The US should support Greece," or "The budget should be balanced." When we discuss politics at the human scale, our grammar becomes active and personal: "We can balance our budget," or "I support Greece."

Civil society—the human scale of politics—is certainly studied, but not sufficiently in ways that combine three matters: *facts, values,* and *strategies.* We need to know facts because we should not try to do something that is impossible, or redundant, or that has harmful but unintended consequences. If, for example, a small group decides to create a co-op to sell local food, but there is no market for their product, or the supply is inadequate, or the law forbids the form of business that they prefer, or their activity will inadvertently destroy natural ecosystems or desirable businesses, or if experiments show that individuals *never* cooperate voluntarily in the way that they dream of, then they had better be aware of these facts.

We need values because otherwise we cannot distinguish between the effective, small group action of Mussolini's *fascisti* in 1922 versus the civil rights movement's leadership in 1955. Both groups were thoughtful and committed, and both won their political battles, but one group was bad and the other was good.

Finally, we need strategies. It is insufficient to wish for better outcomes and determine that those outcomes are possible. We need a path to the desirable results.

Developing a fully adequate strategy is difficult, just as empirical research and moral argument are difficult endeavors. It is not enough to say that something "should be done." People should stop having unprotected sex; if they did, there would be no new cases of HIV/AIDS, and the virus would go extinct. But saying that does nothing to address the HIV crisis. Nor is it sufficient to say that major institutions should change their policies. Many lives would be saved if governments spent more money on HIV education and anti-retroviral medications, but again, saying that achieves nothing. *Sometimes* one can be effective merely by expressing the truth. Usually, however, political success requires more than expression; it takes organization and effective tools that may include laws, votes, payments, electoral campaigns, strikes, boycotts, or lawsuits—depending on the situation. To choose a strategy, one must be smart about what will work and also understand facts and values.

It is ideal to address a real audience that has the capacity to do something, to influence another group to do something, or otherwise to start a helpful chain of events. One must persuade that audience to take beneficial steps, using some effective combination of moral suasion and plausible appeals to self-interest. Sometimes it works to address particularly powerful individuals: billionaire philanthropists, national politicians, or celebrities with huge popular followings. But it is hard to get those people's attention and to persuade them to act differently. Despite their disproportionate power, they are not omnipotent, and they are always asked to do more worthy things than they can manage. Finally, we may not want our strategies to be contingent on the goodwill of an elite. For all those reasons, a fully adequate strategy must address *whomever chooses to listen* and must give those people effective ideas and reasons for action. Engaging anyone who chooses to listen is a civic approach to strategy because it treats citizenship (membership in a community) as a sufficient condition and does not privilege status, expertise, or power. But finding something effective for everyone to do is no easy task.

I believe there is much less scholarship than we need that combines facts, strategy, and values and that deals with the human scale of politics. Empirical social scientists pay relatively little attention to the effects of small-group politics because to do so seems naive. They know that the decisions and strategies of "small groups of thoughtful, committed citizens" generally matter less than economic forces, institutional structures, mass public opinion, and technology. To mention just one example, the outcome of presidential elections in the United States is strongly correlated with the performance of the economy in the previous year.[2] That means that all the deliberate work of campaigns, parties, and independent advocacy groups matters less than the blind, impersonal force of the business cycle.

Nevertheless, working together in small groups is *morally* important—it is what we should do and should care most about. To be a good person is to do this work well. That is reason enough to make it a central question for reflection and research. In addition, deliberate human action has significant impact. Small groups of thoughtful, committed citizens do make a difference under appropriate circumstances, as shown by the civil rights movement, the women's movement, the conservative legal movement, and numerous other examples. Until recently, research on social movements tended to emphasize the external (and uncontrollable factors) that caused some to succeed and others to fizzle. The ones with adequate resources and favorable positions would win; the others would fail. But recent scholarship emphasizes that leaders of movements and other active participants make choices that affect their success. Leadership is emerging as a significant causal factor in the outcomes of social movements.[3] Meanwhile, Elinor Ostrom won the 2009 Nobel Prize in Economic Sciences for demonstrating that the organization and governance of voluntary groups affects whether they can solve social problems. These findings suggest that "small groups of thoughtful, committed citizens" matter, even if other factors matter too.

If the leaders of the South African freedom movement reviewed the scholarly literature on democratization during the apartheid years, they must have found it depressing. Prosperity, economic equality, and ethnic homogeneity were the factors that had been found to increase the odds of a successful transition to democracy. These structural factors were all evidently absent in South Africa. Only the country's heritage of British rule was thought to increase the odds of success, and that was an ambiguous matter in South Africa, where the British influence had been limited.[4] Thus, if the African National Congress and other democratic reformers had been guided by hardnosed, empirical research, they would have chosen a goal short of democracy, something like a negotiated arrangement among separate authoritarian communities. But they were right to ignore the scholarly literature because it was based on empirical data—in a word, on the *past*—and the past can never determine the future. So far, their peaceful revolution appears a monumental work of deliberate human agency. To his credit, one of the leading empirical scholars of democratization, Seymour Martin Lipset, after reviewing the standard preconditions of success (none of which applied in South Africa), said in 1993:

> There are a number of assertions we can now advance, with considerable confidence, about the structural, cultural, and institutional factors that are conducive to the development of democracy. But specific outcomes depend on particular contexts, [including] the abilities and tactics of the major actors. For example, Washington and Lincoln, Lenin and Gorbachev, Nehru and DeGaulle, each had a profound effect on the prospects for democracy in his time and country. Clearly then, we cannot generalize by a formula. The various factors I have reviewed here do shape the probabilities for democracy, but they do not determine the outcomes.[5]

Wise citizens will take into consideration the factors that "shape probabilities," because it is naive to ignore barriers and threats, but they will not renounce their agency just because those factors look daunting.

A master question for social theory during the twentieth century was structure versus agency: whether people's voluntary choices made any difference in politics or underlying structures determined everything. This question divided, for example, French existentialists (who preached the value of intentional political acts) from French structuralists (who thought that political events, including major elections and revolutions, were superficial perturbations on the permanent structures below).[6] But the question for the twenty-first century should be different: not how much impact agency has, but how that impact can be expanded. The reason to expand it is not that agency is intrinsically good. Hitler was an effective political agent. Rather, deliberate and effective human action is one necessary condition of a worthwhile human life. If there is no agency, life is pointless.

Another obstacle to helpful research is the enduring positivist bent of the social sciences. Positivism presumes that there is a sharp distinction between facts, which can be observed and tested, and values, which are sheer matters of opinion. Social scientists acknowledge that they have values but regard them as biases and try to reduce their impact on their own scholarship. They use sophisticated techniques for that purpose. For example, to construct a survey or a test, a researcher often generates many potential questions and then has them screened by several different sets of diverse experts and lay reviewers and tested with a sample of the target population to see which questions correlate with each other. Items that prove controversial or that fail to correlate with others are rejected. The final test or survey then has a patina of objectivity and value neutrality, because the researcher did not control the choice of questions. Often the topics included on the test are drawn from previous literature that has been thoroughly peer reviewed and thus deemed scientific. Finally, careful researchers disclose their remaining biases in the limitations section of their articles.

But having the right values is not a bias; it is the most important achievement. You cannot tell that your values are right simply by asking whether they are uncontroversial or prevalent in the published literature. A whole discipline can be morally misguided, as the examples of Soviet and Nazi sciences clearly demonstrate. Our deepest obligation is to have the *right* values, and that requires being able to propose and assess moral reasons. A good examination, for example, is not merely composed of questions that are scientifically valid and reliable. A good exam tests knowledge and skills that are valuable— that a person really should have or that a just society really needs.

In this book, I draw on several empirical research programs that try to help something good work in the world. For instance, scholars who study positive youth development (PYD) assess initiatives that give young people opportunities to contribute to their communities. Scholars of common pool resources study how communities manage common property, such as fisheries and forests. Scholars of deliberative democracy investigate the impacts on citizens, communities, and policies when people talk about public issues in structured settings.

These are empirical research efforts, committed to facts and truth. They do not seek to celebrate, but to critically evaluate, their research subjects. Nevertheless, an obvious goal is to make the practical work succeed by identifying and demonstrating positive impacts and by helping sort out the effective strategies from the ineffective ones. Underlying these intellectual efforts is some kind of hope that the practical programs, when done well, succeed. Along with hope, another relevant virtue is loyalty to a field of practice that shows promise.

These motives or virtues are largely hidden, because positivist social science cannot handle value commitments on the part of researchers; it treats them as biases to be minimized and disclosed if they prove impossible to eliminate. Often a search for motives is critical and suspicious: one tries to show that a given research project is biased by some value judgment, cultural assumption, or self-interest on the scholars' part. But we can look for motives in an appreciative spirit, believing that an empirical research program in the social sciences is only as good as its core values.

Note that it is not at all obvious why we *should* hope that PYD, common property resource management, and deliberative democracy work. These are expensive and tricky strategies. For instance, the core empirical hypothesis of PYD is that you will get better outcomes for youth if you help them contribute than if you use surveillance and remediation. But it would be cheaper and more reliable if we could cut crime with metal detectors in every school instead of elaborate service-learning programs. So why should we hope that PYD is right?

Likewise, it would be easier to turn all resources into private or state property than to encourage some communities to manage resources as common property. And it would be easier for professionals to make city plans and budgets than to turn those decisions over to citizens. So why do scholars evidently hope that good common property regimes produce more sustainable and efficient economic outcomes than expert management and that citizens' deliberations generate more legitimate and fair policies than governments?

Part of the reason is simply that things are not going very well in the world, and scholars seek alternatives that may be obviously better (for example, more efficient or sustainable and less corrupt and wasteful). That is part of the reason, but it doesn't fully explain the focus of these research projects. If you're worried about violence in American high schools, you should look for something new that works. But why should that new approach include service and leadership programs, instead of better metal detectors and video cameras?

Ultimately, all three of my examples are anchored in commitments that I would describe as Kantian. Immanuel Kant argued that the individual is a sovereign moral agent, and our responsibility to others is always to help them develop their capacities for autonomy and voluntary cooperation. Real

Kantians are willing to defend autonomy even if the consequences for health and welfare turn out to be bad. But real Kantianism persuades few people and has little influence. Thus, I think the research projects I have mentioned here are motivated by a kind of soft or strategic Kantianism. The best initiatives, on this view, are the ones that achieve efficient and reliable improvements in tangible human welfare by enhancing people's autonomy. Strategies like PYD and common property regimes stand out as worthy of study because of their Kantian values. But they deserve critical scrutiny on utilitarian grounds. If they fail to deliver the promised practical outcomes, they should be improved before they are abandoned. The same attention should not be given to surveillance systems or top-down managerial structures. In theory, those solutions might work just as well but helping them succeed would not enhance autonomy. That is the implicit moral theory behind these research programs.

In our time and culture, it is a risky strategy for scholars to admit their core moral commitments. The smartest move is to pretend that a research program is simply scientific and all the outcomes of interest are utilitarian. But those assumptions have the disadvantage of being wrong. They distort research in various subtle but damaging ways. For example, if we try to justify youth service programs because they cut dropout rates and teen pregnancy, we are likely to shift those programs in the direction of noncontroversial service, when the real (but undisclosed) motive is to make young people into political actors. Besides, when we are influenced by an *implicit* moral philosophy, we may make judgments that we would not actually endorse or defend if we spelled them out clearly. Kantian premises may motivate PYD, common property resource management, and deliberative democracy. Those motivations are commendable, but they do not show that Kantianism is *right*. Most people reasonably resist Kant's full-blown moral philosophy. By spelling out our actual views, we can analyze them critically, take responsibility for them, and make them more complex and persuasive. Talking in this way is a form of accountability; a running theme of this book is the importance of accountability as reason giving.

Political philosophy (as practiced in philosophy and political science departments and by some independent writers) directly addresses questions of value. It takes as its central objectives not only to analyze or describe values but also to identify the *best* ones. Political philosophy is often informed by facts: for instance, economics influences it deeply. The problem with political philosophy is that it takes too little account of strategy. Strategy is studied and taught in academia but predominantly in fields far removed from philosophy, such as business.[7]

In the most influential book of political philosophy written in English since the Second World War, John Rawls says that his subject is "justice," which is a feature of "the basic structure of society."[8] This way of thinking about politics can be deeply misleading to an individual who is deciding which groups to join, create, or lead and how to steer those groups. The individual cannot determine "the basic structure of society." He or she might have opinions about the basic structure: for example, Rawls himself favored a more equal distribution of economic goods than actually prevails in the United States today. But if you agree with him about that, it doesn't mean that you should join an association for economic equality. Such an association might gain no traction, or it might provoke a public backlash, or it might divide an existing political coalition, or it might lead to a massive new government program that does not work. Depending on the situation, you might do better advocating a particular reform in the health system that has a real prospect of passage. Rawls's theory by itself would send you in the wrong direction unless you also understood strategy.

In private foundations today, it is popular to ask grantees to articulate a "theory of change": a set of steps that will lead from the existing situation to the desired outcomes. Like any theory, it can be experimentally tested—it will either yield the promised outcomes or not. Sometimes political philosophy has a theory of change. For example, Plato's plan was to develop the blueprint of an ideal state and then persuade the tyrant of a city-state (Syracuse in Sicily) to implement it. This theory did not work—Plato had to flee Syracuse before he was killed there—but it seemed plausible in advance.[9]

Almost 2,000 years later, Machiavelli addressed *The Prince* to another Italian tyrant, Lorenzo the Magnificent. Perhaps Machiavelli's real intent was to give Lorenzo advice, or maybe—as Rousseau believed—Machiavelli was hinting to his fellow Florentine citizens that rule by one man would inevitably turn vicious and tyrannical. In that case, Machiavelli's theory of change was to subvert Medici rule by writing a book that would be read with irony.

In turn, Rousseau addressed his *Discourse on the Origins of Inequality* to the leaders of republican Geneva, with a plea to govern it differently. Since they were sovereign lords, they could change their policies if he persuaded them successfully. Still later, Hamilton, Madison, and Jay addressed their Federalist Papers to Americans who could vote to ratify the Constitution or influence public opinion. Thanks to the American Revolution, the majority of white men collectively held the power of Lorenzo the Magnificent, but they were not yet so numerous or so deluged with media that thoughtful essays would be lost in the noise. It made sense to address and persuade them.

What is the theory of change of modern academic philosophy? John Rawls is a leading example, and his *Theory of Justice* is dedicated to his wife— an appropriate and even touching gesture but interestingly different from the choices made by Machiavelli, Rousseau, Hamilton, and Madison. Either Rawls did not take responsibility for changing the world, or he hoped to change it by the following roundabout strategy: first develop a theory of the best possible society by means of academic scholarship, primarily addressed to colleagues and advanced students, and then popularize (or let someone else popularize) the results so that they might influence public opinion and thereby change influential popular votes.

I see no evidence that this strategy had any impact, despite Rawls's enormous prestige in the academy. Public policy in the United States is less Rawlsian than it was in 1970, and liberal activists and leaders who share some of his principles rarely look to him for arguments or guidance. Nor has any other political philosopher had more success than Rawls or his followers and interpreters.

This is not a refutation of Rawls's philosophy, which may be correct on its own terms. I am not a pragmatist who thinks that the only justification of intellectual work is its impact, what William James used to call its "cash value." A theory can have intrinsic merit. I would, however, assert that Rawls and his colleagues are no longer writing in the same genre as Plato, Machiavelli, Hamilton, and Madison (and many in-between). Contemporary academic political philosophy does not offer a path to a better society but only an indication of what one would be like. It is a highway without the on-ramp.

In political philosophy, "ideal theory" means the effort to define a fully just society. Proponents assert that it is useful for guiding our actual political decisions, which should steer toward the ideal. Amartya Sen, in *The Idea of Justice*, offers one of several recent and prominent critiques of this method. Sen argues that there is no way to settle reasonable disagreements about the ideal state. Knowing what is ideal is not necessary to make wise and ethical decisions. And even an ideally designed set of public institutions would not guarantee justice, because people must be given discretion to make private decisions, and those decisions can always be unjust.

Sen finds an alternative to the tradition of developing ideal social contracts, as Plato, More, Locke, Rousseau, Rawls, Nozick, and many others did. The alternative is to compare on moral grounds actually existing societies or realizable reforms in order to recommend improvements, a strategy epitomized by Aristotle, Adam Smith, Benjamin Constant, Tocqueville, and Sen himself (among many others).

I would push the critique further than Sen does. The non-ideal political theories that he admires are still addressed to some kind of sovereign: a potential author of laws and policies in the real world, a "decider" (as George W. Bush used to call himself). Sen, for example, in his various works, addresses two kinds of audiences: the general public, understood as sovereign because we can vote, or various specific authorities, such as the managers of the World Bank. In his work aimed at general readers, he envisions a "global dialogue," rich with "active public agitation, news commentary, and open discussion," to which he contributes guiding principles and methods.[10] In turn, that global dialogue will influence the actual decision-makers, whether they are voters and consumers in various countries or powerful leaders.

Unfortunately, no reader is really in the position of a sovereign. You and I can vote but not for elaborate social strategies. We vote for names on a ballot, while hundreds of millions of other people also vote with different goals in mind. If I prefer the social welfare system of Canada to the US system, I cannot vote to switch. Not can I persuade millions of Americans to share my preference, because I don't have the platform to reach them. Even legislators are not sovereigns, because there are many of them, and the legislature shares power with other branches and levels of government and with private institutions.

This book has a different theory of change and is meant to exemplify a different approach to scholarship. It is directed at readers who can act to enhance democracy in the United States. But because we are far more effective when we act collectively rather than singly, this book identifies networks of organizations that an individual can join and influence. The book's strategic recommendations, empirical evidence, and moral arguments are all addressed at members (and prospective members) of these networks.

Since the late 1980s, I have had the privilege of working for the Charles F. Kettering Foundation, Common Cause, CIRCLE (The Center for Information & Research on Civic Learning & Engagement), the National Commission on Civic Renewal, the Institute for Philosophy & Public Policy, and the Jonathan M. Tisch College of Citizenship and Public Service at Tufts University. I have served on the boards or steering committees of the American Bar Association's Division of Public Education, America*Speaks*, the Paul J. Aicher Foundation (fiscal agent for Everyday Democracy, which brought Study Circles to America), the Campaign for the Civic Mission of Schools, the Deliberative Democracy Consortium, the State of Maryland's Task Force on Civic Literacy, the Newspaper Association of America Foundation, and Street Law, Inc. I have completed projects for the National Conference on Citizenship, the New America Foundation, the Aspen Institute, and the Corporation for National and Community Service. I have served on advisory committees for America's Promise, Mobilize.org, Generation Citizen, and the Obama campaign's Education Policy Committee and Urban Policy Committee.

These institutions are demonstrably connected—not in one organized structure but as a dense network with many common ties. The same network also encompasses such organizations as Campus Compact, Demos, the League of Women Voters, and the Industrial Areas Foundation, with which I have not worked as directly. Most important, the network touches many citizens who are members of one or more of these organizations or who simply participate in, or follow, civic renewal as individuals.

This book is primarily addressed to that network and to anyone who wants to join it. My theory of change is to try to elucidate the underlying values of the network—anticipating that my analysis will provoke some disagreement—and then to propose strategic next steps in light of the current situation. If the network grows and has political impact, the reasons will go far beyond this book. But if the book contributes to its success, its theory of change will be vindicated.

3

Values

COLLABORATION, DELIBERATION, AND CIVIC RELATIONSHIPS

IN CHAPTER 2, I argued that we need a combination of values, facts, and strategies to think wisely about politics. Chapter 3 turns to values. The core proposition is simple: most Americans should be involved in deliberation and collaboration. In other words, they should talk, listen, and work together on public problems. To do so requires certain kinds of relationships with one's fellow citizens. Thus chapter 3 introduces deliberation, collaboration, and civic relationships as its core concepts. I argue that a combination of these three produces beneficial results, it yields knowledge about what is right, and it enhances the dignity and agency of participants. In other words, the advantages of civic engagement (thus understood) are pragmatic, epistemological, and ethical.

Talking and Listening

The dominant view of political scientists during the 1950s and 1960s was that individuals and organizations *wanted* things. They had options, such as to vote, to contribute money, to run for office, to strike, to sue, or to threaten violence, and they made their choices in order to get as much of what they wanted as possible. Political outcomes were the result of many simultaneous choices. Harold Lasswell's famous book was entitled *Politics: Who Gets What, When, How.*[1]

Since then, "deliberative democrats" have argued that we should not be satisfied with policies that arise because individuals and groups try to get what they want. People may not want good things, their power is starkly unequal, and some of their tactics are unethical. Besides, people often don't know what they want until they have communicated with others. Although our views about matters very close to our own lives may emerge out of private experience, we will not know what to think about Iraq, Social Security, or stem cells until we have heard arguments and formed responses.

Even if you know what you want, you cannot try to get it unless you belong to some kind of political entity that makes decisions. A Parent Teacher Association, a corporate board, a jury, a town, the Supreme Court, the whole United States, and the United Nations General Assembly are examples of political communities with voters and powers. They did not spring fully formed from the air. Creating, defining, and redefining political communities; deciding who belongs in each one; and negotiating among them are essential parts of politics. So is moving from one community to another, which is a common political act for Americans.

We don't even know *who* we are (in a political sense) until we have communicated. Deciding whether you are a Yugoslav, a Serb, a European, or Christian is more fundamental than identifying what you want or what strategies you will choose to get it. You can be persuaded to become something like a Serb or a Croat, and such persuasion is part of politics.

In short, the formation of identities, motivations, goals, and communities are aspects of politics; thus, talking and listening are politically important. That insight does not imply that politics is any better than the political scientists had claimed in the 1950s and 1960s. After all, communication can transform peaceful, tolerant individuals into murderous racists, as the example of Hitler shows. Thus a crucial second step for deliberative democrats is to define some kinds of communication as better than others and to name the better kinds "deliberation." The definition of a deliberation cannot be a conversation that reaches the correct outcome, because a computer algorithm might work just as well for that purpose. Instead, for deliberative democrats, the intrinsic qualities of the conversation are what mark it as valuable.

Typically, those qualities include the diversity of the participants, their equality of influence, freedom of speech, openness and transparency, reasonableness, and civility. A less academic but equally insightful and precise account of good conversation comes from a student at the East Los Angeles Renaissance Academy. Cathy Davidson, a Duke University professor, recalls that she asked a young woman, "What do you mean by 'critical thinking'? She didn't even pause, 'It means being able to see where I am standing and also where you are. It means having enough knowledge and research and discipline not to over-react if you disagree with me or if you dislike me or disrespect me but to pause, and think about who you are, and then help bridge the gap between us.'"[2]

A conceptual distinction is important here. To negotiate is to come into a discussion with predetermined goals. You know what you want, but because others may not permit you to get it, you are prepared to settle for less than the whole. Negotiation can be desirable: it is certainly better than violent conflict, and it is the ideal way to settle issues that truly represent nothing but conflicts among equally valid interests.[3] Negotiation is basically the *only* way that organizations can interact if their fiduciary responsibility is to maximize returns for their owners. Thus negotiation is the main form of political interaction permissible to public companies.

Deliberation, in contrast, means trying to decide what is right to do. Self-interest is relevant to that decision—it is one legitimate consideration—but it is not the only factor. People who deliberate should also consider the implications for other people, as well as abstract considerations of ethics and justice.[4] Deliberation is different from negotiation because the participants' goals, judgments, preferences, and values are open to change. They not only seek what they wanted before they entered the discussion; they are also interested in changing what they want. Deliberation can build legitimacy in a way that negotiation cannot, because it says: This is what is right or just to do. In Michael Sandel's influential phrase, "When politics goes well, we may know a good in common that we cannot know alone."[5]

In the very first paragraph of the Federalist Papers, Alexander Hamilton asks whether "societies of men are really capable or not of establishing good government from reflection and choice, or whether they are forever destined to depend, for their political constitutions, on accident and force."[6] The ideal of deliberative democracy holds that we *can* govern by reflection and choice. It suggests concrete and practical ideas for reforming politics so that transparent, fair, reasonable conversations become more common and more consequential.[7] A whole field (described in chapter 6) is now devoted to organizing tangible public deliberations at a human scale: meetings, summits, citizens' juries, community dialogues, moderated online forums, and various hybrids of these.

Hamilton remarked "that it seems to have been reserved to the people of this country, by their conduct and example, to decide" whether human beings can govern "from reflection and choice."[8] But actually, in other nations, deliberative democratic experiments have gone much further than in the United States. For example, since 1992, the constitution of India has required every rural village to have both an elected council and an empowered open meeting called a *gram sabha* (GS) that allocates funds and makes other binding decisions. Vijayendra Rao of the World Bank and Paromita Sanyal of Wesleyan write, "The GS has become, arguably, the largest deliberative institution in human history, at the heart of two million little village democracies which affect the lives 700 million rural Indians." This experiment has strengthened the confidence, standing, and voice of the poor, of women, and of low-caste Indians.[9]

In practice, "deliberation" means convening a diverse group of citizens and asking them to talk, without any expectation or plan that they will reach one conclusion rather than another. The population that is convened, the format, and the informational materials are all supposed to be neutral or balanced. There is an ethic of deference to whatever views may emerge from democratic discussion. Efforts are made to insulate the process from deliberate attempts to manipulate it.

In contrast, activism or advocacy implies an effort to enlist or mobilize citizens toward some end. At their best, advocates are candid about their goals and open to critical suggestions. But they are advocating *for* something. Many advocates for disadvantaged populations explicitly say that deliberation is a waste of their limited resources.[10] They note that just because people are invited to talk as equals, the discussion will not necessarily be fair. Participants who have more education, social status, and allies may wield disproportionate power.[11] Individuals and groups who are satisfied with the status quo have an advantage over those who want change, because they can use the discussion to delay decisions. (They can filibuster.) Sometimes, the way the topic is defined can benefit one side over the other. If we meet to discuss the *deficit*, the conversation will favor fiscal conservatives, whereas if our topic is *poverty*, liberals will have an edge. When grievances are especially serious, it may be inappropriate to call for discussion among the opposing parties. For instance, the great African American antislavery campaigner Frederick Douglass simply refused to answer arguments in favor of slavery, understandably viewing the whole discussion as offensive.[12]

Talking with people who hold different views can cause us to temper or censor our sincere views in order to avoid confrontation, and such self-editing reduces our passion and our motivation to act.[13] Social movements that oppose injustice seem most likely to arise when there is regular and intense communication among people who share the same opinions.[14]

Iris Marion Young lists some of the tactics that can be more effective than deliberation: "picketing, leafleting, guerilla theater, large and loud street demonstrations, sit-ins, and other forms of direct action, such as boycotts." As she notes, activists may even choose to "make noises outside when deliberation is supposedly taking place on the inside. Sometimes activists invade the houses of deliberation and disrupt their business by unfurling banners, throwing stink bombs, or running and shouting through the aisles."[15]

For their part, proponents of deliberation often see organized advocacy as a threat to fair and unbiased discussion; hence they struggle to protect deliberative forums from being "manipulated" by groups with an agenda. One tactic for this purpose is to select potential participants randomly (like a jury), so that it is impossible for an interest group to mobilize its members to attend. Overall, deliberation seems cool, cerebral, slow, and middle class. Activism seems urgent, passionate, effective, and available to all.

In my view, the main contribution of deliberation is not to allow people to speak (for they may rightly prefer other modes of expression that are more confrontational). Rather, its value is in helping people to *listen*. You don't need to listen if you are correct in all your values, factual knowledge, and strategies. Frederick Douglass was correct that slavery was evil, and he had a winning strategy for ending it. He did not need to listen to slavery's apologists, except perhaps to find weaknesses in their political coalition. But most of us, most of the time, are not in Douglass's position. We cannot know that we are right. Other people's information, values, strategic suggestions, and expressions of interest, identity, and desire may improve our views. So what we get out of deliberation is a chance to learn.[16]

From Talk to Work

Deliberation is most fruitful for learning—and deliberative democracy is a most attractive and realistic political ideal—when talk is embedded in relationships among citizens and connected to their common work.[17] One reason is motivational: we are unlikely to want to talk and listen unless doing so strengthens relationships and leads to action. Another reason is epistemic: we will not know enough to talk *well* unless we gain experience from acting together. To put this point in slogan form: deliberation without collaboration is empty, but collaboration without deliberation is blind.

Consider first the issue of motivation. We know that most people do not actually deliberate. Eighteen percent of the Americans whom we polled in 2007 said (a) they had "been involved in a meeting (either face-to-face or online) to determine ideas and solutions for problems in their community" within the past year, *and* (b) those discussions had included people who held views different from their own.[18] That response implies a substantial amount of deliberation. But the estimate was probably inflated by respondents who exaggerated their behavior; and even if the results were precisely accurate, 82 percent of Americans did *not* deliberate that year. Besides, we used a loose definition of "deliberation": some of the 18 percent who attended diverse discussions may never have listened seriously to other perspectives or tried to reach any kind of conclusion with their peers.

If you are in charge of a government or another important institution, you can create incentives to deliberate. As briefly noted in chapter 1, the former mayor of Washington, DC, Anthony Williams, decided that he wanted more informed public input regarding the budget of the city, which profoundly affects its citizens. So he hired America*Speaks* to organize large, representative "summits" at which thousands of citizens could deliberate about budget priorities. Participants were selected (not randomly, but purposively) to reflect the diversity of the city and to minimize the impact of deliberate mobilization by interest groups. Citizens worked at small tables within the vast expanse of the city's convention center, and the results of each discussion were shared transparently on a computer network. People participated because the few hours they were asked to contribute seemed worthwhile. The event promised to be interesting, and the mayor had committed to incorporate the results into the formal process of budgeting.[19]

Mayor Williams truly wanted to share power with a representative group of Washingtonians, and he genuinely wanted them to be provided with the most neutral possible materials and choices. In theory, however, he had the power to manipulate the process or withdraw his support. In fact, his successor, Mayor Adrian Fenty, chose not to continue the annual citizens' budget summits. Apparently, he calculated that they would not advance his political agenda. When governments or leaders invite citizens to deliberate, they control the process in a way that makes deliberative democracy fragile, at best.[20]

Meanwhile, if you are a citizen with strong views and commitments, a carefully screened deliberative forum offers you no outlet. The whole point of randomly or otherwise purposefully selecting participants is to *exclude* people like you—at least in large numbers—because the substance or the intensity of your views will be atypical. But you have a right to hold intense views and to want to act. In 2009, angry opponents of health care reform deliberately disrupted open "town meetings" convened by Democratic members of Congress. The Stanford political scientist James Fishkin published an argument for randomly selecting citizens to discuss health care instead of holding such open forums. The *New York Times* chose to give his essay the headline, "Town Halls by Invitation."[21] But democratic participation cannot be "by invitation"—it must be a right claimed or created by ordinary people, whether elites like it or not.[22]

Official deliberative forums are helpful innovations in governance. When they are well organized, they provide legitimate input into formal decisions and complement traditional institutions such as legislatures and agencies. They can also offer prominent examples of civil, constructive discourse. Yet running such events should not be our main objective. The fundamental goal is to increase the amount of real listening that occurs in America. Citizens should listen to people different from themselves on topics of mutual concern. Usually, that listening will take place in settings that are not pure public deliberations. The participants will not simply meet, talk, listen, judge, and reach conclusions. Rather, their talk will be sporadic, sandwiched between other activities such as working, playing, advocating, or performing together. Their communication will not be purely civil or rational. They will not merely exchange proposals and reasons but will also give personal testimony, tell stories, form friendships, express self-interest, communicate with anger or irony, and indicate positive emotions such as camaraderie and even love. The groups in which such listening occurs will not be randomly selected or otherwise representative of any larger population; people will tend to know one another already.

Even if people do not rush to deliberate, they like to talk. As the philosopher Anthony Laden argues, an ordinary conversation is not goal directed.[23] On the contrary, a skillful and amiable conversationalist is one who can keep the discussion alive by making comments or asking questions that elicit further remarks from others. There is an art to conversation, and it is a sign of success that a dialogue does not end promptly but continues to engage and please the participants for a long while. Asking and listening are more important to the maintenance of a conversation than speaking. In those respects, natural or everyday conversation is quite different from the formal and episodic deliberations of New England town meetings, citizens' summits, legislatures, and courts, whose purpose is to reach a conclusion efficiently.

By engaging in prolonged or repeated conversations that are not goal directed, we develop ethical obligations to our interlocutors. If you merely pass a stranger on the street, your obligations to him are limited. You may not harm him; you must aid him under certain extraordinary circumstances (for example, by shouting a warning if a brick is falling toward his head), and you must pay taxes that may benefit him. Otherwise, you are free to pass without paying him much attention. But if you have voluntarily spoken for hours to a person about matters of shared interest, you must show greater concern for his welfare. It is not always desirable to incur obligations of this kind; there is such a thing as being over-obligated. Yet a life with very few such relationships would be narrow and impoverished. This is why we respect conversationalists who begin and prolong engaging discussions that are not aimed at reaching decisions. It is also why community organizers, ever since Alinsky in the 1930s, have encouraged citizens to conduct "one-on-one" interviews (exploring one another's interests and values) that lead to "mutual commitments" based on "reciprocal relationships."[24]

Conversations that involve stories, humor, and personal testimony are part of ordinary life—in contrast to deliberative forums, which are rather artificial. But natural conversations are not automatically adequate. If they are to address our serious public problems, conversations must ultimately relate to public or social issues and they must involve politically diverse participants. Three troublingly common phenomena are (1) unreflective people banding together in ideologically homogeneous groups that reinforce their prejudices, (2) diverse groups who avoid any mention of public concerns or issues in order to preserve harmony, and (3) discussions that neglect valid options because a premature and narrow consensus prevails.[25]

Fortunately, people are already motivated to *work* together on public problems. In the United States, one-quarter of the adult population reports volunteer service within any given year, half of us say we belong to at least one voluntary association, and we give 2 percent of our disposable income to charity. People need special incentives to participate in formal deliberations, but they are already quite busy working together. But their work is often disconnected from their talk and vice versa. Thus our goal should be to embed a greater degree of reflection and more diverse discussions in this common work. The tangible experiences that people obtain in service or in their paid work can inform their discussions, and their discussions can move them to serve or work better.

On this definition, "deliberative democracy" does not mean new institutions that look rather like juries or legislatures and that produce decisions. It is not about "neatly packaged episodes of reasoning."[26] It looks more like a busy, heterogeneous civil society, composed of networks and associations, in which there is a relatively high frequency of actual listening among people who do not start by agreeing. This theory blurs the distinctions between decision-making and implementation, talk and work, and state and society. The goal, after all, is not to democratize those special moments when formal policy decisions are made by the government—leaving bureaucrats to implement the decisions and the private sector to follow regulations and pay taxes. Rather, the goal is to democratize the whole process of shaping our common world. To that end, it is just as important to infuse talking and listening into the daily work of the public and private sectors as it is to deliberate periodically about formal policies.[27]

Imagine, for example, that neighbors love a local stream and are concerned about its health. Thanks to them, a pedestrian footbridge is built over it to provide access and to reduce car pollution. It does not matter much whether they cause this bridge to appear by voting at a town meeting to fund it, lobbying the local government to build it, persuading a private company to donate it, or physically erecting it themselves. So long as the bridge was their idea and the fruit of their collective discussion and effort, several advantages are likely to follow: (1) Because they designed it, it will meet their needs and reflect their talents. (2) Because they made it, they will feel a sense of ownership and will be motivated to protect it. (3) Because they are formally equal as neighbors—not ranked in a hierarchy—each will feel a sense of dignity and status. (4) By combining discussion with collaborative action, they will develop skills, relationships, and political power that can transfer to other settings. (5) In shaping their public world together, they will gain a feeling of satisfaction and agency. As the philosopher Hannah Arendt wrote, the Americans of the Revolutionary era "knew that public freedom meant having a share in public business, and that the activities connected with this business by no means constituted a burden but gave those who discharged them in public a feeling of happiness that they could acquire nowhere else."[28]

None of these advantages is guaranteed, nor would I ignore arguments, tensions, and downright failures, which are common enough. But some of the *benefits* are, as Arendt knew, impossible to obtain in other ways. If you work in a construction company, you may take appropriate satisfaction in the bridges that you help build, but they are generally not your ideas nor your property once you are done. If you are asked for input by the local government, and you propose a new bridge, you may feel that your intellect and values have been respected—but the government fundamentally ran the process. It is when you have been part of initiating change in the world, combining talk with some kind of action, that you can attain full civic satisfaction or "public happiness."

The bridge is just a metaphor. We need not burden the earth with unlimited numbers of new structures. Restoring nature is equally valuable, as are various forms of intangible and nonpermanent goods: events, performances, ideas, cultural innovations, and educated children.

Although I have suggested that satisfaction is higher among citizens who gather to create a bridge than among employees of a construction company that builds bridges, I doubt that the fundamental issue is the public sector versus the private sector, in the legal sense of those phrases.[29] A fine example of a publicly created space might be a coffeehouse, papered with posters for local events, populated by a cross-section of the community. That coffeehouse may belong to and profit one person, who (along with his or her customers) can rightly feel responsible for building a common space. Meanwhile, a government-owned underpass nearby may be the most forbidding and hostile, antipublic space in town—whether it was built by a public agency or a private contractor.

As Elinor Ostrom noted in her Nobel Prize Lecture, how people manage a common pool resource depends in part on whether they are organized as (for instance) "private water companies, city utilities, private oil companies, [or] local citizens meeting in diverse settings." Their behavior differs, too, depending on the rules of the game: for example "when they meet monthly in a private water association, when they face each other in a courtroom, and when they go to the legislature."[30] Despite these differences, Ostrom and her colleagues have begun to build one overall framework for understanding the creation and management of common resources—a framework that tends to downplay the dichotomy between the state and private sectors that seems fundamental in other theories. One could say that in this framework, citizens are at the center, and they have available a plurality of institutional forms and combinations of forms.

Still, there is a sense of "public" that makes the creation of public goods particularly precious. My imaginary bridge and coffeehouse may have different legal status, but they share the five advantages enumerated earlier. The outputs of government bureaucracies and private corporations usually lack those advantages, which is why people are alienated from the world that those entities jointly create. Governments can incorporate public discussion, creativity, and work into their operations, which would be the best way to increase trust. Unfortunately, it is not the main trend in public administration anywhere in the developed world.

When diverse people—including truly representative samples of the whole population—are invited to participate in better forms of politics, they rise to the occasion. Here I mention just three examples from a large literature:

Formal deliberation: In 2009, the Congressional Management Foundation randomly invited Americans to deliberate about the contentious issue of immigration with their own members of Congress.[31] Researchers evaluated this experiment carefully, using a randomly selected control group.

Usually, disadvantaged people are relatively unlikely to participate in voluntary political actions, such as voting. But in this experiment, lower income people, racial minorities, women, individuals who do not attend religious services, and people with weak or no partisan affiliations were *most* likely to accept the invitation to deliberate.

In keeping with many other experiments, these discussions proved substantive, civil, and well informed. Participants liked them: "95 percent Agreed (72 percent Strongly Agreed) that such sessions are 'very valuable to our democracy' and 96 percent Agreed (80 percent Strongly Agreed) that they would be interested in doing similar online sessions for other issues." Participants' opinions of the politicians with whom they deliberated rose dramatically. Participants also came closer to agreeing with these politicians about the issue under consideration. They were more likely to vote in the next election (compared to the randomly selected control group), and more likely to vote for the politician with whom they had deliberated. This example is just one of many in which representative groups of citizens perform exceptionally well when asked to deliberate about serious matters.[32] It is an episodic interaction, however, and not likely to build lasting relationships among the participants or lead to civic action. The next two examples are stronger on those dimensions.

Youth service: Teenagers have a reputation for being disrespectful, unruly, and damaging to themselves and others. Adolescents from poor communities are especially likely to be seen that way—and not simply because of prejudice: many low-income urban high schools are actually disordered places. Yet when young people from disadvantaged or marginalized backgrounds are enlisted in constructive service projects, they regularly act with discipline, solidarity, respect, and ethics. The atmosphere in a room devoted to service or activism is virtually the opposite of the atmosphere in a high school cafeteria or in many conventional classrooms, even when the individuals are the same.

Reed Larson, a distinguished psychologist, is one of several scholars who explains this difference in terms of "agency" and "initiative." Most activities available to adolescents are either required by authorities (like homework assignments) or voluntary but episodic and ultimately pointless (like video games). Neither type of experience encourages or even permits long-range planning, strategic thinking, and deliberation about means and ends. When teenagers are encouraged to address significant public problems, many of them rise remarkably well to the challenge.[33] Richard F. Catalano and colleagues have identified 22 programs that include elements of service or youth contribution to society, that have been rigorously evaluated, and that "showed significant improvements in problem behaviors, including drug and alcohol use, school misbehavior, aggressive behavior, violence, truancy, high-risk sexual behavior, and smoking."[34]

Participants as evaluators: The assessment of public employees creates a dilemma, illustrated by the example of teachers. Everyone who has ever been inside a school knows that teachers differ in their skills, relevant knowledge, and motivation. It seems appropriate to measure these differences and use the results to guide decisions about hiring, retention, promotions, and assignments. But raw student test scores are poor measures because they do not take into account students' backgrounds and other external factors. Measuring the change in individual students' scores also poses technical problems. Besides, it is not clear that even an accurate measure of a teacher's impact, if such a statistic were available, would have beneficial results. When teachers use standardized test scores to modify their own performance, they often "teach to the test" and narrow the curriculum. When administrators use such data, they do not consistently enhance the strength of their teaching staffs; they certainly don't make the workplace more desirable for talented teachers.[35] Evidence from other fields shows that when self-accountability is replaced with external measures and sanctions, people often become less motivated to do good work.[36]

The civic alternative is "internal accountability": processes that allow the members of a community to assess themselves and encourage them to improve.[37] The most civic approach would be an internal accountability process not only *used* by a community but also *created* by it.

Consider, for example, the Constructive Feedback Forms that all Boston high school students complete for each teacher each semester. These carefully constructed surveys do not ask the students to rate their teachers as good, bad, nice, smart, or by any overall measure. Instead, they ask a series of specific questions about teaching practices. How soon after the bell does the class get down to work? How many students participate in discussions? In what ways does the teacher provide feedback on homework?

The union and school system endorsed this policy, which is modest so far because only the teacher receives the anonymous results to use in self-improvement. The next step might be to share the survey results in some form with administrators, mentors, other colleagues, students, or parents.

An important aspect of this policy is its origin. Students on the Boston Student Advisory Council developed it—both the outline and the details— and succeeded in persuading the Boston School Committee to approve it. Those students are supported by Youth on Board (a nationally recognized nonprofit) and by the school system's Office of High School Renewal, so they perform excellent, well-informed, and effective work as public leaders. I saw the survey before I knew anything about its origin and assumed it was the product of highly trained professionals.

The initiative represents a shift to internal accountability: participants in the educational process—including the "clients" (in this case students) develop a sophisticated tool that they use for continual self-improvement.

The Content of Our Conversations

The examples given so far are all about deciding what is right to do. But how can we tell what is right? Moral intuitions are unreliable: for many centuries, almost everyone's intuitions told them that women were unsuited to public life. General principles may help: for example, "Do unto others as you would have them do unto you." But such principles cannot resolve subtle and complex cases, and plausible moral principles conflict in particular instances. We cannot reason our way privately to acceptable conclusions, because we are too prone to bias, and because no individual knows enough to make valid judgments about social issues. We must reason *together*, deciding what is right by sharing ideas and perspectives and, in the process, building a common life, which will be richer and more satisfying than a purely private one. In this section, I argue that reasoning together is not merely a matter of exchanging arguments, but must be embedded in shared activity.

Actual public discussions are messy and often indecisive. So many perspectives, interests, reasons, and opinions are in play that it seems impossible to reach any principled or organized resolution. We talk for some arbitrary amount of time, and then a decision must be made by the pertinent authorities or by a popular vote. It is not clear whether the decision was correct based on the discussion that preceded it.

It seems beneficial to organize and systematize public discussion, and several kinds of experts stand ready to help:

- Social scientists propose to organize public discussions by identifying reliable causal relationships among concepts that can be empirically identified in the world. For instance, *success* comes to mean passing a test or graduating on time, and *class size* is found to influence (or not to influence) success. The hope is—if not to end the discussion—at least to focus and rationalize it.
- Managers (both actual administrators of our institutions and experts on management) hope to limit or organize public discussions by pronouncing on which *strategies will work* and which are *permissible* under the current rules and policies.
- Ideological thinkers try to simplify the discussion by putting heavy weight on certain moral concepts, which then trump others. (For example, *personal liberty* is a trump card for libertarians; *equal welfare*, for social democrats.)
- Lawyers are trained to guide public discussions by explaining which options are *legal* or *obligatory* under laws, precedents, and constitutions.

- Moral and political philosophers have less public influence than the other groups mentioned so far, but they hold the most subtle and sophisticated views of how public discussions ought to be improved. Contemporary academic philosophers are often disarmingly modest about their contributions, yet a core professional goal is to improve discussions by identifying morally clear and invariant concepts that should then influence decisions. Depending on which philosophical school one defends, those concepts might include *rational autonomy*, *maximum utility*, or *virtue*.[38]

All these forms of expert and disciplined guidance can be useful. But they often conflict, and so the very fact that they *all* help should tell us something. There is no methodology that can replace or discipline our public discussions or bring them to a close. This is because of the nature of moral reasoning itself.

Moral concepts are indispensable. We cannot replace them with empirical information. Even if smaller class sizes do produce better test scores, that does not tell us whether our tests measure valuable things, whether the cost of more teachers would be worth the benefits, or whether the state has a right to compel people to pay taxes for education.

But moral concepts are heterogeneous. Some have clear moral significance but controversial application in the world. (Fairness is always good, and murder is always bad.) Others have clear application but unpredictable moral significance. (Homicide is sometimes murder, but sometimes it is justifiable.) Still others are morally important but are neither predictable nor easily identified. (Love is sometimes good and sometimes regrettable, and whether love exists in a particular situation can be hard to say.) A method that could bring public deliberation to closure would have to organize all these concepts so that the empirically clear ones were reliably connected to the morally clear ones.

That sometimes happens. For instance, waterboarding either happens or it does not happen. The Bush administration's lawyers defined it in obsessive detail: "The detainee is lying on a gurney that is inclined at an angle of 10 to 15 degrees to the horizontal. . . . A cloth is placed over the detainee's face and cold water is poured on the cloth from a height of approximately 6 to 18 inches."[39] Waterboarding is, in my considered opinion, an example of torture. Torture is legally defined as a felony, and the reason for that rule is a moral judgment that torture is always wrong (in contrast to punishment or interrogation, which may be right). Therefore, waterboarding is wrong as well as illegal. This argument may be controversial, but it is clear and it carries us all the way from the concrete reality of a scene in a CIA interrogation room to a compelling moral judgment and a demand for action. The various kinds of concepts are lined up so that moral, legal, and factual ideas fit together. There is room for debate: Is waterboarding torture? Who waterboarded whom? But the debate is easily organized and should be finite.

If all our moral thinking could work like that, we might be able to bring our discussions to a close by applying the right methods—usually a combination of moral philosophy plus empirical research. But much of our thinking cannot be so organized, because we confront moral concepts that lack consistent significance. They are either good or bad, depending on the circumstances. Nevertheless, they are morally indispensible; we cannot be good human beings and think without them. Love and freedom are two examples. To say that Romeo loves Juliet—or that Romeo is free to marry Juliet—is to say something important, but we cannot tell whether it is good or bad until we know a lot about the situation. There is no way to organize our thinking so that we can bypass these concepts with more reliable definitions and principles.

A structured moral mind might look like the blueprint of a house. At the bottom of the page would be broad, abstract, general principles: the foundation. An individual's blueprint might be built on one moral principle, such as, "Do unto others . . ." Or it might start even lower, with a metaphysical premise, like "God exists and is good." At the top of the picture would be concrete actions, emotions, and judgments, like "I will support Principal Jones's position at the PTA meeting." In-between would be ideas that combine moral principles and factual information, such as, "Every child deserves an equal education," or "Our third grade curriculum is too weak." The arrows of implication would always flow up, from the more general to the more specific.

Our actual moral thinking is much more complex than this.[40] Grand abstractions do influence concrete judgments, but the reverse happens as well. I may believe in mainstreaming special needs children because of an abstract principle of justice, and that leads me to support Mrs. Jones at the PTA meeting. Or I may form an impression that Mrs. Jones is wise; she supports mainstreaming; and therefore I begin to construct a new theory of justice that justifies this policy. Or I may know an individual child whose welfare becomes an urgent matter for me; my views of Mrs. Jones, mainstreaming, and justice may all follow from that. For some people, abstract philosophical principles are lodestones. For others, concrete narratives have the same pervasive pull—for example, the Gospels, or one's own rags-to-riches story, or *Pride and Prejudice*.

We must avoid two pitfalls. One is the assumption that a general and abstract idea is always more important than a concrete and particular one.[41]

There is no good reason for that premise. The concept of a moral "founda-tion" is just a metaphor; morality is not really a house, and it does not have to stand on something broad to be solid. Yet we must equally avoid thinking that we just possess lots of unconnected opinions, none intrinsically more impor-tant than another. For example, the following thoughts may all be correct, but they are not alike: "It is good to be punctual," "Genocide is evil," and "Mrs. Jones is a good principal." Not only do these statements have different levels of importance, but they play different roles in our overall thinking.[42]

I would propose switching from the metaphor of a foundation to the met-aphor of a network. In any network, some of the nodes are tied to others, producing an overall web. If moral thinking is a network, the nodes are opin-ions or judgments, and the ties are implications or influences. For example, I may support mainstreaming because I hold a particular view of equity; then mainstreaming and equity are two nodes, and there is an arrow between them. I may also love a particular child, and that emotion is a node that con-nects to disability policy in schools. A strong network does not rest on a single node, like an army that is decapitated if its generalissimo is killed. Rather, a strong network is a tight web with many pathways, so that it is pos-sible to move from one node to another by more than one route. Yet in real, functioning networks, all the nodes do not bear equal importance. On the contrary, it is common for the most important 20 percent to carry 80 percent of the traffic—whether the network happens to be the Internet, the neural structure of the brain, or the civil society of a town.[43]

A healthy moral mind is similar. It has no single foundation, and it is not driven only by abstract principles. Concrete motives, emotions, and judg-ments (such as love or admiration for a particular individual) may loom large. Yet the whole structure is network-like, and it is possible for many kinds of nodes to influence many other kinds. My respect for Mrs. Jones may influence how I feel about the concept of the welfare state, and not just the reverse. I need many nodes and connections, each based on experience and reflection.

To have a complex moral network is not a fully reliable sign of good moral thinking. A fascist might have an elaborate mental map composed of many different racial and national prejudices and hatreds, each supported by stories and examples, and each buttressing the others. That would be a more complex diagram than the ones possessed by mystics who prize purity and simplicity. *Purity of Heart Is to Will One Thing*, wrote Søren Kierkegaard, and the old Shaker hymn advises, "'Tis the gift to be simple / 'Tis the gift to be free / 'Tis the gift to come down where we ought to be." A righteous Shaker would do more good than a sophisticated fascist. But even if complexity is not a sufficient or reliable sign of goodness, a complex map is both natural and desirable. It reflects the actual complexity of our moral world, it reduces the odds of becoming fanatical, it hems in self-interest, and it is resilient against radical doubt.

Let us assume that we learn what is right through interactions with other people. It is easier to converse with individuals who hold many different interests, commitments, and beliefs, because each such idea is a point of contact. A person with diverse beliefs is like an organic molecule with lots of surfaces for other molecules to bond to. Reasonable conversationalists may hold very strong commitments, including general philosophical or religious beliefs that they consider fundamental. But if they constantly and immediately cite those beliefs, it is impossible to deliberate with them. To put the point in network terms, your map can include nodes that are fixed points for you, but they ought not carry all the traffic; it should be possible to route around them.

Four conclusions follow from this discussion. First, we should banish a certain kind of moral skepticism which arises from thinking that moral conclusions always rest on foundations, but alas there is nothing below our biggest, most abstract ideas. For example, you may believe in the golden rule but be unwilling to say *why* it is true. You may feel that there is no answer to the "why?" question, and therefore morality is merely prejudice or whim. Your moral house has a foundation (the golden rule), but the foundation is floating in air. Fortunately, our whole morality does not rest on any such rule, nor must a principle rest on something below it to be valid. The golden rule is part of a durable network. It gains credibility because it seems consistent with so many other things that we come to believe. If it or any other node is knocked out of the network, the traffic can route around it.

Second, moral thinking is influenced by worldly experience, by practice and by stories, and not only by abstract theories and principles. The business leader who enters public debates having struggled to meet a payroll while paying taxes speaks from authentic experience. So does the soup kitchen volunteer who has faced a long line of homeless people with insufficient welfare benefits. Civil society functions best when both kinds of people (and many others) bring their experience into a common conversation and then take what they learn from discussions back to their work in an iterative cycle. In Laden's terms, moral reasoning is a "deeply social activity."[44] It is less about offering arguments that go all the way from premises to conclusions than about trying to form a common view of the world that integrates many people's perspectives and experiences so that they can live and work effectively together.

Third, we can handle diversity. If individuals' conclusions derived from the foundations of their thought, we would face a serious problem whenever we encountered people who had different foundations from our own. It is hard to tolerate them, let alone deliberate with them. The existence of a different foundation can even provoke vertiginous skepticism. If my worldview rests on utilitarianism, and yours depends on faith in Jesus's resurrection, then perhaps I should doubt that my own fundamental premise is valid. But if our respective worldviews are more like networks, then they probably share many of the same nodes even though they differ in some important respects. What's more, each person's network must be slightly different from anyone else's—even his twin brother's. Thus when we categorize people into cultures, we are crudely generalizing. There is actually one population of diverse human beings who are capable of discussing their differences even though they may not reach agreement. Since my moral network map shares many nodes with yours, we can think of a whole community as one elaborate, interpersonal moral network (full of tension as well as consensus), and civic engagement as a process of enriching and enhancing that shared network. Danielle Allen reaches a similar conclusion by a different route, arguing for friendship among strangers as the basis of democracy. "Friendship is not an emotion, but a practice, a set of hard-won, complicated habits that are used to bridge trouble, difficulty, and differences of personality, experience, and aspiration. Friendship is not easy, nor is democracy. Friendship begins in the recognition that friends have a *shared* life—not a 'common' nor an identical life—only one with common events, climates, built-environments, fixations of the imagination, and social structures. Each friend will view all these phenomena differently, but they are not the less shared for that."[45]

Finally, expertise plays a limited role in reaching good decisions. The moral network in my mind cannot be—and should not be—radically simplified by applying any sophisticated methodology. I can learn from experts about causation and about how we should define various concepts and principles. But at the end of that process, I will still have my own moral network map, nourished by many sources other than the experts, and I will have to make decisions both alone and in dialogue with my peers. There is no substitute for thinking together about problems and solutions.

The most important intellectual resource for citizens to possess is a set of considered judgments about how public institutions should run. People do and should disagree about that question, but everyone's judgments should be based on informed and reflective thoughts about how to balance equity, participation, minority rights, voice, and efficiency; how much to reward innovation and hard work versus protecting people against failure; when to preserve traditions and when to innovate; how much to demand of individuals and when to leave them alone; what to do about the lazy and the disruptive; and how to relate to newcomers and outsiders. They should also know how to participate in constructive debates about such issues when people disagree.

To some extent, those matters can be discussed in classrooms and informed by readings. But much of our civic learning is and must be experiential. From Jefferson's idea of ward republics that would manage "the small and yet numerous and interesting concerns of the neighborhood" and give "to every citizen, personally, a part in the administration of the public affairs,"[46] to Tocqueville's observation that juries and voluntary associations were schools of government, to John Dewey's notion of democracy as a set of learning opportunities, our wisest thinkers have always understood that the American system depends on knowledge and virtue that must be learned through experience. Our problem today is that such experience is sorely lacking.

Civic Relationships

Participants in politics and civic life frequently say that they prize relationships with other participants. Civic relationships generate power, they build communities, they reflect values and principles, and they are intrinsically rewarding.

In 2001, Doble Research Associates conducted focus groups for the Kettering Foundation on the topic of testing and accountability in schools. That year, the No Child Left Behind Act codified the national movement toward regular measurement of students and schools and promised parents choices if their schools were deemed to have failed. In short, the relationship between a public institution (the school) and its citizens was defined in terms of information and choice. But in the Doble focus groups, parents were highly resistant to the idea that testing would improve education. For one thing, they wanted to hold other parties accountable, starting with themselves. A Baltimore woman said, "If kids don't pass the test, is that supposed to mean that teachers are doing a lousy job? That's not right. I mean where does the support come from? You're pointing the finger at them when you should be supporting them." Another (or possibly the same) Baltimore woman explained, "When I think about accountability, I think about parents taking responsibility for supervising their children's learning and staying in touch with teachers." This respondent not only wanted to broaden responsibility but also saw it in terms of two-way communication.

Many participants wanted to know whether schools, parents, and students had the right values. They doubted that data would answer that question. And although the Doble report doesn't quite say this, I suspect they envisioned knowing individuals personally as the best way to assess their values. The focus groups turned to a discussion of relationships:

FIRST WOMAN: People don't know people in their communities anymore.
SECOND WOMAN: That's right. I was raised in an area where you knew everyone. That's just the way it was. But you don't know your neighbors anymore.
THIRD WOMAN: I have neighbors that lived next door to me for nine years and they don't even wave or talk to anybody in the neighborhood.

And so on—the conversation continued in this vein. Note that this was supposed to be a focus group about accountability in education. One Atlanta woman summed it up: "What we've got to do is develop a stronger sense of community between the schools and families in the community." I suspect that she envisioned a situation in which school staff and parents knew one another, shared fundamental values, and committed to support one another.

Similar results emerged from focus groups conducted ten years later, after American parents had gained access to a deluge of new data on test scores and school spending. According to the Public Agenda Foundation's summary, "Typically, people know almost nothing about specific [accountability] measures, and they rarely see them as clear-cut evidence of effectiveness. For most people, the best evidence that a system is working is its responsiveness and the personal interactions they have with it. 'You can't even get a human being on the phone' is perhaps the chief indicator of failure."[47]

Implicitly, these citizens understand the concept of "social capital." In fact, when the Harvard political scientist Robert Putnam revived that technical term in his scholarly article entitled "Bowling Alone" (1995), he hit such a chord with the public that within a year he was featured in *People* magazine. Depending on one's theoretical framework, social capital can be understood as a public good or resource that people *produce* by engaging civically, as a *measure* of their engagement, or as a *precondition* of active citizenship. In any case, it means the strength, distribution, and quality of relationships in a community. In the book version of *Bowling Alone*, Putnam defines social capital thus:

Whereas physical capital refers to physical objects and human capital refers to properties of individuals [such as their own skills], social capital refers to connections among individuals—social networks and the norms of reciprocity and trustworthiness that arise from them. In that sense social capital is closely related to what some have called "civic virtue." The difference is that "social capital" calls attention to the fact that civic virtue is most powerful when embedded in a dense network of reciprocal social relations."[48]

Before Putnam, the most influential scholar of social capital had been James S. Coleman, who had found that young people benefited tangibly from "the social relationships that exist among parents," the structure of those relationships, and "the parents' relations with institutions of the community."[49] If social capital predicts important outcomes, such as success in school, then enhancing relationships becomes a promising strategy. In keeping with the work of Coleman and Putnam, many grassroots organizing groups now explicitly aim to reform education by strengthening relationships that involve educators, parents, and students themselves.[50]

In traditional issue-based organizing, an organizer "already has an issue such as education reform in mind." He or she may believe that a particular change in official policy (such as more or less testing) would benefit the students. But "in relational organizing, an organizer builds a one-on-one relationship with individuals, trying to know everything about these leaders and members—even things that might at first seem to be irrelevant to education reform. The ideas for campaigns come about more slowly that way, but some argue that groups engaging in relational organizing can be more successful in the long term."[51]

Even in Saul Alinsky's day, community organizing was explicitly concerned with creating and building relationships among diverse residents of poor neighborhoods. Alinksy, however, was skeptical about relationships with the government, which he treated mainly as a distant target of public pressure. His skepticism was evident in his writing and in his daily practices. The Industrial Areas Foundation (IAF), which he started, would never take government grants, because Alinsky wanted to retain its fundamental independence. However, in the decades after his death, the IAF has broadened its conception of relationships to include government officials and corporate executives. Sirianni and Friedland report that "IAF 'accountability nights' with public officials have undergone a significant shift, from confrontational meetings designed to embarrass and expose leaders in the 1970s to forums designed to consolidate incipient relationships in full public view."[52] More generally, the modern IAF now teaches a "relational" view of organizing and of power.[53]

Similar ideas pop up in other networks. Helen Johnson, who organizes in Mississippi, observes, "The whole idea of community organizing is really about relationship building."[54] Often community organizers say that when they seek new recruits, they are looking for people with a "relational" sense.[55]

This vocabulary is not limited to community organizing but is also seen in kindred fields, such as civic engagement for youth. Sistas and Brothas United in the Bronx works on school reform but devotes time to cultivating relationships among youth and between young people and adults. Nathaniel, a teenage organizer, reports, "We have fun things. We do trips. And, on a personal level, we chill with each other . . . We definitely relate differently." And one of his colleagues observes that these relationships have made her "able to understand people better, not only personally, but what they're trying to say when they speak at meetings."[56]

Of all the strands of civic renewal, formal public deliberation seems the most remote from "relational" politics, because individuals are recruited to talk for a limited time and then disband. But participants in juries and policy deliberations often develop strong emotional ties. Further, the organizers of deliberations tend to believe that their own role is to strengthen relationships among citizens.[57] Thus Harold Saunders describes the West Virginia Center for Public Life, which organizes statewide deliberations on public issues, as having a "relational paradigm."[58]

For democracy, reciprocal relationships of concern and support are not sufficient. A *civic* relationship has the following specific features: (1) Unlike a family tie, a deep friendship, or a romantic partnership, a civic relationship is nonexclusive. In fact, a community's social capital is higher if diverse residents are connected by a broad and dense web of relationships. Citizens ought to expand and diversify their own relationships; exclusion and partiality are problematic in civic life. (2) Although civic relationships involve identities, interests, private concerns, and personal stories, they are not *simply* personal. For a relationship to be "civic," it must involve talking, listening, and working on public issues or problems. (3) A civic relationship need not be "civil," if that implies politeness and frequent expressions of positive emotions. It can rather encompass sharp disagreements. But the relationship must be predicated on the value of the other person as a fellow citizen, seen as someone who should be encouraged to participate in the common life.[59]

Thus civic relationships are connected to particular civic virtues, starting with loyalty. In his short, classic book entitled *Exit, Voice, and Loyalty*, Albert Hirschman argued that we have two basic options when we are dissatisfied with any institution or group, whether it is a restaurant, a church, a railroad company, or a nation-state.[60] We can leave it and join a different institution ("exit"), or we can try to persuade our fellow members to change it ("voice"). Exit is a human right: except in extraordinary situations, people should not be trapped in institutions. Besides, exit can improve the world, because institutions that lose members are forced to reform. That is the logic of market competition, and it works.

But voice is also valuable, and it is the harder path. When a city is deindustrializing or a school system is failing, exit will simply strip it of members and resources. It will not die completely—American Rust Belt cities and their school systems are not going to vanish like ancient Carthage and Thebes— but it will suffer from shrinking. Those who are left behind will be the weakest and the most vulnerable. These communities need internal reform and rebirth, and that requires voice. As Hirschman argued, *loyalty* is what causes people to exercise voice when exit is an option.

It would be difficult to measure the ratio of exit to voice in modern America, especially if one tried to assess the quality as well as the mere frequency of voice. Since I do not know how to measure this ratio, I cannot demonstrate that we are substituting exit for the voice and loyalty that we once had. But problematic examples of exit are widely visible. Wealthy parents exit public school systems, and middle-class families exit cities for suburbs. Partisans exit politically heterogeneous communities in favor of homogeneous ones so that they do not have to persuade fellow citizens to agree with them. (Bill Bishop argues in *The Big Sort* that Americans now live in counties—and other fixed geographical jurisdictions—that are far more politically homogeneous than they were in previous generations, because we "vote with our feet."[61]) During the last third of the twentieth century, the composition of American civil society changed profoundly as people exited associations that were diverse in terms of occupation, social class, and ideology (but rooted locally) and instead joined single-issue organizations that advanced causes they favored. You need not use voice within a single-issue organization: it speaks for you. You can exit as soon as you cease to agree with its agenda.[62] Finally, millions of Americans have exited public life altogether in favor of purely private concerns and networks. Overall, it is my impression that we are substituting exit for voice. That may be a natural (although undesirable) process, because voice is the more difficult mode.

But there are countertrends, particular efforts to enhance voice. I have already noted the revival of practical deliberative democracy: efforts to engage citizens in open-ended discussions of public issues. I have also mentioned positive youth development (PYD): the theory that institutions can enhance the welfare of adolescents by giving them opportunities to contribute to their societies. To read the scholarly literature on these two strategies, one would think that their main justification is that they "work": in other words, they produce better concrete outcomes than alternative strategies, such as top-down public administration or didactic instruction. But to the extent that they work, that is thanks to the committed people who have designed interventions, raised the funds to implement them, struggled to make them succeed, and refined their original plans to address challenges. Why would anyone go to all that trouble?

Underlying both deliberative democracy and PYD is a similar moral commitment. We should develop relationships with the other people who inhabit our communities, treating them as fellow citizens, not as threats or problems. We should use voice to engage them, which means both talking to them and genuinely listening. We should invest in their civic skills: leadership, effective speaking, and organizing. Those premises apply even if our fellow citizens happen to be younger than 20. Thus deliberative democracy and PYD are manifestations of civic loyalty.

The same could be said of several other movements described more fully in chapter 6. For example, proponents of asset based community development (ABCD) recommend taking a positive inventory of the good things in any community before attempting to change it; their underlying value is loyalty to places. Relational community organizers try to include everyone in their discussions and work, instead of simply mobilizing people who might agree with them. Again, an underlying value is loyalty to the place and its people.

A related virtue is *hope*, meaning a belief that collaborative and deliberative initiatives (such as ABCD, relational organizing, or PYD) can work and that their participants can improve their world. Hope is not mere optimism or a sunny disposition. It does not presume that matters are likely to improve, but only that we have a chance to improve things if we develop appropriate relationships.

Arendt saw hope and loyalty as a pair of related political virtues that matter because human beings are born and develop from infancy. Martin Heidegger, one of her teachers, had seen mortality—the inevitable movement toward death—as the fundamental metaphysical fact. Human beings were defined by our finitude and our one-way journey through time. In politics, Heidegger had been a Nazi. Whether his death-centered philosophy and his Nazi politics were related is a controversial question, but Arendt thought they were. Without naming him, she replied to him in *The Human Condition*: "Since action is the political activity par excellence, natality, not mortality, must be the central category of political, as distinguished from metaphysical thought."[63]

This was the response of a little-"d" democrat, someone who believed that we should create the world freely but together. ("Action," in her lexicon, meant talking with peers and acting in common.) Her democratic commitment arose from the fact that human beings are constantly being born, thus renewing the world and making its future basically unpredictable and up to us. Racism, to name just one example, is not written in nature but is produced by people, and the new people who arrive on earth every few seconds do not have to reproduce it. We are free to remake the world in a way that would be impossible if our earthly lives were immortal. Our finitude is a blessing if we consider it as an opportunity for births.

History is the story of the tens of billions of people who have lived so far. Many were killed by other people, and many died well before their natural life spans because of human-created social injustices. History, from one perspective, is a vast slaughterhouse. But all those people were also born: they came into the world as infants whose possibilities were radically open. From that perspective, history is a vast nursery.

Newborns compel our love. There are physical, biological causes of that response, the same with us as with all warm-blooded animals. But an appropriate interpretation of our human love for infants is our knowledge that each new baby represents the possibility of a better world. This is its meaning, in our terms. Arendt elaborates:

> The miracle that saves the world, the realm of human affairs, from its normal "natural" ruin is ultimately the fact of natality, in which the faculty of action is ontologically rooted. It is, in other words, the birth of new men and the new beginning, the action they are capable of by virtue of being born. Only the full experience of this capacity can bestow upon human affairs faith and hope, those two essential characteristics of human existence which Greek antiquity ignored altogether, discounting the keeping of faith as a very uncommon and not too important virtue and counting hope among the evils of illusion in Pandora's box. It is this faith in and hope for the world that found perhaps its most glorious and most succinct expression in the few words with which the Gospels announced their glad tidings: "A child has been born unto us."[64]

For Arendt, our highest calling is to love the world. To love the world is to remake it in each generation with our contemporaries. We count on the newly born to replenish our efforts, and we owe them the virtues of hope and loyalty. We must welcome each new generation to common action, which is "politics."

Whether or not we accept Hannah Arendt's whole philosophy of politics rooted in natality, I think we must treat our fellow human beings in a developmental way. A developmental ethic is fundamental to many of the concrete, practical projects I describe in this book, from civic education to community-based economic development.

A theory of development expects constant change, as opposed to any stance that assumes stability, ignores the dimension of time, or overlooks the potential for bad things to improve. Development is not random change, but it also is not fully predetermined and predictable. When something develops, we can say that changes occur *because* the object is moving toward some kind of objective or end, whereas ordinary physical objects change only as a consequence of what is done to them. In the case of a biological organism, we are able to talk about development and change *toward* objectives or ends because the physical structure of the object includes guidelines for its own growth and transformation (mostly encoded in its genome). In contrast, we would not say that a mountain develops, even though it changes, because there is no design encoded in it that makes it change in a particular direction.

Human beings' development is more complex, because we are able to reflect on our own trajectories and strive to change them. Not every influence is random or encoded in our genes. On the other hand, we are never fully free, because our developmental course up until the present influences our efforts to change. Thus development can involve intentions and self-consciousness, but it is not simply a matter of choice.

Nor do human beings pass through automatic "stages." Personal decisions and external events and opportunities disrupt the standard progression and can produce wide variation.[65] Nevertheless, some sequences of development are encoded genetically, or are deeply embedded in our cultural traditions, or flow logically. For example, there are important reasons that individuals typically babble before they talk, learn to read before they become sexually active, attend school before they vote, fill the roles of children before they are parents, and hold jobs before they retire. Some of these sequences are biologically necessary; others are wise conventions; and some might be mistakes. To think developmentally is to pay attention to the typical (and atypical) sequences and the timing of opportunities and experiences. The usual course of human development is open to critique but it cannot simply be ignored.

Human beings are distinctive because we can have ordinary desires plus desires concerning our desires. For example, I may want to put down a difficult scholarly book that I am reading so that I can watch a trivial television show, and at the same time want *not* to have that desire. Such "second-order volitions," as the late philosopher Harry Frankfurt named them, are important for several reasons.[66] A form of freedom only comes into play when we have second-order volitions. I may be free to read academic books or to watch TV (in other words, to *do* what I want), but I do not have freedom of the will unless I am also free to want what I want to want. In turn, my freedom of the will makes me morally responsible. We say that an addict who wants to quit and fails is more responsible than an addict who doesn't even care whether he is addicted. Meanwhile, freedom of the will permits certain satisfactions that cannot come from ordinary action.[67] That is because it is possible to change our basic desires in line with our second-order volitions, which is a deeply satisfying achievement. If I turn myself into someone who enjoys scholarly books more and trivial TV shows less, I am not only entitled to believe that I have done the right thing with my time, but that I have also improved myself. In that way, the self (personal identity) is connected to second-order volitions.

I introduce this concept here because we are capable of assessing and altering our own second-order volitions in ways that produce conscious development, not just random change. In the words of the Port Huron Statement that inaugurated the New Left in America, we "have unrealized potential for self-cultivation, self-direction, self-understanding, and creativity." The Statement proceeds to note that this process of self-cultivation is not individualistic, on the model of a Romantic artist developing his or her own genius. "This kind of independence does not mean egoistic individualism—the object is not to have one's way so much as it is to have a way that is one's own.... Human interdependence is contemporary fact."[68]

Indeed, most of the effective techniques for improving our second-order volitions are relational and collaborative. Religious congregations, study circles and other deliberative forums, internally democratic associations, and participatory social movements convene people to decide on what they should want and then to hold one another accountable for changing their identities by changing what they want. In the Book of Proverbs, it is written, "Be not thou envious against evil men, neither desire to be with them.... Eat thou not the bread of him that hath an evil eye, neither desire thou his dainty meats" (Prov. 24:1–3; 23:5–7). I would not claim that these verses are especially famous or influential, but they are representative of an important kind of discourse—one that asks us to change our desires as well as our actions.

Meanwhile, as a whole country, we have both desires and second-order volitions. We want to drive our big SUVs to work, and we want to be the kind of country that does not want to do that. Whereas individual consumer choices elicit our ordinary desires, civic acts such as making arguments in public and voting make us think about our second-order volitions. A good law is not a reflection of what we want but of what we think we should want.[69]

Like individuals, communities and institutions have developmental trajectories that are shaped by their initial designs, constrained by logic, affected by random events, and yet susceptible to deliberate alteration by the group itself. Sun Belt boom towns are at a different stage of development from Rust Belt inner cities. The government of the United States has developed rapidly since the ratification of the Constitution and cannot now reverse course. To think developmentally about a community is to take its past seriously, and not imagine that it can simply start over from scratch, but recognize the potential for deliberate change.

An ethic of development, then, is a particular way of making judgments and intervening in the world. It does not presume that every person, community, or institution has equal merit and virtue: some are better than others once they develop past their infancies. But if we think developmentally, we are alert to the ways that the past has shaped each one's present, the limits of choice, and the potential for any person or community to change, for better or worse, in and through relationships with others.

For example, some college professors are offended that their students are relatively superficial and undisciplined thinkers. That perspective fails to view students as individuals in development; their thinking will change rapidly. On the other hand, if you are a college teacher who simply tolerates and expects your students to think immaturely, you are not contributing to their development. You fail to exhibit hope in their potential and loyalty to them as fellow citizens. If you try to *make* them think better, you ignore the inevitable responsibility of human beings for their own development. But if you leave them to do and think whatever they want, you forget that healthy development requires guidance and support. If you treat a 12-year-old just like your college students, you are unreasonable. But if you try to shepherd a fellow adult intellectually, as you would your own students, you misunderstand your limited rights and responsibilities for other people's development. In short, thinking developmentally is not easy—it raises a host of empirical, strategic, and ethical questions—but it is indispensable in politics based on human relationships.

Youth Build USA can serve as a model of the core values illustrated in this chapter. It enlists young people who have dropped out of high school, assigns them public work (building houses for the homeless), engages them in conversation about strategy and policy, invests deeply in their individual development, and emphasizes loyal relationships among the participants and between participants and staff. As one graduate told us in an evaluation interview, "All the staff—it wasn't just one person—but they would sit down and have a one-on-one conversation with you throughout the year. It wouldn't be just a classroom, you know. If they saw you outside, they would just stop and ask you how it's going. It wasn't just asking the question, and not really caring. They actually listen, they actually respond."

4

Values

THE LIMITS OF EXPERTISE, IDEOLOGY, AND MARKETS

TO PARAPHRASE BOTH Emerson and Dewey, we lie in the lap of an immense collective human intelligence that we can tap through collaboration, deliberation, and civic or public relationships. But that doctrine (the thesis of chapter 3) requires a defense against several significant criticisms. If you believe that technical expertise generally reveals the best policies, that one particular ideology is correct, that markets are the best means of organizing human interactions, or that civic engagement is impossible under conditions of economic inequality, then you cannot endorse the core propositions I have defended so far. Thus, in chapter 4, I summarize these critical views and respond to them in turn. Along the way, I develop the positive position in more detail and draw out more of its implications.

Technical Expertise

We need expertise to make wise public decisions. You wouldn't ask any citizen to operate on your heart; you would find the best-trained and most experienced cardiologist. In the same way, if you want to fix public schools or the justice system, you need professional educators, economists, psychologists, criminologists, and other experts to advise and perhaps decide.

Everyone finds some merit in this argument, but it is widely exaggerated to the detriment of public engagement. For example, Donna Shalala was the president of the University of Wisconsin in the 1980s and went on to eight years as secretary of Health and Human Services under Bill Clinton. She epitomized the policy expert who attains public influence. In a major speech that she gave in 1989, she began by citing scientific discoveries that had "improved human life, prolonged human life, enriched and protected human life. The great plagues are basically behind us," she said, thanks to "scientific research done under the sheltering arms of research universities." She went on to defend an "idea of a disinterested technocratic elite" that had arrived in America before 1900 and shaped both the modern research university and government:

> It persisted because everyone—farmers and professors and business owners and politicians and homemakers and workers—basically agreed on some important ideas: That those *without* wealth and power must be protected. That government must be open. That there must be some social control over those with huge economic strength. And that the government ought to be used as a tool to achieve social equity—to level the playing field for everyone. All acknowledged that the university's experts could help secure those goals. And the rightness of those goals was held to be a notion that transcended politics.

Shalala ended her speech with a call for the university's experts to take on the pressing challenges of the late twentieth century, especially persistent poverty and educational failure, with "grand strategies" grounded in apolitical social science.[1] Four years later, she was running a huge federal agency responsible for health care. The administration she served devised a complex health reform bill, presented to voters as the work of a "disinterested technocratic elite." It was defeated (although not necessarily because it was too technocratic), and the major trends in public health remained basically unaffected.

When Donna Shalala was a young scholar in the 1970s, the "moon-ghetto" metaphor was popular. This was the idea that engineers and other specialists had put human beings on the moon (and brought them safely home), so it should be possible to tackle the problems of the so-called ghetto in much the same way. It was all a matter of scientifically diagnosing the causes of poverty and efficiently deploying solutions.

Actually, the moon and the ghetto are very different. The moon is almost perfectly detached from all other human issues and contexts, because it is 240,000 miles away from our planet (although NASA's launch facilities in Florida and Houston might have some local impact). The goal of the Apollo program—whether you endorsed it or not—was clear and easily defined. The challenges were physical; thus Newtonian physics allowed engineers to predict the impact of their tools precisely in advance. The costs were also calculable—in fact, the Apollo program was completed under budget. The astronauts and other participants were highly motivated volunteers, who had signed up for a fully developed concept that they understood in advance. The president and other national leaders had committed enough funds to make the Apollo program a success, because its value to them exceeded the costs.

In contrast, a low-income urban neighborhood is enmeshed with other communities. Its challenges are multidimensional. Its strengths and weaknesses are open to debate. Defining success is a matter of values; even how to measure the basic facts is controversial. (For example, how should "race" be defined in a survey? What are the borders of a neighborhood?) Everyone involved—from the smallest child on the block to the most powerful official downtown—has distinct interests and motivations. Outsiders may not care enough to provide adequate funds, and residents may prefer to leave than to make their area better. When social scientists and policymakers implement rewards or punishments to affect people's behavior, the targets tend to realize what is happening and develop strategies to resist, subvert, or profit from the policies—a response that machines can never offer. No wonder we could put a man on the moon, but our poor urban neighborhoods persist.

Thanks to personal computers, spreadsheets, and the World Wide Web, the resources and skills necessary to analyze social data have fallen by orders of magnitude since Donna Shalala was first trained in social science. Now anyone with a computer and basic knowledge of statistics can copy columns of numbers from official websites and look for correlations or more complex statistical relationships. Yet, if anything, we feel less confident about our ability to diagnose and cure social problems than we did in 1970. Shalala's "grand strategies" have receded from view.[2]

Although I acknowledge the value of expertise, we can identify several important general reasons why it is never enough, and we always need citizens' participation to tackle social problems.

First, professions cannot be trusted to make decisions for the public, even when their tools and techniques are appropriate and effective. Professionals are human, and if people outside their group turn to them for guidance but do not closely scrutinize their work, they are sure to become lazy, biased, careless, or even corrupt. In 1913, George Bernard Shaw wrote about the reluctance of doctors to testify against one another in malpractice suits. "The effect of this state of things is to make the medical profession a conspiracy to hide its own shortcomings. No doubt the same may be said of all professions. They are all conspiracies against the laity."[3] Unless professionals are forced to justify their methods, assumptions, and conclusions in frequent, detailed, open discussions with laypeople, corruption is inevitable.

Second, social issues involve inescapable questions of value. It is not enough to know that A causes B. An engineer, an economist, or a biochemist might tell us that with some reliability. But we must also know whether B is desirable, whether A is an ethically acceptable means to B, and whether the cost is worthwhile. For example, you can often cause a low-income neighborhood to vanish by building a mass-transit station that links it to the downtown business core. Rents will rise around the station and poor people will move out. Crime will fall and investment will follow. Whether those changes count as success depends on your values, not on the data alone.

Third, experts are trained to think in terms of categories: to classify situations and then to recommend the rules, methods, solutions, or "best practices" that apply to each classification. There is value to thinking in categories, and experts do it better within their own fields than other people do. However, there are also serious limitations to categorical thinking, and laypeople often see a *particular* situation better than experts do.[4]

Told a story about specific people interacting in a particular context, any professional will look for abstractions. For instance, in medical school, one learns the signs and definitions of diseases, and when a disease is present, a physician knows which treatments to offer. When more than one condition is involved, or when the diagnosis is uncertain, the decision becomes complex, and good physicians fully understand the roles of judgment and luck. Doctors could never be replaced by machines that simply took in data and spat out treatment plans. But diseases and other general health conditions remain central to physicians' analysis. They look for the necessary and sufficient conditions that define conditions, and then apply general causal theories that say *this* medicine reduces *that* illness.

Lawyers, meanwhile, try to apply general rules from statutes, constitutions, and court rulings. Their advice may be controversial or uncertain if no single, definitive legal rule covers the situation—and they understand that—but their professional thinking involves rules. For engineers, economists, psychologists, and virtually all other professionals, the important abstractions may be different, but the basic habits of mind are alike. Professionals have achieved monumental advances (and prestige) by discovering generalizations that apply widely. For example, the polio vaccine reliably prevents polio, and that is extremely valuable to know. Members of each profession are trained and socialized to focus on one aspect of all cases and are oriented toward one set of social outcomes: health for physicians, legality for lawyers.[5]

You can also hear ordinary people generalize if you listen in public spaces. They say things like, "Of course Amtrak is always late, it's a government monopoly." Or, "You're getting a cold, you should take vitamin C." Research and data disprove these assertions, and a trained professional would not make them. Even an economist who was hostile to monopolies would not draw a direct line from Amtrak's monopoly status to the tardiness of its trains. (Other countries have monopolistic railroads that run on time.) Instead of being too quick and bold with generalizations, a good professional is fully aware of complexities and nuances.

Even so, there is a deeper alternative to using general concepts as the main units of analysis. Instead, a person, a situation, an institution, or a community can be apprehended as a whole object. We can assess it, judge it, and form opinions about how the situation should change. Evaluating a whole situation need not be any harder or less reliable than analyzing general categories abstracted from such situations. If we can say something valid and useful about a generality (like diabetes, tax incentives, or free speech), we can talk just as sensibly about *this* patient, *this* school, or *this* conversation. The particular object or situation is not just an aggregate of definable components. It has distinctive features as a whole, and we human beings are just as good at understanding those as we are at generalizing abstractly.

The form that our understanding takes is often narrative: we tell stories about particular people or institutions, and we project those stories into the future as predictions. We may find generic issues and categories embedded within a story: King Lear, for example, was a king and a father, and there are general truths to be said about both categories. But the story of *King Lear* is much more than an aggregate of such categories, which are not especially useful for understanding the play.[6]

Nonprofessionals are often better at the assessment of whole objects than experts are. That is because ordinary members, clients, or neighbors of a school, a park, a clinic, a district, or a firm know its whole story better than an outsider who arrives to apply general rules.

Often, professionals have in the back of their mind an empirical finding that is valid in academic terms, but that should not tell us what to do. Even when results are statistically significant, effect sizes in the social sciences are usually small, meaning that only a small proportion of what we are interested in explaining is actually explained by the research.[7] Statistical studies shed some light on why individuals differ but can tell us nothing about why they are all alike. In research based on surveys or field observations, the sample may not resemble the population or situation that we face in our own communities. Much experimental research is conducted with volunteers (often current undergraduate psychology majors) in artificial settings. Even if a particular finding is strong, and the sample does resemble the population that concerns us, there is always a great deal of variation, and any particular case may differ from the mean. Measures are always problematic and imperfect, and some important factors are virtually impossible to measure. Unmeasured factors may be responsible for the relationships we think we see among the things we measure.

All this is well known and may be thoughtfully presented in the limitations section of a published paper. When carefully and cautiously read, such a paper can be very helpful. But the professional's temptation is to focus on a statistically significant, published result even if its practical import and relevance are low. Besides, it is rarely the author of a paper who tries to influence a practical discussion. Often professionals have not even *read* the original paper that influences them. They rely instead on their graduate training or abstracts and second-hand summaries of more recent research. The limitations of the original studies tend to be forgotten.

Of course, people with professional credentials can be excellent observers and assessors of whole objects like schools, neighborhoods, or firms. In some affluent communities, practically everyone holds an advanced degree and is therefore a professional. But their judgments of whole objects and situations are best when they think as experienced laypeople, not as specialists. They should draw on professional expertise but only as one source of insight (and should not rely on only one profession).

Arguments about the proper role of generalization take place within professions, not just between professionals and laypeople. Physicians, for example, are being pressed to adopt "evidence based medicine," which deprecates doctors' intuitions and personal experiences in favor of general scientific findings, especially those supported by randomized experiments. Some medical doctors are pushing back, arguing that experimental findings rarely yield reliable guidance for complex, particular cases. What matters is the whole story of the particular patient.

The same argument plays out in education. The No Child Left Behind Act favors forms of instruction proven in "scientifically based research," and the gold standard is a randomized experiment. (Second-best is a statistical model, which can be understood as an estimate of what would be found in a randomized experiment.) Like physicians, some educators resist this pressure, on the ground that an experienced teacher can and should make decisions about individual students and classrooms that are heavily influenced by context and only marginally guided by scientific findings.

This debate will never be fully resolved, but there is a logic to the idea that if we are going to train people in expensive graduate schools and rely on their guidance to shape general policies, they should be the bearers of scientifically based research. In other words, the most optimistic claims about the value of expertise rely on a notion of the expert as an abstract and general thinker. When professionals are seen instead as experienced and wise craftspeople, no one exaggerates their role in public life. The physician who is a seasoned healer is left to treat his or her patients; it is the medical researcher with general findings who is invited to influence policy.

In this section, I have argued that professional expertise has serious limits and should not be allowed to eclipse broad public engagement. Albert Dzur reaches a similar conclusion, but he argues that *"deprofessionalization* is a mistake."[8] Society needs expert knowledge. Professionals who address difficult public issues often feel beleaguered rather than dominant. We will not get the maximum benefit from professionals if we seek to limit or curtail their power or teach them to be more humble and reserved. A better strategy is to recognize the value of genuine collaborations that involve experts.

Traditionally, the justice system was an example: jurors brought human empathy, concern for individuals, fresh eyes, and local knowledge into the courtroom, but lawyers and judges contributed general rules and principles and experience from prior cases. That balance has been lost with the decay of the jury, but other professional fields, such as medical ethics, environmental stewardship, city and county management, and community-based research, are developing elaborate methods and principles for engaging citizens.[9] Because those methods require training and experience, they are appropriately understood as "professional" attainments. Collaborating with citizens can benefit professionals at least as much as it helps the laypeople. For example, lawyers involved in the mainstream criminal justice system risk burnout when their jobs become defined as processing huge numbers of seemingly identical cases, but lawyers who work in problem-solving courts report much more satisfaction as they work with laypeople to address underlying social problems.[10] Harry Boyte argues that "public professional work frees the powers not only of ordinary citizens but of professionals as well."[11]

Ideology

One kind of generalization is an expert's. A credentialed professional applies general research findings (or legal rules) to a particular situation and generates a recommendation. Another kind of generalization comes from ideology. In fact, I would define an "ideology" as a collection of generalizations that its proponents use to make judgments and decisions. In the network terminology introduced in chapter 3, an ideological thinker is one who directly connects many of his or her beliefs to a small number of very general premises, thus producing a centralized mental network. Marxists who see everything in terms of class struggles over the means of production, philosophical libertarians who decide almost all cases based on the principle of liberty as noninterference, and politically engaged religious fundamentalists of many faiths are examples of ideological thinkers. They stand at one end of a spectrum. At the other end are people who try to decide each case on its own merits and are not upset to find that their various judgments are rather miscellaneous.

Experts' generalizations are supposed to be different from ideological premises. Social scientists claim neutrality and openness to the facts as they happen to be, whereas ideologues are openly committed to values and are often accused of ignoring empirical evidence that complicates their views. Yet the apparent gap between expert and ideological thinking looks narrower once you realize that almost all empirical research rests (and *should* rest) on value judgments. Empirical research programs in the social sciences always have core commitments about what is important to study and what outcomes we should welcome. Meanwhile, ideologies are built on empirical evidence, albeit selectively presented. What ideology and expertise have in common is generalization.

To be sure, we must generalize, or else we would be confronted constantly with situations that required completely new thinking. And we *do* generalize, whether we admit it or not. Judges, politicians, administrators, and lay citizens who claim that they are immune to ideology—that they just call each situation on its merits—are almost always mistaken or lying about their own thinking. An example (although I do not know whether it illustrates a mistake or a lie) was John Roberts's claim during his confirmation hearings for the Supreme Court that his judging would be like an umpire's calling balls and strikes. "Umpires don't make the rules; they apply them," he said.[12] As a justice, he has participated in making dramatic new laws to advance his own social goals. Moral principles, causal theories, and archetypal stories are always in the back of his mind, and anyone's. But there remains a great deal of variation in the degree to which our various conclusions and judgments follow from foundational premises. Some people make a wide range of decisions automatically on the basis of a few general assumptions—I call them ideologues—and others are much more flexible and pragmatic. It is worth considering the relative advantages of each style before recommending an approach for citizens to use.

An ideology is helpful for people who are marginalized and disadvantaged. Making a decision from scratch about each policy and situation is hard for anyone, but it is somewhat more manageable if you are paid to think about public issues, if you have plenty of leisure time, if your education has prepared you to reflect politically, if you have a great deal of confidence in your ability to think independently, and if you have been recruited into conversations and networks with other people who fit all those criteria. Those advantages typically accompany wealth, status, and education. In the Supreme Court's chambers or at the faculty club over lunch, discussants have the time, the motivations, and the skills to deliberate about issues without strong preconceptions. Harried working-class parents have no such advantages. For them, an ideology is a valuable shortcut that enables them to cast a vote or make a consumer decision without having to deliberate endlessly. We know from survey data that people who have ideological (or partisan) commitments vote at higher rates than other people, which suggests that ideology is a resource that can compensate for a lack of time and education.[13]

If we force people to make decisions about individual candidates or policies instead of choosing among ideologies, the cognitive demands will rise and the rate of participation will fall. Indeed, during the Progressive Era (1900–14), reformers tried to deemphasize ideology and partisanship by creating ideologically neutral newspapers, allowing the people to vote on separate candidates and referendum questions instead of choosing between the major parties, and promoting open deliberation. Voter turnout plummeted from 73 percent in 1900 to 49 percent in 1920, and the active electorate narrowed to a more educated and wealthier slice of the population.[14]

To be sure, poor and working-class people have built organizations and forums in which they can deliberate at length about social issues, without taking the shortcut of quickly applying an ideology. Sara Evans and Harry Boyte named these venues "free spaces"; they have included Grange Halls, union meetings, working people's reading circles, churches during the civil rights movement, and consciousness-raising discussions during the women's movement, among many others.[15] But those free spaces have waxed and waned over the decades—shrinking, in general, since 1960—whereas ideology always confers advantage.

Looking back on his days as a persecuted dissident, Czech president Vaclav Havel recalled, "The dissident movement was not typically ideological." His recollection may be incorrect and even self-serving: from an outsider's perspective, the anticommunist dissidents did have common beliefs and goals that constituted a kind of ideology. But Havel was onto something when he expressed nostalgia for those ostensibly nonideological days, when a type of politics prevailed that "cannot be enshrined in or guaranteed by any law, decree, or declaration. It cannot be hoped that any single, specific political act might bring it about and achieve it. Only the aim of an ideology can be achieved." He added that the best form of politics has a goal that "is never completely attainable because this politics is nothing more than a permanent challenge, a never-ending effort that can only in the best possible case leave behind it a certain trace of goodness."[16]

Havel, by his own admission, failed to bring the dissidents' open-ended, deeply ethical politics into the world of power when he became head of a state that split into two independent nations just days after this speech. One could even say that the dissidents were free from ideology *because* they lacked power and therefore the responsibility to choose and govern. It was only because they lacked the rights of citizens, one might argue, that they were able to avoid politics as a "technological competition for power, limited to that which can be practically achieved and seeking primarily to satisfy this or that particular interest."[17] Once they had votes and free speech, not to mention the control of ministries and states, they naturally began to try to achieve or prevent various outcomes and to support or block various interests. They inevitably split into right and left, Czech and Slovak, and began to compete for power.

In our vast country, power is distributed across layers and branches of government and split between the public and private sector. All intentional change is hard. Therefore, ideological and manipulative politics generally works best. We cannot gather everyone together and ask, "What should we do?" "Everyone" means more than 200 million busy adults. If you hope to make a difference, you must seek efficient strategies for getting what you have decided in advance that you want. These strategies may have to include simplified and compelling messages that can cut through the clutter and command attention.

But even though ideological thinking increases citizens' engagement and helps them to change the world, it also has serious drawbacks. Applying a few rules or principles to a wide range of cases can distort and mislead. An empirical research finding comes originally with various caveats and limitations, but ideological premises tend to be categorical. "The history of *all* hitherto existing society is the history of class struggle," wrote Marx and Engels in the *Community Manifesto*. From the opposite end of the spectrum, today's Libertarian Party holds, "A free and competitive market allocates resources in the most efficient manner . . . *All* efforts by government to redistribute wealth, or to control or manage trade, are improper in a free society." I have italicized "all" in both statements because the logic of universals is fundamental to ideological thinking.[18] But I would submit that both statements are wrong, just because they ignore many exceptions.

Being strongly committed to an ideology leads to a kind of manipulative engagement with others. If you know the right answer in advance, you have incentives to select favorable evidence, simplify proposals, exaggerate arguments, ignore complications, and choose examples or controversies that allow your side to win while ducking issues that are more problematic for you. Ideological thought is good for talking but much worse for listening and learning.

The past few pages have identified a dilemma. Ideological thinking distorts and manipulates, but avoiding it spells political defeat, especially for poor people and those who lack robust political organizations. I think the solution is to differentiate between two varieties of ideology, one helpful and the other dangerous.

The dangerous kind of ideology is highly intellectual. It proceeds from a few ideas—the fewer the better, for the sake of elegance. Its foundational principles are mutually consistent; contradictions would be embarrassing. Adherents of such ideologies make concrete, practical judgments by applying principles. Classical libertarians and Marxists are excellent examples, but sometimes utilitarians, nationalists, and religious fundamentalists also fit the bill. Such ideologies are quaintly irrelevant when they operate in democratic societies whose citizens are unmoved by their arguments. They are deadly when they seize control, because then people, organizations, and institutions that are inconsistent with their ideas are at grave risk.

A healthy, helpful kind of ideology emerges in a different way. Diverse people struggle with related social problems that involve tradeoffs and conflicting values. They experiment with concrete solutions—specific programs, organizations, institutions, or curricula. Their lives of struggle become compelling stories, enriched by their efforts to balance conflicting goals and values. Their disparate contributions are embraced by one or more political parties—or by other major political forces, such as coalitions within civil society. Laws are passed that expand the scale of their original experiments and codify some of their principles. The ideology now consists of programmatic examples, heroes (both living and dead), organizations and their members, diagnoses and explanations, ethical principles, legislative victories, reform proposals, and related cultural expressions, such as novels and music. The whole ideology has a name and some coherence, yet it embraces tensions.

For example, American liberalism was ascendant in the mid-twentieth century, from the election of Franklin Roosevelt until the end of the Lyndon Johnson administration. In that period, it had everything that an ideology should: millions of active adherents, heroes and leaders, supportive organizations (from the AFL-CIO to the ACLU), legislative victories and an unfinished legislative agenda, empirical theories and supportive evidence, and moral principles. The principles could be summarized as the famous Four Freedoms that President Roosevelt announced in 1941 (freedom of speech and expression, freedom of religion, freedom from want, and freedom from fear), but we could spell them out a bit more as follows. The individual liberties in the Bill of Rights trump social goods, but it is the responsibility of the national government to promote social goods once private freedoms have been secured. The chief social goods include minimal levels of welfare for all (the safety net, or freedom from want); equality of opportunity (achieved through public education, civil rights legislation, and pro-competitive regulation in the marketplace); and consistent prosperity, promoted by Keynesian economic policies during recessions.

These ideas had empirical support from sociology and economics and could be developed into a whole philosophy. Franklin Roosevelt constructed a temple to Thomas Jefferson because he wanted to show liberalism's debts to that enlightenment philosopher; the interior of the Jefferson Monument is bedecked with quotes favorable to the New Deal. Other parts of the liberal synthesis can be traced back to Jefferson's less popular contemporary, Alexander Hamilton. John Maynard Keynes, Louis Brandeis, Gifford Pinchot, and Felix Frankfurter were more proximate intellectual sources. We could understand the New Deal as a development of Victorian liberalism that added arguments in favor of federal activism to combat monopoly, environmental catastrophe, and the business cycle.

But I would tell the story an entirely different way: as the scaling up of concrete examples and experiments that were undertaken originally in a highly pragmatic vein. Think, for example, of Jane Addams in 1889. She is a rich and well-educated person who has no possibility of a career (because she is a woman) and who is deeply troubled by poverty in industrial cities. She is impressed by the concrete example of Toynbee Hall, a settlement house in London. She and Ellen Gates Starr move into a house in a poor district of Chicago without a very clear plan for what to do. They launch projects and events, many of which have a deliberative flavor—residents come together to read challenging books, discuss, and debate. They work in a pragmatic intellectual milieu that encourages people to set assumptions aside. For example, their frequent visitor John Dewey wrote:

There is no more an inherent sanctity in a church, trade-union, business corporation, or family institution than there is in the state. Their value is . . . to be measured by their consequences. The consequences vary with concrete conditions; hence at one time and place a large measure of state activity may be indicated and at another time a policy of quiescence and *laissez-faire* . . . There is no antecedent universal proposition which can be laid down because of which the functions of a state should be limited or should be expanded. Their scope is something to be critically and experimentally determined . . . The person who holds the doctrine of "individualism" or "collectivism" has his program determined for him in advance. It is not with him a matter of finding out the particular thing which needs to be done and the best way, under the circumstances, of doing it.[19]

Out of the pragmatic, problem-solving discussions in Hull-House come a kindergarten, a museum, a public kitchen, a bathhouse, a library, numerous adult education courses, and reform initiatives related to politics and unions. Some 2,000 people come to Hull-House every day at its peak, to talk, work, advocate, and receive services.

In the 1920s, when progressive state governments, like New York, start building more ambitious social and educational services, they fund settlement houses and launch other institutions (schools, state colleges, clinics, public housing projects, welfare agencies) modeled on Hull-House and its sister settlements. Then, when Roosevelt becomes president and decides to stimulate the economy with federal spending, he creates programs like the Works Progress Administration (WPA) that are essentially Hull-House writ large.

I do not think the result was especially coherent, intellectually. Liberalism in its golden age incorporated a populist commitment to majority rule along with civil libertarian principles that protected minority rights. It empowered professionals within government agencies and yet often criticized expertise and bureaucracy. It had one foot in "good government" reform movements that were hostile to bosses and parties, and another in big-city urban machines. It inspired people who advocated decentralization, smallness, and local control along with enthusiasts of great national programs. Often those ideas coexisted in the same mind, as when President Lyndon Johnson declared a national war on poverty, asked for huge federal appropriations, and said, "This program asks men and women throughout the country to prepare long-range plans for the attack on poverty in their own communities. These are not plans prepared in Washington and imposed upon hundreds of different situations. They are based on the fact that local citizens best understand their own problems and know best how to deal with those problems."[20] Rather than criticize the Great Society for inconsistency, I would salute its balance. An ideological movement that promises to improve the world and that is built on experience will embrace exceptions, tensions, and even contradictions; it will not be pure. To use the network analogy introduced in chapter 3, a healthy ideology is a complex web of many nodes that does not rely too heavily on a few assumptions. Each adherent holds a unique set of opinions, but they share enough to cooperate.

By emphasizing liberalism's pragmatic, experimental roots, I do not mean to deny its intellectual achievement. Jane Addams, for instance, was an extremely learned and insightful writer. But I suggest that in a healthy ideological movement, intellectual reflection follows practical experimentation, not the reverse. Even John Rawls can be read as a defender of the concrete reforms of 1930–70. *The Theory of Justice* looks like a refined exercise in philosophy, in which you imagine yourself ignorant of your social position and reason your way to a set of principles that would apply to anyone, anywhere. Rawls appears to be discussing justice with eighteenth- and nineteenth-century philosophers who might be his contemporaries. But timeless philosophical arguments are not what make his theory plausible. Rather, Rawls has observed a real government helping people by guaranteeing the First Amendment; taxing citizens to a substantial but not overwhelming extent; and spending the proceeds on education, welfare, and health. He has not observed a government abolish or even reform families with any success. Thus, even though he concedes that families have enormous and unequal effects on children, he concludes in favor of welfare rights but against reforming families.[21] His reasons are thoroughly experiential. He is codifying the New Deal.

One could write a somewhat parallel story about American conservatism in the period from Ronald Reagan's election to Newt Gingrich's "Contract with America." The conservative movement had intellectual forebears, writers like Friedrich von Hayek, Milton Friedman, and William F. Buckley. But its signature policies were not necessarily consistent with any of these authors' ideas (which, in any event, conflicted with one another). That is not a criticism but a respectful acknowledgement that conservatism was a balance of diverse principles, heroes, examples, and cultural expressions—not a simplistic application of ideas.

I argued in chapter 1 that no ideology currently exists that is commensurate to our intertwined and stubborn problems: climate change, terrorism, deindustrialization, crime, the lack of social mobility over generations, the close association between economic security and educational attainment, and rising health care costs. We have available some good policy ideas and supportive arguments and evidence, but those are only *elements* of a worthy ideology. Take, for example, the proposal to expand Medicare to all Americans, thereby enacting a single-payer health care system (one in which the government funds, but does not provide, all medical treatments). There are plausible economic and moral arguments for such a policy. It rests, to a degree, on experience, because Medicare has been fairly successful as a single-payer system for retirees. But it would require citizens to entrust more than 10 percent of their income to the federal government, which would make life-and-death decisions about their health. Contemporary liberalism emphasizes the duty of the government to provide services such as health insurance. At the same time, it stresses the deep corruption of government, its oppression of children in factory-like schools and degradation of welfare recipients, its susceptibility to capture by special interests, its dependence on Congress, which is riddled with lobbyists' money and outrageous procedures. Scratch a liberal who wants to expand the government's role and you will find someone who is deeply angry at government. Liberalism must include—not only proposals for new programs—but also plausible strategies for government reform, powerful and trusted organizations that support these ideas, examples of successful programs, and living leaders and role models. By that standard, contemporary liberalism is (at best) just at the start of a comeback. Conservatism, at the same time, seems almost devoid of positive ideas.

If it is right to understand the main twentieth-century ideologies as expansions of pragmatic experiments, then we should be looking to today's charter schools, innovative clinics and health plans, land trusts and co-ops, and socially minded businesses for the concrete cases that merit expansion. We are less in need of ambitious theories than of what the Brazilian theorist and cabinet member Roberto Mangabeira Unger calls a "culture of democratic experimentalism."[22] The experimentation will have to be decentralized, participatory, and driven by citizens, not just experts. They will be most creative if they can set ideology aside and think anew about problems and solutions.

Experimentalism

In a campaign speech at Oglethorpe University in Atlanta during the depths of the depression (May 22, 1932), presidential candidate Franklin Roosevelt said:

The country needs and, unless I mistake its temper, the country demands bold, persistent experimentation. It is common sense to take a method and try it: If it fails, admit it frankly and try another. But above all, try something. The millions who are in want will not stand by silently forever while the things to satisfy their needs are within easy reach. We need enthusiasm, imagination and the ability to face facts, even unpleasant ones, bravely. We need to correct, by drastic means if necessary, the faults in our economic system from which we now suffer. We need the courage of the young. Yours is not the task of making your way in the world, but the task of remaking the world which you will find before you. May every one of us be granted the courage, the faith and the vision to give the best that is in us to that remaking!

FDR's words apply today—to the letter—because our problems are again very serious, and our understanding of what will fix them is just as tentative and preliminary. Once again, we especially need a new generation to be social innovators. But I would distinguish between two forms of experimentation.

The first is the search for *cures*, replicable programs and strategies that are proven to work. This is a very popular goal today: consider the Department of Education's What Works Clearinghouse website, "a central and trusted source of scientific evidence for what works in education," which describes program models that have been proved effective in randomized controlled experiments or their close equivalents. The master analogy is to bench science, and the hope is to find treatments for social ills that work as reliably as chemicals that kill harmful microbes on contact. A social entrepreneur is someone who invents a new solution, proves that it works, and helps it spread through society, rather like Jonas Salk with the polio vaccine.[23]

The alternative is *tinkering*: setting up programs that embody one's profound ethical commitments and theories of society and then experimenting in order to improve their impact or—if they consistently fail—scrapping them and moving on. (As FDR advised, sometimes you have to "admit [failure] frankly and try another" approach.) On this view, a "social entrepreneur" is a tinkerer who launches or leads some kind of practical experiment that is always subject to revision and improvement.

Experiments are actually rather simple and accessible tools for practitioners to use in program improvement. Imagine, for example, that you are running a program that depends on regular meetings, and you need good turnout. Who shows up seems to depend on when you schedule the meeting, but you aren't sure whether recent changes in the meeting time have helped because there are many other factors in play (the weather, the subject of the meetings, and so on). You can answer the question with a simple experiment. Randomly divide the next ten meetings into two groups: say, evenings and Saturdays. Count the total number of people who attend the two categories. If one is much better than the other, go for that. No fancy math, survey design, or other research skills are required.

If many organizations routinely applied experimental designs, they could become more effective, and that would help society. Randomization is merely a tool; they would also need a general ethic of experimentation and rigorous self-review.

But often randomized experimentation is motivated by a faith in a shorter path. The hope is to identify big cures that can be quickly taken to scale after experiments prove they work. This hope is likely illusory.

A randomized experiment can prove that a social intervention works; its success was not caused by other factors, such as the participants' enthusiasm. But an experiment cannot prove that the same intervention would work in different contexts. To find real cures, one would have to replicate success in many contexts. But experimental results rarely replicate when human beings and communities are involved.

One reason is that the roots of problems lie in human motivations and choices. Often, the chief culprits are not the people directly in view as one experiments, such as the delinquent adolescents who are enrolled in a program. The real fault may lie with policymakers, business leaders, and other people out of view. But in any case, human intelligence and will are involved. So when one intervenes, all the affected parties adjust and seek their own goals, often frustrating the intervention. Microbes don't respond that way. It is true that bugs can evolve to develop resistance, but human change is deliberate and immediate, not evolutionary.

Besides, many of the most important factors that determine human well-being are not programs or interventions that we can possibly offer to people or assign them to. An example of a program would be a community-service opportunity that students can be required to take or else rewarded for choosing. That is worth assessing with a randomized experiment. But consider a community service activity that kids develop completely on their own. That might be more important and valuable than a program, yet there is no point in assigning individuals to such an experience; it is essential that they created it. Or consider a community, like the city of Somerville, Massachusetts, where I am writing this paragraph. There are good things and bad things about Somerville as a context for human development, and we should understand its pros and cons and tinker with its elements. But Somerville was never designed by anyone, nor can people be assigned to live there (without changing it dramatically). Somerville has emerged from three centuries of choices and work by countless powerful and relatively disempowered people. If you try to replicate its positive aspects elsewhere, you will be creating something entirely different.[24]

A tinkering approach to social change is compatible with the ideals of open-ended and particularistic deliberation defended in chapter 3. An example will bring out the connection. The Washington, DC, public school where my daughter used to study and my wife used to teach is a little chaotic, inefficient, and inequitable, but it is also diverse, participatory, and tolerant. It has its successes: academic, ethical, and cultural. In other words, it is a public institution (and a community) that can easily flourish or fail—or do a bit of both at the same time. Many adults devote attention and passion trying to make it flourish, rarely in unison but with overlapping values and goals.

One of the most obvious problems that this particular school faces is the system's bureaucracy, which is often arbitrary and wasteful. Charter schools are permitted to operate independently of downtown and have become very common. So whether to turn our school into a charter was an obvious issue for discussion. As a matter of fact, I didn't notice much talk about charters— partly because many parents were ideologically opposed to them, and partly because a group of parents had actually left the school to launch a charter. (They had opted for exit over voice.) Still, it is easy to imagine a conversation about charters arising within this school.

With that background, consider two ways that a charter debate might unfold within such a community:

1. Strategic politics: Advocates favor charters (in general) for several quite different reasons.[25] Some see them as means to introduce competition into education. Others see them as opportunities for teachers to obtain professional autonomy and dignity. For either group, an individual charter school is an *experiment* designed to test a general principle. That principle can generalize, not only beyond the individual school, but beyond education altogether. For instance, libertarians have seen charters as a way to demonstrate that competition can improve outcomes even for one of the most traditional and accepted functions of government—the school. If charters work, libertarians feel they gain an argument in favor of a different kind of society, which is also why some of their opponents try to block charters. Again, libertarians provide only one example; there are also leftist charter advocates who want to test principles of localism and teacher control.

Unless you are an unethical ideologue, you must care about local issues, such as the impact of any policy on individuals and the proper timing, risk, cost, and inconvenience of a particular change. You should also be open to the possibility that your experiment will fail. Yet, if you are strategic—that is, you believe that society as a whole would be better off if your theory were applied more generally—then you are right to look for opportunities to test it responsibly. From that perspective, a school is a chance to try the theory.

    2. Open-ended politics: Members of our school community might not be interested in charters, pro or con. They might care instead about what is good and bad in their own school and how to improve it. In other words, their unit of analysis might be the building and the people in it, not something as general as charters, let alone competition or professionalism. Each participant in such a debate would have slightly different objectives and different beliefs about what works. But they would share a primary loyalty to the particular institution.

Most people will bring into such particularistic discussions some prior opinions about general concepts, such as bureaucracies, charters, teachers, competition, and liberalism and conservatism. But if their focus is on the school itself, such concepts will arise as just one type of consideration among others. Instead of debating whether charters advance a general cause, they may be concerned about the school principal (who happens to be good at her job), and ask how she would fare if the school became a charter. Or they might worry about the effects of any controversial change on the cohesion of their community. For them, turning the school into a charter competes for attention and credibility against modest, everyday changes, such as tinkering with the fifth-grade curriculum or raising more money at the annual auction. Instead of considering incentives and rules imposed from outside, they look inside the black box of the school and want to improve each classroom, curriculum, test, and rule.

Citizens are entitled to develop, test, and strategically promote general political doctrines. But open-ended politics is a valuable alternative and it is understudied, notwithstanding important scholarship by Harry Boyte, Lewis Friedland, Archon Fung, Jane Mansbridge, Carmen Sirianni, Mark E. Warren and others cited in this book. Incalculably more research is available about formal institutions, interest groups, and ideologies than about particularistic, open-ended, public work. Open-ended politics is also underresourced, because vast quantities of money and skill are devoted to various kinds of strategic politics, but hardly anyone subsidizes or rewards open-ended politics. It is countercultural, because a group of Americans who assemble today to discuss an issue are quick to seize on a general cause and look for messages and data to persuade others. Finally, it is disfavored by modern laws and policies, which often implement general theories. Under these circumstances, we need strategies to enhance deliberative and pragmatic forms of local civic engagement. To say that we need strategies to protect non-strategic politics is not a contradiction. On the contrary, the civic renewal movement has been hampered so far by its failure to develop just such strategies.

Civic Engagement in a Market Economy

The previous sections have considered the tension between civic engagement and two abstract and general forms of thinking: expertise and ideology. Engaged citizens provide an important corrective by offering their experience of particular situations.

A different tension arises between civic engagement and markets. From one direction, libertarian or laissez-faire thinkers argue that civic engagement is incompatible with functioning markets that yield maximum prosperity. An economy cannot grow unless the people who control capital and make investment decisions have broad discretion to put their money where it will produce the best returns. Their ability to choose where to invest (or remove their investments) gives them power over the government and civil society alike. To hamper them greatly would stifle innovation and prosperity.

This is correct, but it is a matter of degree. Putting all investment decisions to majority vote would destroy an economy, but companies and private investors can be circumscribed and guided by popular regulations and social norms. The degree to which we accord business a privileged position is something that a democratic people can debate and negotiate over time. There is no evidence that Americans are prone to underestimate the value of private business or to forget the needs of investors; quite the contrary.

A pragmatic kind of libertarianism says: Market solutions might work better than government programs, and we should try them. For example, we ought to experiment by giving vouchers to parents to buy education from public or private schools, instead of using government money only to finance government-run schools. This experiment will either work or not (under various circumstances), but it is perfectly compatible with popular government. The people can assess the voucher program, disagree about it, and make collective decisions through their political institutions. Thus pragmatic libertarianism and civic engagement are not incompatible.

A voucher system would not, however, bring about true philosophical libertarianism. The government would still collect mandatory taxes to fund education and would still make certain educational experiences mandatory for every child. In fact, voucher systems are standard in some of the Western European countries that we call social democracies.

True philosophical libertarianism says: Government taxation and regulation are affronts to personal liberty. My life is mine, and no one can take goods from me or direct my actions without restricting my freedom.[26] At most, minor restrictions on my liberty are acceptable for truly weighty reasons, but they are always regrettable. Unlike pragmatic libertarianism, true philosophical libertarianism is incompatible with civic engagement and civic renewal, because it demands sharp restrictions on collective decisions, even if they happen to be popular. It presumes that it is wrong to take people's things, and it does not matter whether the taker is a mugger with a knife or a tax official with a valid warrant; it is theft either way.

Because such libertarianism is incompatible with the premises of this book, it deserves a response. Imagine that all levels of government in the United States reduced their role to providing national defense and protecting us against crimes of violence and theft. Gone would be an interventionist foreign policy, criminalization of drugs and prostitution, and—more significantly—publicly funded schools, colleges, medical care, retirement benefits, and environmental protection. As a result, a family like mine could probably keep 95 percent of the money we now have to spend on taxes, paying only for a minimal national defense and some police and courts. We would have perhaps one-third more disposable income, although we would use most of it to purchase schooling for our children, a bigger retirement package, and more health insurance; and we would have to pay the private sector somehow for things like roads and airports.

I have my doubts that we would be better off in sheer economic terms, but that is a matter for debate and personal preference. I am fairly sure that I would not have more *freedom* as a result of this change. And freedom (not economic efficiency or impact) is the core libertarian value, the reason that libertarians want to restrain popular role.

I do not think one-third more discretionary income would make me more free because I know plenty of people who already have that much income, and they don't seem especially liberated. With an extra *billion* dollars, I could do qualitatively different things from what I can do now; but an amount under $100,000 would just mean more stuff. Meanwhile, when I consider the actual limits to my freedom, the main ones seem to fall into two categories. First, I lack the time to do what I want. Not having to pay taxes would give me a bit more time because I could work fewer hours. But my work is a source of satisfaction to me (and is also somewhat competitive with others' work). I would be very unlikely to cut my hours if the opportunity arose nor would doing so feel like an increase in my freedom. The way to get more time is to stop wasting it.

Second, I feel limited by various mental habits: too much concern with material things, too much fear of disease and death, and too much embroilment in trivialities. I hardly think that being refunded all my taxes would help with those problems, especially if I then had to shop for schools, retirement packages, and insurance. That sounds like a perfect snare.

I have been talking about me and my family. Whatever the impact on us of a libertarian utopia, it would be worse for people poorer than us. Unless you take a *very* dim view of the quality of government services such as Medicaid and public schools, you should assume that low-to-moderate income citizens get more from the state than they could afford on the market. They would have reason to worry if they could afford basic services at all, and such insecurity would decrease their freedom as well as their welfare.

Economic Determinism

Libertarians are skeptical of civic engagement because it can be an impediment to market exchange. A criticism from the opposite direction also merits serious consideration. This view holds that civic engagement is desirable, but it remains impossible or specious as long as capitalist markets prevail.

Justice Louis Brandeis is supposed to have said, "We can have democracy in this country, or we can have great wealth concentrated in the hands of a few, but we can't have both." Like the quotation from Margaret Mead about "small groups of committed citizens," this one may be apocryphal.[27] But it is repeated often, and apocrypha can be more illuminating than actual statements by long-dead luminaries. It is reasonable to fear that democratic participation is fruitless and frustrating whenever a small number of people control major employment and production decisions through direct ownership and influence government by literally paying for the decisions they seek (through campaign finance contributions) and implicitly threatening to move their investments if they dislike policies.

In 2007, just before the recent recession, the wealthiest 1 percent of American households held 34.6 percent of the nation's wealth. The assets of that top percentile consisted mainly of investments that gave them power over other people. Almost 90 percent of their assets took the form of non-home real estate (mainly business facilities and rental properties), business equity, stocks, and other securities—in other words, stakes in firms that employed their fellow citizens and made things. In contrast, typical families (those between the 20th and 80th percentiles) had sunk two-thirds of their modest wealth in their own homes and were deeply in debt.[28]

One could conclude that it is naive to expect ordinary (not to mention poor) Americans to participate in the demanding ways I recommend elsewhere in this book. If their participation threatens the economic interests of the rich, one would expect them to fail. It would appear that economic reform must precede political engagement.

A different version of the argument focuses not on the top 1 percent and their control of the "commanding heights" of the economic and political battlefields, but rather on the bottom 20 percent, who ostensibly cannot participate because they have more pressing and immediate needs than civic engagement. According to Abraham Maslow's theory of a "hierarchy of needs," people will not participate in politics until they have sufficient safety, welfare, and love. "When millions lack health insurance, live at or below the poverty level, face racism in their lives, it is no wonder there is disengagement."[29]

The difficulties that this analysis presents are severe. First, it is not clear how we can attain higher levels of economic equality unless lower income people do engage politically, using their votes and other forms of influence to change policies in their own favor. Strategies that rely on some kind of political vanguard to look out for their interests have usually been disastrous, not only in the notorious case of state communism but also in many machine-dominated American cities, where ostensibly progressive leaders who claim to represent the poor have become corrupt.

Even if our political system does enact redistributive legislation, the resulting spending will benefit lower income people only to the degree that it funds programs that genuinely serve their needs. Taxing the rich benefits the poor only if the revenues support programs that work. Programs are most effective and sensitive (and popular) when citizens engage with them, holding agencies accountable and contributing their own talents and energies. Thus, until there is more and better public participation in institutions, it is not clear that governments can promote equality. I would personally favor expanding certain tools of financial redistribution, such as the Earned Income Tax Credit. But such programs do not address inequality that emerges from gaps in literacy, nutrition, mental health, residential segregation, and neighborhood-level violence and crime. To address those causes of inequality, one needs effective programs, and such programs rely on active citizens as well as tax dollars.

Finally, it is difficult to use an open-ended, deliberative style of politics if one is convinced from the start that an essential goal is to reduce the share of wealth controlled by the top 1 percent of Americans. Many citizens do not share that goal. The General Social Survey regularly asks people to place their opinions on a scale between two statements: (1) "the government in Washington ought to reduce the income differences between the rich and the poor, perhaps by raising the taxes of wealthy families or by giving income assistance to the poor," and (2) "the government should not concern itself with reducing this income difference between the rich and the poor." The mean answer is always slightly closer to the latter than the former, and between 10 and 20 percent of the sample consistently place themselves at the antiredistributionist extreme of the spectrum.[30] This is not evidence that Americans are overwhelmingly against modest amounts of additional redistribution. It is evidence that their opinions vary. The issue can be discussed, but to *assume* that more redistribution is needed is no way to invite all kinds of people to participate.

The dilemma that I have introduced here is real, but it can be overstated. The poorest 20 percent of Americans—not to mention the middle 50 percent—have considerable potential power in politics and the marketplace. They do not own very many securities, but they do make important discretionary decisions about where to live and work and which consumer goods to buy. They also have a lot of potential votes. They do not *actually* vote or join political organizations and movements at nearly the same rate as wealthier Americans, but that disparity isn't inevitable.

Consider India, the world's largest democracy, where "scheduled castes" are groups (including the traditional Untouchables or Dalit caste) that are recognized as subject to historic deprivation and discrimination. Although 30 percent of scheduled caste members lived below the Indian poverty rate, in the national elections of 1996, voter turnout among the scheduled castes was 89.2 percent, and turnout among the upper castes was about three points *lower* than theirs.[31] In the same year, the United States held a presidential election in which 58 percent of all adult citizens voted—31 points lower than the scheduled caste members in India. Even Americans who held college degrees (a privileged minority) voted at rates far below the scheduled castes.[32]

Sometimes this kind of comparison is offered to chastise Americans. Why can't we vote like Indians? Indeed, why do Americans choose to vote at lower rates than in all other democracies except (sometimes) Switzerland? Voting may be an ethical obligation, like many other forms of civic and political participation. But personal virtue does not explain enormous differences in participation by social class, by nation, and within the United States over time. (As noted earlier, 73 percent of American men voted in 1900, even though most African American men were still blocked from voting.) Nor can moral exhortation raise the turnout rate or encourage other forms of civic and political participation. Structural factors, such as the competitiveness of elections; the issues that are open to debate; the functioning of parties, interest groups, and the mass media; and the prevailing political culture, affect the rate of participation.

In the next chapter, I analyze the structural reasons for declining engagement in the United States and suggest reforms. In the present context, the point of invoking India is simply this: *economics does not determine political participation*. People who experience absolute deprivation and profound relative disadvantage sometimes vote at rates far above privileged Americans.

Voting is by no means the only form of civic engagement, but similar conclusions can be drawn regarding democratic participation in general. The proportion of people who say they take "local community action on issues like poverty, employment, housing, [and] racial equality" is higher in some poor countries, such as Bangladesh and Tanzania, than it is in rich countries such as Germany, Singapore, and the United States. The correlation between economic development and grassroots political participation is weak but negative at the global level—more participation occurs in poorer nations.[33] In a study of highly demanding and effective forms of grassroots political action, Gaventa and Barrett find successful examples no less common in poor countries, war-torn countries, and dictatorships than in peaceful and developed democracies.[34] In the United States, voting and volunteering are strongly correlated with social class: wealthy people are the most likely to participate. But attending community meetings and working on local problems are different: rates of participation are almost the same for low-income people as for rich people.[35]

Robert Sampson and his colleagues involved in the massive Project on Human Development in Chicago Neighborhoods found that concentrated poverty decreased residents' "collective efficacy": the likelihood that they would take action to stop crimes and other local problems. But collective efficacy was not *tightly* linked to poverty: in some poor Chicago neighborhoods, efficacy was high, and those neighborhoods saw strikingly lower levels of crime and other social problems. What seemed to boost their collective efficacy was the strength of their local nonprofit organizations, which local citizens had built. Chicago neighborhoods that had strong networks of civic leaders saw less homicide, teenage parenthood, and infant mortality, after other factors were controlled. Poverty and race did not determine the strength of their local leadership networks. Based on the Chicago study, and many others around the world, Sampson argues that collective efficacy "transcends poverty and race and in many cases predicts lower violence and enhanced public health."[36]

Overall, we can conclude that economic disadvantage is not an insuperable barrier to participation. In fact, economic need can *spur* engagement and make it more common in poor and even undemocratic contexts than it is in affluent communities. Some of our most impressive and innovative civic movements have originated with our poorest and most oppressed people, starting with slaves in the 1800s.

Experience shows that justice is much more likely when reform begins with changes in the mentality and organization of citizens, not the rules of markets and other institutions. Gaventa, former director of the Highlander Folk School and author of a classic book about the enforced "quiescence" (or lack of engagement) of oppressed people in Appalachia, nevertheless believes that active citizenship should come first. "Civic participation does not need democracy; in fact, the weakest states often have the highest levels of civic participation," he says. "It is in these turbulent communities where grassroots efforts take hold and flourish—it is in weak states where civic participation is most needed." He adds: "There's a tendency to put civic participation last—to say, 'let's get the model and the institutions right, then worry about engaging the people. But that approach is intrinsically flawed—you should start with a citizen-based approach and then build the institutions out of their needs and interests."[37]

Although civic engagement is possible even under conditions of deep economic inequality, that does not mean that we can be complacent about the contexts in which we expect citizens to talk, work, and form relationships. Contemporary American governments, markets, and communities are inequitable and structured in ways that frustrate civic engagement. Havel movingly recalled the open-ended, deliberative, creative, and ethical relationships that had arisen in opposition to communism. But he recognized that the values of the dissident movement would not easily translate into regular politics in modern Europe or North America. In fact, reviving such values in a capitalist society would demand "infinite tenacity, infinite patience, much ingenuity, iron nerves, great dedication, and last but not least, great courage."[38]

Havel meant to inspire, but if any form of politics literally requires *infinite* virtue, we cannot reasonably hope for it. We may even do more harm than good by striving for the unattainable. The goal of this book is to develop practical strategies for expanding and rewarding open-ended politics under difficult circumstances, so that acting in the ways that Havel described would *not* require infinite patience, courage, and dedication. An important step is to understand why civic engagement is relatively rare and marginal in our times.

5

Facts

THE STATE OF AMERICAN DEMOCRACY

IN KEEPING WITH the methodology proposed in chapter 2, I am moving deliberately from values to facts and then to strategies, intending to show how individuals and small groups of Americans can improve their world through deliberate action. As I turn to facts, the first question concerns the condition of our democracy and civil society, which I address in this chapter. In chapter 6, still concentrating broadly on facts, I consider the organizations and practices that are emerging to revive civic engagement in America.

The Collapse of Traditional Civil Society

In the middle of the twentieth century, the United States had a decent civil society, an array of organizations and venues in which people could do the kinds of civic work that I defended in the previous chapter. This civil society supported reasonably high levels of political participation, reasonably healthy political discussion and problem solving, and a satisfactory relationship between the public and their government. It was far from perfect, but it offered clear paths to reform. For example, racial minorities and women faced severe discrimination in civil society and in political discussions (as well as in government and in the private sector), but it was clear what fights they would have to win to make democracy more equal. And they did win many battles.

That whole structure is now shattered. We have building blocks with which to construct a new civil society, and many Americans are doing their best to rebuild. But the collapse of the old order is a serious problem. It weakens democracy and closes the obvious paths to reform. The responses have so far been inadequate.

The old civil society consisted primarily of voluntary associations: religious congregations, labor unions, fraternal societies, civil rights organizations, service clubs, and political party organizations. They held face-to-face

meetings at which members gained and exercised skills of rhetoric, deliberation, and problem solving, along with more concrete and practical skills such
as balancing budgets and taking minutes. At their meetings, participants also
built trust and relationships that would prove useful in their business, personal, and civic lives. Associations had cash, buildings, volunteers, newslet-
ters, and alumni—resources that gave power to their members. They used
some of their resources to recruit young members and to build their skills and
interests. They provided ladders that a young person could climb if he or she
was lucky, popular, and talented—ultimately becoming a priest, a union stew-
ard, a Rotary president, or the party's nominee for public office.

Individuals typically did not join these associations because they were
interested in political discussions, civic engagement, or democracy. You
joined a religious congregation because your family belonged to it or
because you had a personal conversion experience and believed that the religion offered a path to your salvation. You joined a union because you took
a job; the business was unionized; and there were social, emotional, and
political advantages to joining the union rather than paying a representation fee in lieu of union dues. You joined the Knights of Columbus, the
Urban League, or the local Republican club because of some mixture of
support for its principles and desire to socialize with like-minded people.
(Often, a member had recruited you, and the real reason you joined was
to say "yes" to this friend.)

But once you were in, the organization had incentives to engage you in
political and civic affairs. These groups had political agendas and faced
public challenges; they needed their members to vote, to argue in public for
their positions, to raise money, and even to run for office. Because you could
enter without a political or civic motivation but gain such motivations as a
member, associations *made* people interested in politics and public affairs.

Many voluntary associations were internally homogeneous and thus prone
to groupthink, parochial views, and narrow self-interest. Those were genuine
problems, but Theda Skocpol has identified three mitigating factors.[1] First,
associations tended to encompass a fair amount of *class* diversity, something
that has been largely lost since then. Second, many associations formed pyra-
midal structures, with local clubs or chapters, state and regional bodies, and
national headquarters. A Democratic Party club in Brooklyn or in Montana
might be quite homogeneous and parochial, but delegates from both places
had to meet and negotiate at the Democratic National Convention. The same
was true of big religious denominations, fraternal associations, and unions.
The state- and national-level meetings brought diverse people together, but

the grassroots chapters made these organizations authentically democratic and connected their agendas to lived experience.

Third, associations had incentives to venture beyond their own membership into the public sphere, interacting with other associations in ways that produced robust public dialogue and considered public opinion.[2] After all, they would have to persuade or negotiate with other groups or they would not get what they wanted. At first, their most important means for distributing information and opinions were newspapers. Associations needed newspapers to communicate, and sometimes they formed in response to the news. Thus, as Tocqueville had written in the 1830s, "There is a necessary connection between public associations and newspapers: newspapers make associations and associations make newspapers."[3] In fact, we could identify newspapers (and later, broadcast news programs) as another part of the mid-twentieth-century civic infrastructure, along with associations. Some news organizations aspired to be neutral spaces, fair to all organized groups in the society. Others represented particular groups and were proud of it. As long as a community had either neutral news media or a range of partisan outlets, the whole discussion could be healthy.

Often the associations overlapped. For example, if you were born to a family of French Canadian origin in Lewiston, Maine, in the early twentieth century, you were destined for a textile mill, the union, the Democratic Party, and the Catholic Church. You had a *right* to enter these organizations and a perceived *duty* to do so. These institutions might (or might not) serve you well, and you were less likely to benefit if you were female, gay, an atheist, or an economic conservative. But the three overlapping institutions of union, party, and church had motives to recruit you; they were accountable (at least to the majority of their members); and they had an interest in helping some of their new recruits become leaders. They also had enough collective power to make the city government, industrial companies, and the local newspaper highly responsive to their members. In fact, local governments and various public boards and offices often resembled powerful local voluntary associations, such as unions and churches. The parish priest, the newspaper editor, the mayor, and the union local president were peers with similar constituents.

In Lewiston today, the industrial unions are gone, because the factories have shut down. St. Mary's Church, a traditional bastion of French Catholic life, was closed in 2000 and has become the Franco-American Heritage Center. The Lewiston *Sun Journal* is unusual in that it remains an independent company with an ambitious newsroom, yet both the paper and the local Democratic Party have lost constituents and impact compared to 50 years ago.

Lewiston is certainly no civic wasteland. In fact, it won an All-America City award from the National Civic League (NCL) in 2007, an award that recognizes national excellence in civic engagement. In explaining the prize, the NCL cited a Lewiston program that integrates Somali refugees into the local economy and schools; a nonprofit association called Lots to Gardens that uses abandoned industrial sites to produce food for the poor; municipal support for residents who want to claim the federal Earned Income Tax Credit; and a structure for youth leadership in city affairs, called the Lewiston Youth Advisory Council.[4] These are excellent projects, characteristic of civic renewal efforts in our time (see chapter 6 for other examples). But such small, voluntary projects—dependent on volunteers, grants, or support from local elected officials—cannot replace the traditional infrastructure that once recruited *most* residents, provided them with an effective *right* of participation, honed their civic skills, and helped them exercise collective political power.

Lewiston is also the home of Bates College, which offers excellent service learning, community-based research, grants for community associations, and other forms of civic engagement through its Harward Center for Community Partnerships. No such center would have existed 50 years ago. Knowing the Center's staff, I believe they are truly and skillfully committed to "collaboration and dialogue with our community partners."[5] But Bates is a well-endowed private college that enrolls mostly affluent students from out of state. It is not compelled to collaborate with Lewiston's citizens but does so optionally, out of an ethical commitment or a highly enlightened sense of self-interest. The power to *compel* accountability is gone, as are the structures that once recruited and educated working-class citizens for democracy. The most impressive democratic programs in town originate in a selective, private institution. That is not a healthy situation.

Clearly, Lewiston is not the United States. It has lost its industrial base and shrunk, much like Syracuse and Detroit, but not at all like Houston, Atlanta, or Phoenix. In Lewiston, it is plausible to explain the decline of the traditional civic infrastructure in economic terms as a direct result of deindustrialization. That explanation makes little sense in Phoenix.

Yet the trends I have used Lewiston to illustrate are national in scope. Figure 5.1 shows that attendance at community meetings and reading the newspaper fell in lockstep from 1975–2005.[6] Meanwhile, the rate of working together on a community project has also fallen, albeit not as steeply.

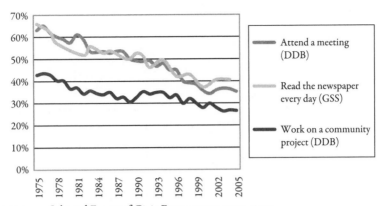

FIGURE 5.1 Selected Forms of Civic Engagement, 1975–2005

Source: General Social Survey (GSS) and DDB Needham Life Style Survey (DDB). Age range of survey population is 18 years and older. Analysis by the author. Data from DDB © 1975–98 by DDB Worldwide.

(Unfortunately, the data used in this graph were not collected after 2005, but somewhat similar Census questions on civic engagement, collected only since 2008, show low rates of participation and no improvement over time.)

This decline occurred before the Internet was widely used for virtual discussions and news. Thus it cannot be the case that people deliberately renounced face-to-face meetings and newspapers because they had online alternatives. But it may be that after the old order had badly decayed, people began to find online substitutes not shown in this graph.

The number of people who belong to at least one group has been relatively steady, compared to the steep decline in meeting attendance.[7] That pattern suggests that groups are no longer playing their traditional roles in civil society. The grassroots, face-to-face associations of Tocquevillian civil society have yielded to various kinds of transactional organizations. Today you may pay an annual fee to a professional association or a lobby, like Common Cause or the National Rifle Association, to become a member, when previously you had to attend meetings and work on projects to be part of groups.

Meanwhile, as shown in Figure 5.2, the rate of membership has diverged by social class. People without any college experience are much less likely to belong to groups and to work on community projects than their fellow citizens who hold college degrees. (I use these two categories as crude proxies for the working class and the middle class, respectively.)

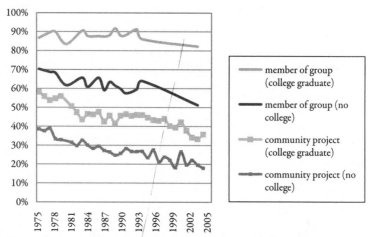

FIGURE 5.2 Group Membership and Meeting Attendance by Educational Status, 1975–2005

Source: General Social Survey. Analysis by the author.

In the case of group membership, the rate is basically flat for people with college degrees, but steeply downward for their non-college-educated peers. (Just over half of the latter group report having any memberships at all: the rest are on their own.) In the case of community projects, the trends are parallel for the most-educated and least-educated groups. But since both have declined in tandem, the proportion of the working class that participates in community projects has now dropped to a critically low level. Whereas poor and working-class neighborhoods once saw a great deal of community work, that is mostly gone today.

Note that these trends did not occur because the population became better educated and the non-college-educated became a shrinking and marginalized minority. On the contrary, rates of college attendance and completion were fairly steady from 1975–2005. Instead, the working class has lost most of their organizations.

A Growing Class Divide

The most evident and serious consequence of these trends is inequality. Working-class people have less political impact than college graduates—and less than the working class had thirty years ago. In poor and moderate-income communities, too few people are organized to address common problems, which worsens concrete outcomes such as crime and poverty. And because civic engagement has psychological and educational benefits for people who participate, the decline in engagement means that working-class Americans are missing opportunities for personal growth and fulfillment.

There is a subtler consequence, too. Civil society is increasingly dominated by people who have received relevant professional training or who officially represent firms and other organizations. In local discussions about schools, for example, a significant proportion of the participants may hold degrees in education, law, or a social science discipline or represent the school system, the teachers' union, or specific companies and interest groups. Such people can contribute valuable sophistication and expertise. But if the arguments of chapters 3 and 4 are correct, we should not be satisfied with public discourse that is merely technical or that reflects negotiations among professional representatives of interest groups. We should want broad deliberations, rooted in everyday experience, drawing on personal values and concrete hopes for the future as well as facts and interests, and resistant to the generalizations of both professionals and ideologues.

Technically trained professionals already intervened powerfully in public policy and institutions a century ago. The ratio of professionals in the United States doubled between 1870 and 1890, as society became more complex and urbanized and scientific methods proved their value. More than 200 different learned societies were founded in those two decades, and learned professionals specialized. For example, physicians split into specializations in that period.[8] The historian Robert L. Buroker describes the implications for politics and civic life: "By 1900 a social class based on specialized expertise had become numerous and influential enough to come into its own as a political force. Educated to provide rational answers to specific problems and oriented by training if not by inclination toward public service, they sensed their own stake in the stability of the new society, which increasingly depended upon their skills."[9] At best, they offered effective solutions to grave social problems. At worst, they arrogantly tried to suppress other views. For instance, the American Political Science Association's Committee of Seven's argued in 1914 that citizens "should learn humility in the face of expertise."[10]

One of the great issues of the day became the proper roles of expertise, specialization, science, and professionalism in a democracy. The great German sociologist Max Weber interpreted modernity as a profound and unstoppable shift toward scientific reasoning, specialization, and division of labor. One of Weber's most prominent students, Robert Michels, introduced the "iron law of oligarchy," according to which every organization—even a democratic workers' party—would inevitably be taken over by a small group of especially committed, trained, and skillful leaders. In America, the columnist Walter Lippmann argued that ordinary citizens had been eclipsed because of science and mass communications and could, at most, render occasional judgments about a government composed of experts. Thomas McCarthy, author of the *Wisconsin Idea*, asserted that the people could still rule through periodic elections, but expert managers should run the government in between. John Dewey and Jane Addams (in different ways) asserted that the lay public must and could regain its voice, but they struggled to explain how.

Thus the contours of the debate were established by 1910. If dominance by experts is a problem, it was already evident then. But even if the conceptual issue (the role of specialized expertise in a democracy) is the same today as it was in 1900, the sheer numbers are totally different. This is a case in which quantitative change makes a qualitative difference.

Just before the Second World War, the Census counted just 1 percent of Americans as "professional, technical, and kindred workers": people who according to Steven Brint's definition, "earn[ed] at least a middling income from the application of a relatively complex body of knowledge."[11] This thin slice of the population was spread fairly evenly. There was usually a maximum of one "professional" per household, and even in a neighborhood association or civic group, there might just be one physician, one lawyer, and one person with scientific training. Often these people (mostly men) had been socialized into an ethic of service. They had valuable specialized insights to offer, but they were obliged to collaborate with nonexperts on an almost daily basis to get anything done. Without romanticizing the relationship between professionals and their fellow citizens, I would propose that the dialogue was close and reciprocal.

Today, in contrast, there are so many professionals that particular neighborhoods, and even whole metropolitan areas, can be dominated by people who make a good living by applying specialized intellectual techniques. As holders of professional degrees, these people possess markers of high social status that were much more ambiguous a century ago when gentlemen were still expected to pursue the liberal arts, and the professions still smacked slightly of the trades. When wealthier and more influential communities are numerically dominated by people with strong and confident identities as experts, the nature of political conversation is bound to change.

In 1952, of all Americans who said that they had attended a "political meeting," only about one-quarter held managerial or professional jobs. Many more (41 percent) worked in other occupational categories: clerical, sales, and service jobs; and as laborers and farmers. The rest were mostly female home-makers. In short, professionals and managers—people trained to provide specialized, rational answers to problems—were outnumbered three-to-one in the nation's political meetings. By 2004, however, 44 percent of people who attended political meetings worked in managerial or professional occupations, and 48.5 percent held other jobs. The ratio nationally was now almost even, and professionals were the dominant group in affluent communities.[12]

These are crude categories that do not tell us how people talk in meetings. A clerical worker could argue like a technocrat; a physician could tell rich, personal stories, laden with values. But I think the increasing proportion of professionals and managers in meetings tells a story about a society dominated by people with specialized training and expertise. Thomas Webler and Seth Tuler quote a citizen who had participated in an official advisory council on the management of public lands:

> I think, in many instances, people in a certain profession, whether it is medicine or education or logging, there is a certain terminology that goes with that profession. And many times people, when they are trying to explain or get a point across, they talk over people who are not familiar. . . . What is a "widow-maker," "basel area"? We use those terms very fluently if you are into industrial logging and that sort of thing, but other people have no idea what "basel area" is. And that does happen when you go to meetings.[13]

Skocpol notes that traditional fraternal associations like the Lions and the Elks, which once gathered people at the local level who were diverse in terms of class and occupation (although segregated by race and gender), have lost their college-educated members. But non-college-educated or working-class people continue to join this type of group. It is not so much that working-class people have left fraternal associations, but that professionals have left *them*—moving from economically diverse local associations to specialized organizations for their own professions and industries.[14]

The proportion of all Americans who are professionals or managers has roughly doubled since the 1950s. That is a benign shift in our workforce, reflecting better education and more interesting jobs. It largely explains why highly educated specialists have become more numerous in meetings. They bring sophistication and expertise to community affairs. Still, two-thirds of people do *not* classify themselves as professional or managers, and it is important that their values and interests be represented. The steep decline in traditional civil society leaves them poorly represented, at their cost and to the detriment of public deliberation.

The Big Sort

Another change in civil society deserves attention: the "sorting" of Americans into increasingly homogeneous geographical communities. When we move, we now choose states, metropolitan areas, counties, neighborhoods, and blocks where the other residents share our overall worldview, including our political opinions. The psychologists Nansook Park and Christopher Peterson find that cities now differ markedly on how residents rate themselves on a battery of strengths that are "intellectual and self-oriented" (such as curiosity, judgment, and appreciation of beauty) and a different set of "strengths that are emotional and interpersonal" (such as love, prudence, bravery, and hope). In the 2008 presidential election, cities that ranked themselves high on "strengths of the head" chose Barack Obama. Cities that prided themselves on "strengths of the heart" preferred John McCain. It appears that America has hard-driving, competitive, creative, and cerebral cities that like Democrats, and warm, friendly, emotional, and devout cities that prefer Republicans.[15] Likewise, Bill Bishop and colleagues find that counties have become far more politically homogeneous since the 1970s.[16] The explanation must be shifts in population, because county borders are fixed.

One word to describe this change would be "fragmentation." Another word would be "diversity." The sorting of people into like-minded communities is a result of freedom, and it makes America as a whole more heterogeneous. Bishop puts the tradeoff well:

> It would be a dull country, of course, if every place were like every other. It's a joy that I can go to the Elks lodge pool in Austin to see the H2Hos, a feminist synchronized swimming troupe accompanied by a punkish band, or that I can visit the Zapalac Arena outside my old hometown of Smithville, Texas, to watch a team calf roping. Those sorts of differences are not only vital for the nation's democratic health, but they are also essential for economic growth. Monocultures die.
>
> What's happened, however, is that ways of life now have a distinct politics and a distinct geography. Feminist synchronized swimmers belong to one political party and live over here, and calf ropers belong to another party and live over there. As people seek out the

social settings they prefer—as they choose the group that makes them feel the most comfortable—the nation grows more politically segregated—and the benefit that ought to come with having a variety of opinions is lost to the righteousness that is the special entitlement of homogeneous groups. We all live with the results: balkanized communities whose inhabitants find other Americans to be culturally incomprehensible; a growing intolerance for political differences that has made national consensus impossible; and politics so polarized that Congress is stymied and elections are no longer just contests over policies, but bitter choices between ways of life.[17]

The cultural and political fragmentation that Bishop laments has worsened just as civic participation in general has declined, and that combination is particularly toxic. It means, first of all, that we have sorted ourselves into participatory communities and communities where hardly anyone engages. In Miami, less than 15 percent of adults report volunteering, compared to 37 percent in Minneapolis-St. Paul.[18] Within those two metropolitan areas, some neighborhoods see almost no organized civic activities, while other districts (even in Miami) are full of voluntary organizations, events, and discussions.

Second, when we engage, we tend to do so with like-minded people. Bishop begins his book with a vignette from his own neighborhood's e-mail discussions. A rare conservative resident endorses a political candidate who, in turn, opposes gay marriage. Numerous participants write to denounce—not this position—but the very presence of their neighbor on the e-mail list. "Stephen," one person writes, "you're in the minority politically on this list and in this neighborhood, and while your opinions are your own to have, this list isn't the place for them. [Travis Heights, in South Austin, Texas] is my home, and this list is an extension of that. . . . I hope we can all agree to prevent it from becoming a battleground."[19]

It is almost always easier to exit from a discussion that includes diverse perspectives than to listen and speak with others who are different. When a heterogeneous discussion sounds like a "battleground," and a homogeneous place sounds like "home," people will do their best to avoid controversy. Thus homeowners' associations frequently ban public political expression in the form of yard signs, flags (other than the national flag), and bumper stickers. This is a use of private contract rights to ban civil liberties voluntarily. The results include less listening, less learning, less trust, and an environment less conducive to the civic education of young people.[20]

In short, we must address four forms of pervasive exit: the exit of most Americans from traditional, face-to-face associations and discussions; the exit of credentialed specialists from associations favored by working-class Americans; the exit of working-class Americans from public life; and the exit of millions of people from communities where they might encounter opposing views.

Measured by the values defended in chapters 3 and 4, our current civil society looks deeply flawed. It does not promote deliberative talk by diverse people and especially not talk that leads to (or is enriched by) hands-on action. It does not favor or reward loyalty. It does not take a developmental approach, providing opportunities for individuals and communities to learn civic skills and values. And it is deeply inequitable.

The Corruption of Our Public Institutions

The previous section summarized troubling developments in civil society and in ordinary life. I now turn to government and argue that our political institutions are corrupt in ways that discourage civic engagement.

In making this argument, I will avoid two shortcuts. One would be to show that people *believe* the government is corrupt. In 2008, 70 percent of Americans said the government was "run by a few big interests"; 30 percent said it was "run for the benefit of all." That sounds like a public verdict of corruption.[21] Alexander Hamilton thought that low public confidence in the government was a sure sign that its performance was actually poor.[22] If he was right, then recent survey data suggest that the government is corrupt.

But such surveys cannot tell us exactly what is wrong with our political system. People could correctly declare the government corrupt but not know what reforms would fix it. Also, there is little evidence that perceptions of corruption dampen civic engagement. On the contrary, respondents who said that the government was "run by a few big interests" were somewhat *more* likely to vote and to follow the news in 2008 than those who thought it was "run for the benefit of all."

A second shortcut would be to list egregious recent examples of corruption, perhaps in conjunction with graphs showing upward trends in the amount of private money spent on campaigns, the number of convictions for public malfeasance, or the proportion of news stories devoted to political scandal. Each of these measures could be criticized as evidence of corruption. But I leave them aside for a different reason. There is *always* a gap between official rules, standards, and laws (on one hand) and actual behavior (on the other). To show that politicians act badly proves little, even if they acted somewhat better at times in the past.

My claim is a subtler but more serious one. There is not only a gap between norms and politicians' behavior (that much is inevitable), but our norms themselves have become corrupt in ways that undermine democracy. High republican principles remain embodied in the Constitution and other foundational documents. Laws still constrain leaders' behavior and impose sanctions when they stray. But the political system has another layer of norms as well. This layer consists of principles that guide discretionary action, that make some decisions seem dishonorable even though they are legal, that commend certain kinds of speech and action, that set standards for excellence in public life, and that shape congressional procedures and other malleable rules of the game. It is my claim that these principles have been distorted and degraded to the point that there is not just a gap between aspirations and performance; our aspirations themselves are now unworthy. The result is not always less political engagement—2004, 2008, and 2012 saw high voter turnout—but our engagement is qualitatively worse because of our low expectations.

The government we have is mostly the result of massive expansion between 1930 and 1970, the era of mid-twentieth-century liberalism and the administrations that named themselves the New Deal, the Fair Deal, the New Frontier, and the Great Society. Idealistic principles undergirded this structure, and majorities of Americans voted in favor of it. As that era came to an end in the 1970s, a "liberal" was someone who wanted to preserve the institutions that liberalism had already created and to fill certain cracks (such as the failure of Medicare and Medicaid to cover lower income workers before retirement). A "conservative" was someone who wanted to trim the existing structure or roll back some of its provisions.

Harry Truman provides an example of liberalism as the application of high moral principles. In the 1949 State of the Union address, he told Congress:

> We have rejected the discredited theory that the fortunes of the Nation should be in the hands of a privileged few. We have abandoned the "trickledown" concept of national prosperity. Instead, we believe that our economic system should rest on a democratic foundation and that wealth should be created for the benefit of all. The recent election shows that the people of the United States are in favor of this kind of society and want to go on improving it. The American people have decided that poverty is just as wasteful and just as unnecessary as preventable disease.

Truman then offered a whole series of diagnoses and prescriptions that he believed followed from his opening statement of principles. For example: "In a nation as rich as ours, it is a shocking fact that tens of millions lack adequate medical care. We are short of doctors, hospitals, nurses. We must remedy these shortages. Moreover, we need—and we must have without further delay—a system of prepaid medical insurance which will enable every American to afford good medical care."

Truman's ideological style of politics was clear and understandable; people could render a verdict on it. If they did *not* want their government to "see that every American has a chance to obtain his fair share of our increasing abundance" (as Truman promised), they could vote against him in the 1952 election. If the president failed to enact his priorities (such as universal health insurance), they could hold him responsible. Thirty years later, Americans could render a similarly clear judgment when a critic of liberalism, Ronald Reagan, took office proposing to roll it back.

In short, this style of government—announcing general principles and governing accordingly—had virtues for democracy. But it also had disadvantages. The ideals of any given philosophy were bound to conflict with other values that also had some merit. Abstract principles could not actually tell leaders what to do in complex, concrete situations. And the nation could not long sustain a habit of reforming society to match consistent ideals, no matter how worthy those ideals might be.

The best tools for implementing ambitious, abstract theories were landmark acts of Congress. By definition, passing a landmark bill is a rare event in any given field or domain. (If a law is frequently revisited and revised, it is not a landmark.) However, Congress deals with an enormous range of issues, so it can frequently pass landmark acts. That is just how it operated from 1932 to 1975, and especially in the mid-1960s. For example, the 88th Congress met for a matter of months in 1963–64. It passed the Economic Opportunity Act of 1964 (launching the War on Poverty and creating Head Start, Job Corps, and many other programs), the Food Stamp Act (institutionalizing food stamps as a permanent federal welfare program), the Federal Transit Act (providing federal aid for mass transportation), the Library Services and Construction Act (offering federal aid for libraries), the Community Mental Health Centers Act (deinstitutionalizing many mental health patients), the Clean Air Act (the first federal environmental law allowing citizens to sue polluters), the Wilderness Act (protecting nine million acres of federal land), the Equal Pay Act (addressing wage discrimination by sex), the Civil Rights Act of 1964 (ending de jure racial segregation in the United States), and the Tonkin Gulf Resolution (rapidly escalating the Vietnam War).[23]

This pace was unsustainable, and the frequency of landmark legislation clearly fell after 1975.[24] Whereas Congress passed at least ten momentous bills in 1963, in 1997–98, 70 percent of the issues it took up went nowhere at all, and the *Washington Post* decried "the barrenness of the legislative record" at the end of the session.[25] Another way to describe the change would be to say that from 1932 until 1975, Congress was almost always considering some kind of landmark legislation, whether conservative or liberal, that drew the attention of the nation and that plausibly promised to change America. Hardly any landmark legislation has been passed since then. In its tentativeness, its delegation of hard choices to agencies and panels, and its internal compromises, the Affordable Care Act of 2010 exemplifies modern lawmaking. And yet it was the boldest change in decades and seems to have exhausted the whole system.

But that did not mean that the government stopped governing after 1975. Washington still faced innumerable choices about which activities and programs to fund, purchase, permit, require, measure, ban, and punish. It is just that those decisions were no longer made in major bills, widely publicized, debated on the floor of Congress, and signed or vetoed by presidents. Instead, the decisions were made by administrative agencies in the form of regulations; by administrative law judges in their determinations; by federal judges hearing lawsuits against federal agencies; by congressional subcommittees (and even individual members) in appropriations bills, riders, earmarks, and filibuster threats; by the administrators who negotiated contracts with private organizations that implemented most federal policies; by the same contractors in their own policies and procedures; and by state and local officials, who now were deeply implicated in national policy—thanks to large federal grants—and who often had similar powers to their counterparts at the federal level.

The ratio of ordinary administration to landmark lawmaking rose dramatically. This was virtually inevitable, because each statute produces a mountain of regulations and lawsuits and requires regular appropriations. The momentous reforms of the 1960s and early 1970s would take some time to be absorbed. In fact, settling controversies and setting priorities through negotiation could be defended as the best way to govern. There are, after all, many interests in society; and most have official representatives. Each interest wants something and brings some combination of votes, money, and influence to the table. Policy can be analyzed as the outcome of interactions among such interests. *Good* government can be defined as negotiation that is reasonably balanced and equitable, efficient, harmonious, and inclusive. If a particular interest is not represented at all, that is a flaw in the system, but it can be remedied by organizing them.

This philosophy of governance predominated by the time the great liberal movement ran out of energy. In a prescient book entitled *The End of Liberalism* (first published in 1969 and revised a decade later), Theodore Lowi called the new philosophy "interest-group liberalism." It started with the definition of "politics" as negotiation among interest groups and added a very modest reform agenda. All interests should be formally represented by groups, and groups should be treated equitably. They all should, for example, have equal rights of access to administrative agencies and courts.

Lowi saw interest-group liberalism as the predominant *actual* theory of his day. Although important speeches and preambles to legislation still invoked a transparent, principled, deliberated, public philosophy, the real action was in deals among interest groups. The Democratic Party controlled the House of Representatives from 1948 to 1994, but as a loose coalition of interest groups, including white conservatives from the rural South and West and urban northeastern liberals. Members of Congress made the institution work by logrolling: voting for one another's programs without supporting them in principle. Urban liberals would vote for the farm bill, and rural conservatives would help fund the National Endowment for the Arts, with no one sincerely endorsing the whole package. Logrolling is inevitable and can even be a desirable way to get complex legislation through a diverse legislature. But, as Lowi put it, logrolling turned "from necessary evil to greater good" once a *deal* was seen as evidence of good government.[26]

In a republic, "law" classically means consistent, durable, binding principles that are enacted after public deliberation. Laws should not change unless substantial events in the outside world demand change, nor should they be subject to exceptions and negotiations after passage. The Constitution (article 1, section 1) vests "all legislative powers" in Congress, although the president's veto power gives the White House a role in lawmaking as well. Thus, under our system, Congress and the president are supposed to make laws that are as durable and coherent as possible. Interest groups and party blocs will inevitably negotiate before a law is passed, although there is also supposed to be a public deliberation about matters of principle and philosophy. Once the president signs the bill, it should be fixed until significant changes in the world require reform.

But meeting those standards would be hard for elected politicians. They could be held accountable for their own momentous decisions, and they would have nothing to offer interest groups once they had passed an important law. They are tempted to act in quite a different way. First, instead of deliberating and passing coherent, durable statutes, they issue voluminous and constantly amended laws—too long for anyone to read before the vote. That may be inevitable in a complex modern society, but Congress compounds the problem by delegating its lawmaking role—not so much to the president and the cabinet as to administrative agencies, civil servants, and special courts and panels within the executive branch. They do this by passing statutes that empower regulatory agencies to make policy within very broad outlines. In 2004, federal agencies generated 78,851 pages of proposed rules, filling 69 volumes of the annual *Federal Register*. The number of pages has crept almost steadily up, from one volume of 2,620 pages in 1936, when the government was a more assertive regulator but a less prolific author of regulations than it is today.[27]

Every major reform act of the 1960s and 1970s created or gave new powers to at least one regulatory agency that would then begin to govern in a routine sense. In turn, the administrative agencies tended to delegate their powers further down, to various boards and committees that were forums for negotiations among stakeholders. For example, during the 1970s, Congress created within the US Department of Agriculture a Cotton Board, a National Potato Promotion Board, and an Egg Board: official venues for ongoing negotiations.[28] Agribusinesses, supermarkets, consumer lobbies, and other groups could be given space at these tables, but a process of continuous negotiations inevitably favors *organized* interest groups, especially the ones that physically appear in Washington. Negotiated decisions could then be appealed in court or taken back to the myriad House and Senate subcommittees on agriculture, which then issued a new farm bill every other year.

Agriculture is an industry notorious for interest-group pressure and for federal subsidies, but the arts can serve as another example. In the 1970s, Congress delegated to the National Endowment for the Arts the responsibility for deciding what forms and works of art to support with public money. The NEA, in turn, delegated its authority to committees representing the "Art World" (professional artists, curators, and critics, mostly based in New York City). The Art World explicitly denied that the public had any appropriate influence over its decisions.[29]

Delegation allows elected officials to take credit for general principles, even if they conflict, and then blame bureaucrats who actually make choices.

A classic but not atypical example is the "dual mandate" that Congress gave to the Federal Reserve: to maximize employment *and* control inflation. Those goals often conflict in practice, but Congress claims to have mandated both and can critically question any Federal Reserve chairman who fails to achieve both. Another example is the section of the Clean Air Act that empowers the EPA administrator to set ambient air quality standards at levels "requisite to protect the public health" with "an adequate margin of safety."[30] *No* amount of air pollution has zero potential impact on safety or health. "Adequate" safety means some amount of risk that is greater than zero—but not too much. That is not a scientific or technical judgment; it's a value judgment about what level of safety is worth the cost. Congress avoids making such value judgments, because then it would be responsible when some people suffer—or even die—from whatever pollution is left in the air. But Congress would equally be responsible for the financial cost of any regulation. So it passes the responsibility to the EPA, which can then be blamed for both the costs of a regulation and the environmental harms that result.

By the 1960s and 1970s, America had a large and intrusive national government, matched by comparable governments in states like New York and California. One could certainly justify their scale and scope with public reasons. But no public philosophy guided their everyday decisions, which were ad hoc, opportunistic, mutable, and voluminous. By that time, we lacked a confident language or intellectual framework for discussing the public interest.[31] Many political scientists argued that there was no such thing, that politics was simply a clash of special interests. Certainly, hard-boiled political reporters depicted politics that way. The press routinely described lawmaking as a contest among politicians to gain the support of interest groups and to win the next election.

This transformation of governance caused momentous changes in civil society. As long as important decisions about a given topic (such as health, civil rights, or labor) were made only occasionally in landmark federal statutes, then the best way to influence politics was to build a national, popular advocacy movement and consult its members about what to do.[32] Only by finding active supporters in many congressional districts could one hope to influence Congress. Once an issue came to the floor, it was easy to notify concerned citizens all across the country, and they would have an opportunity to contact their own representatives. The vote would be clear and definitive; citizen-members could decide whether to fight on or declare victory.

On the other hand, if policy was made continuously by congressional appropriations committees, regulatory agencies, quasi-independent boards, administrative law judges, and federal courts, then it would be impossible to sustain public interest and keep everyone adequately informed. At the same time, it was *unnecessary* to have large numbers of active supporters outside Washington. More effective would be a small office of professional lobbyists and litigators who could track all the important action and sit at the various negotiation tables. A small outfit like that could be funded by foundation grants, wealthy individuals, or the proceeds of litigation, not by members.

"What ensued," as Matthew A. Crenson and Benjamin Ginsberg write, "was an 'advocacy explosion.'" Most of the new groups that sprung up in the 1970s and thereafter "had no arrangements for democratic participation or consultation with their own presumed constituents." Many groups were just mailing lists with staffs in their national offices. "In fact, the concentration of interest groups based in Washington now includes a sizable population of organizations without any members at all."[33] Some were funded by liberal foundations and donors who actively endorsed "interest-group liberalism." They presumed that constant negotiation among official interests was compatible with good government as long as every valid interest had a group. Other lobbies were funded by industry or by conservative donors. Regardless of their ideologies, all these groups contributed to the trends described in the previous section on civil society. Professionalism and expertise increasingly dominated; discussion and action at the grassroots level was becoming irrelevant.

Trends within the civil service were congruent with these changes. By now, the people who administered federal policy had been trained, as Robert Reich observed in 1988, to facilitate negotiations among organized interests.[34] Whenever government officials see their job as facilitating negotiations among stakeholders, they have abandoned the goal of identifying or defending the public good. They may not believe that there is any such thing, or they may doubt their ability to identify it, or they may simply feel that they lack the right to make major moral decisions.

Public servants are also trained to identify the most beneficial policy through science and economics. This process implies that the public good *can* be known: it is the policy that enhances social outcomes at the lowest cost. That could be a very demanding moral doctrine; if it is right, we ought to consider radical policies, such as taxing Americans heavily to pay for education in the developing world (because a dollar spent on primary schooling in Africa does much more good than a dollar spent on consumer goods in the United States). But federal civil servants never propose such policies. They correctly feel that they have no right to do so, since major moral questions are for the public to decide. But that means that the professional analysis of policy within government agencies is highly constrained and does not reflect a coherent moral view. For example, regulators in the EPA can decide to ban a given pesticide but cannot critically assess the whole system of agriculture in which pesticides are used.

As Lowi wrote, the modern methods of public administration "impair legitimacy by converting government from a moralistic to a mechanistic institution."[35] Deliberation about principle looks naive and becomes an obstacle to smooth logrolling, stakeholder negotiation, negotiated rulemaking, and cost-benefit calculations within statutory limits. The characteristic ethic of governance—deciding together what is right to do—is lost. And when governance turns into negotiation, the organizations with big bank accounts have a huge advantage.

While government was turning into a venue for private negotiations, elections were increasingly understood as opportunities for interest groups to transmute money into political influence. Throughout American history, political campaigns have always been privately financed, and the actual impact of money was more pronounced in the Gilded Age than after the Second World War, and especially after the post-Watergate reforms of the 1970s. But a new public philosophy was emerging that understood market-like behavior as *appropriate* in politics. An election was deemed fair if many private interests officially registered as political action committees (PACs) or otherwise as donors, announced what they wanted from government, gave limited amounts of money to a range of candidates, and disclosed what they had spent. "Corruption" meant a quid pro quo or a massive, undisclosed gift. Private financing of politics was not corrupt but an example of free speech and debate.

From the 1970s through the 1990s, the political scientists who specialized in campaign finance held generally positive attitudes toward the existing system, finding that special interests cancelled one another out and that politicians as well as donors exercised power in the marketplace.[36] A task force of nine leading experts, for example, depicted organized donors as legitimate participants in civil society.[37]

Corporate PACs are required to pursue policies economically beneficial for their own companies. To accept them as fully legitimate participants in electoral politics, one would have to assume that there is an organized group for every interest; that each group genuinely represents its whole constituency; that the appropriate way to address any issue is to bargain; and that equilibrium among interest groups is evidence of good government. One would have to ignore such questions as, "What is good for the republic as a whole?" "What is just?" "What is a good reason?" And "Is our political arena open and attractive to all?"

By the 1970s, the large and expensive structure of mid-twentieth-century liberalism had ceased to address those questions in a credible way. The federal government seemed incapable of addressing major current challenges, from "stagflation" to illegal drugs. It also lacked the mechanisms and practices that create genuine democratic legitimacy, instead operating as a kind of market for organized interest groups. In 1958, 73 percent of Americans had said they trusted the government in Washington to do the right thing, either "just about always" or "most of the time." By 1980, trust had fallen to 25 percent.[38]

Scholars have explained the collapse in trust as a result of declining economic growth rates, the spectacular failure in Vietnam, scandals at home, and a breaking of the relationship between people (organized in diverse, participatory, civic associations) and their government. There is persuasive empirical evidence for each of these explanations, but I don't find any scholarly account as perceptive as Ward Just's Washington novels, such as *Echo House* and *City of Fear*. A common theme is the shift from Washington as the seat of *government* to the modern city of dealmakers and negotiators. Just (who was the *Washington Post*'s lead reporter in Vietnam) certainly does not regard the old Washington as benign. It was a city of power, and the powerful sometimes lacked wisdom and ethics. Yet their job was to govern. Their titles, their powers, and their paychecks were federal. In *Jack Gance*, Just's eponymous narrator recalls the end of the 1960s:

> The clamor and racket ceased, but the echoes were still in the ears of the population; many in the capital were ashamed and stricken, comforting each other as family members customarily do in times of great grief. It seemed that not everything was possible after all. The capital turned a sullen face to the country, stung by the accusation that it had failed and was unworthy of trust, that it had lost its nerve. . . . Frightened, mesmerized, it resolved to hold fast—consolidating, performing quotidian chores. . . . Besieged, we came to resemble the corporate world we had despised and derided. The city grew, the culture thickened, and the custodians multiplied.[39]

We have considered two styles of liberal government: bold reform through landmark legislation (which was clearly unsustainable after 1975); and constant negotiation inside regulatory agencies, congressional subcommittees, and

courts. A third alternative would have been pragmatic, decentralized, participatory government. Instead of trying to implement grand principles and strategies by statute, the government could have created small deliberative bodies
to make ad hoc choices and reflect on their own decisions in a continuous
process. In Ostrom's terms, this would have been "polycentric" governance, or
rule by numerous, small, overlapping, participatory bodies.

A pure version of pragmatism would be skeptical of momentous principles and bold, enduring reforms but would instead ask citizens at any given
moment to consider the status quo, including the various problems and limitations in their environment at that time and the programs and institutions
that had the best records of ameliorating problems. At each point, communities would experiment with expanding the most promising programs and
pruning the least successful ones.[40] Decentralization and citizen participation
would be hallmarks of pragmatic policymaking. In chapter 4, I argued that a
pragmatic spirit was an important component of mid-twentieth-century liberalism, for the New Deal and even the Great Society can be read as expansions of programs like Jane Addams's Hull-House.

But pragmatism cannot be value free. What counts as a problem to be
remedied or a successful program to be expanded is a matter of debate and
judgment. Making those decisions requires either a wise and trustworthy class
of rulers or an engaged, deliberating public, or both. In the heyday of American liberalism, reformers tried to make our leaders wiser and more ethical by
changing congressional procedures, requiring open meetings and public access to records, and revising the rules of the civil service. They also created
structures in which ordinary citizens could deliberate and make decisions locally. Two examples of empowered, hyper-local, democratic assemblies created by federal law were the Community Action Agencies in the War on
Poverty and the Title One Parent Advisory Councils in schools that received
federal aid. In both cases, residents who were not professional politicians were
elected or selected to set priorities and spend public funds.[41] These experiments had value, but they faded in importance and lost funding in the 1980s.
Decentralization and deliberative government by citizens were never the central pillars of liberalism; they were decorative ornaments.

A libertarian-leaning Republican president was elected in 1980 with another alternative. Ronald Reagan said, "The government is not the solution to
our problem; government is the problem."[42] He could have offered libertarianism as a coherent political theory, subject to public debate and review.
Although I believe the public would have rejected libertarianism in time, it had
a legitimate place on the public agenda as an alternative. Landmark libertarian

legislation would have moved the country in a different direction from the landmark liberal legislation of the 1960s, but the process would have been the same. However, no landmark legislation was really offered. The Reagan years actually saw increases in federal spending, along with tax cuts, leading to deficits that were never part of the president's promise.

The Immigration Reform and Control Act of 1986 was supposed to combine amnesty for immigrants who were already in the country with provisions to prevent hiring of undocumented workers. The latter half of the act was basically unenforced "owing to the complexity of undertaking such regulation and the political resistance by employers." Although it remained enshrined in federal law, "in effect, one-half of this major bill was repealed during the implementation process."[43] The same Congress passed the Gramm-Rudman-Hollings Balanced Budget and Emergency Deficit Control Act with great fanfare, but the law did not actually balance the budget. In subsequent years, government essentially returned to being an equilibrium of interest groups, albeit with business better represented than it had been during the New Deal and Great Society.

We can now take the story forward to the present. A political system that no longer honors deliberation about the public good, even in principle, is bound to react dishonorably in a crisis. Thus consider how Congress responded to the financial catastrophe of 2008–10. First, legislators negotiated for months to produce a reform bill that was 2,000 pages long, full of special exemptions and breaks that no individual could even count or understand prior to passage. The legislative process offered rich opportunities for professional lobbyists and their clients. Steven Brill estimates that $15 million was spent to lobby on one particular technical provision that reduced corporate tax obligations by $10 billion—an excellent return on investment. Brill observes:

> Complexity is the modern lobbyist's greatest ally. Three lobbyists showed me three different proposals for rewording what may be the bill's biggest-money section: a provision in the Senate version that would force the five major banks that do most of the country's trillions of dollars of trading in derivatives—and make nearly $23 billion a year doing so—to spin off those operations. Even holding the dueling paragraphs side by side by side, I found it difficult on first read to appreciate the differences. But with some pointers from the lobbyists, it was clear that billions in profits depended on the variations in this nearly impenetrable language.[44]

The passage of the bill by no means ended the process of negotiation. Binyamin Appelbaum wrote in the *New York Times*, "Well before Congress reached agreement on the details of its financial overhaul legislation, industry lobbyists and consumer advocates started preparing for the next battle: influencing the creation of several hundred new rules and regulations. The bill . . . is basically a 2,000-page missive to federal agencies, instructing regulators to address subjects ranging from derivatives trading to document retention. But it is notably short on specifics, giving regulators significant power to determine its impact—and giving partisans on both sides a second chance to influence the outcome."[45]

James Madison's words about mutable government by now seemed prophetic:

> To trace the mischievous effects of a mutable government would fill a volume. . . . It poisons the blessings of liberty itself. It will be of little avail to the people, that the laws are made by men of their own choice, if the laws be so voluminous that they cannot be read, or so incoherent that they cannot be understood; if they be repealed or revised before they are promulgated, or undergo such incessant changes that no man, who knows what the law is to-day, can guess what it will be to-morrow. Law is defined to be a rule of action; but how can that be a rule, which is little known, and less fixed? Another effect of public instability is the unreasonable advantage it gives to the sagacious, the enterprising, and the moneyed few over the industrious and uninformed mass of the people. Every new regulation concerning commerce or revenue, or in any way, affecting the value of the different species of property, presents a new harvest to those who watch the change, and can trace its consequences; a harvest, reared not by themselves, but by the toils and cares of the great body of their fellow-citizens. This is a state of things in which it may be said with some truth that laws are made for the FEW, not for the MANY.[46]

In the same year that Congress struggled to respond to the Wall Street crisis (2010), the Supreme Court found—for the first time—that corporations have First Amendment rights to spend unlimited money to influence campaigns. The *Citizens United* decision was the logical conclusion of a half century of retreat from notions of the public good. The majority justified unlimited spending as a matter of fairness toward corporations, understood as associations. "Wealthy individuals and unincorporated associations can spend unlimited amounts on independent expenditures. Yet certain disfavored associations of citizens—those that have taken on the corporate form—are penalized for engaging in the same political speech." Striking down those prohibitions and penalties, the court confidently predicted that "shareholders and citizens [will have the] information needed to hold corporations and elected officials accountable for their positions and supporters."[47] The court applied the theory that people are adequately represented by organized interest groups, that politics is negotiation, and that money is a legitimate source of political influence.

Before *Citizens United*, corporations could already purchase "issue" advertisements that would benefit or harm particular candidates; they simply could not make explicit appeals to vote for or against those individuals. By removing that relatively subtle and technical obstacle, *Citizens United* arguably did not change the rules as profoundly as press coverage suggested. Yet corporate campaign spending increased at least fivefold in the wake of the decision (if we compare 2010 to the previous midterm election of 2006). The conservative activist Steven Law observed, "The principal impact of the Citizens United decision was to give prospective donors a general sense that it was within their constitutional rights to support independent political activity. . . . That right existed before, but this Supreme Court decision essentially gave a Good Housekeeping seal of approval."[48] The Supreme Court said that corporations had been "disfavored associations of citizens" before the *Citizens United* decision restored their equal rights. The Court meant that it was entirely appropriate for corporations to exercise power in their own interests by spending money to influence elections. This decision capped a century-long process in which special interests became "civil society," Madison's factions became "constituencies" or "stakeholders," propaganda became "public relations" and "communications," corporate pressure became "government relations," and lobbying morphed from a disreputable matter of hanging around hotel lobbies and button-holing politicians into a white-collar profession.

It is important to acknowledge several valid points in favor of special interests. They arise whenever people are free, and therefore to suppress them, as Madison said, would be a treatment "worse than the disease."[49] When we form distinct interest groups, society becomes diverse and plural; we are then a rich mosaic instead of a monotonous mass. When interests take the form of parties, unions, and pressure groups that advance sharply dissenting views, citizens gain choices and can govern by picking one clear path. And finally, justice sometimes demands the strong defense of discrete interests and values.

Picture, for example, members of the United Farm Workers Union marching for 340 miles from the grape fields of Delano to Sacramento behind the image of the Virgin of Guadalupe, arriving on Easter Sunday 1965 to say, in the words of César E. Chávez, "We want to be equal with all the working men in the nation; we want just wages, better working conditions, a decent future for our children. To those who oppose us, be they ranchers, police, politicians, or speculators, we say that we are going to continue fighting until we die, or we win."[50]

This was a manifestation of a "special interest," in the sense that the workers demanded legislation that would benefit them, they identified adversaries whose interests they decried, and they did so proudly in their own cultural and religious idioms, deliberately putting their distinct identity into the public domain and demanding recognition. Yet Chávez was surely right that they marched for justice. The public interest was served by their struggle. Their voices contributed to the broad public deliberation in at least two ways: by providing information to other Americans about their interests and needs (the population was overwhelmingly ignorant about migrant farmworkers), and by developing their own positions and demands, which would otherwise have no chance to be considered.[51]

The Farm Workers' struggle was one kind of politics, but it is rare. Far more common is a routine controversy among economic interests. For example, optometrists and ophthalmologists frequently clash over the right to perform particular procedures. Their disputes become policy questions because state and federal governments license medical professionals for specific roles and also decide which procedures to reimburse through Medicare and Medicaid. Optometrists and ophthalmologists are organized and employ lobbyists and litigators. Although they often cooperate, they also clash. In recent years, optometrists have lobbied Texas, Florida, California, and Oklahoma for the right to perform eye surgery not requiring anesthetics.[52] In 1987, optometrists won changes in federal Medicare rules which caused their share of the Medicare market almost to quadruple in one year.[53]

Of course, there are other interests at stake, beyond the optometrists and the ophthalmologists—including patients and taxpayers. Somehow, all their competing claims must be adjudicated. Here are four solutions that have been defended theoretically:

1. Implement the policy that maximizes the benefits and minimizes the costs to society as a whole. In this example, we would define "benefits" as high-quality medical services and "costs" in terms of money and adverse medical outcomes. Presumably, letting optometrists compete would lower prices

for patients, but it might also lower quality. The American Academy of Ophthalmology asserts (ostensibly on scientific grounds) that "surgery should be performed by physicians with a medical or osteopathic education and training"—in other words, *not* by optometrists.[54] In addition to the science, there is also an underlying moral premise here: policies should maximize the social cost-benefit ratio. That is one form of *utilitarianism*.

2. Implement the most popular policy. Then the goal is to satisfy as many people's preferences as possible, perhaps weighted for how much they know or care about the issue. Ideally, policymakers would hold focus groups or even polls or referenda to find out, but in the absence of those tools, a good policy is the one that people would support if someone asked them. This is a second form of *utilitarianism* (preference-satisfaction), and it also appeals to *populists*.

3. Minimize the role of the state and maximize individual freedom. Milton Friedman argued that all licensing laws were corruptly monopolistic. Patients and other consumers should be "free to choose" whatever medical procedures they wanted from anyone who offered to provide them. He thought that if there were no medical licenses, most people would seek care from large group practices—"department stores of medicine, if you will"—that would attract patients because of their reputations for reliability. But some people would prefer unlicensed "individual practitioner[s]," and that would be their right.[55] Friedman opposed Medicare altogether, but assuming it existed, he might favor reimbursing surgeries by anyone whom patients endorsed. His view is a type of *libertarianism*.

4. Maximize the benefits—not for society in the aggregate—but specifically for the poor and marginalized, because they are not served by the market or because they would benefit most. Instead of calculating how many total high-quality procedures can be performed per million dollars of government money under each policy, calculate how many poor people would gain access to such services. That is *egalitarianism*.

In addition to those four approaches that have defenders, here are four methods that seem indefensible theoretically—but that are very common:

5. Split the difference between the optometrists and ophthalmologists, or give one interest what it wants and make a side payment to the other interest.

6. Preserve the status quo, whatever it may be.

7. Create a permanent process of bargaining within the executive, legislative, and judicial branches of both federal and state governments and allow policies to vary by year and place. That way, no one loses outright, and the professionals involved in lobbying, litigation, regulation, advocacy, policy research, and public relations can remain permanently employed.[56]

8. Let the interest that wields the most effective political power win.

I would call options 5–8 "corrupt"—not to cast aspersions but in a sober, technical sense. The public good that is the root meaning of "republic" is subverted when these methods prevail.

Each of the first four options, by itself, has some potential to solve the corruption problem (although not without creating new problems). For example, libertarians argue that money would lose its corrupting influence over politics if the government stopped regulating and left people free to choose. Populists since William Jennings Bryan have argued that popular rule (referenda and other voting mechanisms) would make government clean. And many good-government reformers believe that an insulated, professional, scientifically informed civil service could maximize benefits and minimize costs. Donna Shalala, as quoted in chapter 4, defended that view.

I have grave doubts about each of these positions. Not only is their practical feasibility questionable, but they rest on moral foundations that, in each case, seems simplistic. There is truth in libertarianism, utilitarianism, populism, and egalitarianism, yet in many situations each of these doctrines does *not* seem satisfactory. The very fact that there are four plausible approaches to addressing conflicts among interests suggests that we have an intellectual problem—and of course, one could lengthen the list of moral theories to include various kinds of environmentalism, religious doctrines, conservative respect for traditions, and group rights. If the critique of expertise in chapter 4 was correct, none of these doctrines will solve our problems. Instead we need:

9. An ongoing dialogue in public forums about what the public interest requires.

But what actually prevails is some combination of the four indefensible options. One reason for this corruption is suggested by rational choice theory (the formal study of how people and groups pursue their own interests). Everyone is affected by the struggle between optometrists and ophthalmologists, but most of us are affected to a very limited extent. The optometrists and the ophthalmologists are deeply affected. It therefore pays for them to lobby in their own interests, but it does not pay for the rest of us to organize on this issue. In founding Common Cause, John Gardner said, "Everybody is organized but the people."[57] Maybe he was just stating an inevitable fact.

Of course, not all groups are equally able to form effective lobbies. For instance, the homeless are a discrete group of modest number who share important interests. In those respects, they are comparable to realtors. Both groups should organize in their own interests. But according to the Center for Responsive Politics, "the real estate industry gave $135 million to federal candidates and campaigns in 2008, with the National Association of Realtors contributing the most by far, at $4.3 million."[58] The homeless presumably gave approximately zero dollars to federal candidates in that year. The reason is not the size or structure of the two interests, but simply that realtors have a lot more money than homeless people. Since economic inequality is more pronounced in this decade than at any time since at least 1929, it would not be surprising if—to quote E. E. Schattschneider—the choir of interest groups sings today with a "strong upper-class accent."[59]

The promise of interest-group liberalism was to remedy such inequality by forming and strengthening organizations that represented the poor and the marginalized, and by revising government procedures and rules so that these groups would have access to decision-makers. The Ford Foundation was especially active in launching new official interest groups. But any such strategy must overcome profound structural causes of inequality. Even if it could do so, the idea of a *public* interest would still be lost.

It is worth returning to César Chávez, who served as my example of an interest-group leader. He did fight for an interest group, but his rhetoric was intentionally universal. "We seek our basic, God-given rights as human beings. . . . We seek the support of all political groups and protection of the government, which is also our government, in our struggle. . . . At the head of the pilgrimage we carry *La virgen de la Guadalupe* because she is ours, all ours, Patroness of the Mexican people. We also carry the Sacred Cross and the Star of David because we are not sectarians, and because we ask the help and prayers of all religions."[60] This was a moral claim on the public as a whole, which is the essence of good politics and what we have largely lost.

Measured against the values defended in chapters 3 and 4, our political institutions fall far short. They are deeply inequitable, and they fail to exemplify or promote deliberation, either in Washington or in local communities. But their corruption has certainly not gone unnoticed, and in chapter 6, I turn to remedies.

6

Facts

A CIVIC RENEWAL MOVEMENT EMERGES

AS NOTED IN chapter 5, most of the large-scale trends affecting our democracy are destructive. Fortunately, some citizens know what is happening and are responding with creativity, skill, discipline, and ethics. They form a civic renewal network whose main contributions, so far, are concrete, practical experiments that could be the basis of a national movement. After describing their work, I examine civic engagement in the 2008 Obama campaign and the first Obama administration to illustrate that we have made progress but also seem to have reached an impasse that requires new strategies to break through.

Practical deliberative democracy. The theory of deliberative democracy says that all citizens should discuss important issues before public decisions are made. Citizens' discussions should conform to principles of fairness, civility, and reason and should affect public policy.

Those are utopian ideals, but various nonprofits currently organize groups of citizens at a human scale (say, five to 500 people) to discuss specific public issues in ways that influence policies or communities. An organization's role may be to recruit or help recruit participants, to provide neutral background materials, to moderate or facilitate the meeting (or to train local people to moderate), and to report the results. Practitioners of deliberative democracy differ on several dimensions, including:

- **How to recruit participants.** Some argue that only a random sample ensures legitimate results;[1] others are open to non-random recruitment to obtain representative samples; and still others see themselves as community organizers who convene self-selected activists for discussions that are intentionally diverse and open-ended, but not necessarily representative of the local population.[2]
- **The format and structure of the discussions.** Organizers use and recommend highly diverse formats. For example, Citizens Juries require at least

five full, consecutive days of deliberation among small groups of representative citizens. The America*Speaks* Twenty-First Century Town Meeting draws hundreds or thousands of people into a large space, such as a convention hall, for a few hours of discussion connected by computers at each table. Study Circles, as promoted in the United States by Everyday Democracy, are informal but structured conversations, dispersed throughout a community, that normally meet on numerous occasions over months. In 2009–10, the White House built a public website for online discussion of its proposed rules regarding transparency as a formal source of public comment on the rules. These examples illustrate the wide range of formats that have been tried in recent decades.

- **The purpose of the exercise**. Some deliberations are opportunities for formal participation in the policymaking process of a government (or another major institution). Normally, the policymakers organize—or at least welcome—the public's deliberation in advance, so that citizens can be confident that there is a purpose to their discussions. For example, in 2009, the federal Centers for Disease Control and Prevention (CDC) asked more than 1,000 Americans to deliberate about what should be done in the case of an avian influenza pandemic. Because moral tradeoffs as well as technical matters were at stake, CDC officials were glad to share their decision-making responsibility with citizens. A deliberation was more useful to the CDC than a poll would have been, because participants were informed by the process and changed their views as a result of discussion.[3]

In participatory budgeting (PB), the goal is not just input: citizens actually *decide* in the meeting how to spend portions of a local government's capital budget. Modern PB originates in Brazil but has been adopted in several American communities, and it has a rough kinship to the town meetings that still govern some New England jurisdictions.

In contrast, some public deliberations are disconnected from the government but aim to educate citizens about the specific issues under discussion, teach civic skills, or enhance the capacity of a community to govern itself. For example, the National Issues Forum Institute disseminates guides on several issues each year for use across the United States, often in educational settings.

A robust example is the elaborate system for public deliberation that has been constructed in Hampton, Virginia, an old, blue-collar city of about 145,000 people. When Hampton decided to create a new strategic plan for youth and families in the early 1990s, the city started by enlisting more than

5,000 citizens in discussions that led to a citywide meeting and then the adoption of a formal plan. "Youth, parents, community groups, businesses, and youth workers and advocates . . . met separately for months, with extensive outreach and skilled facilitation." These separate groups converged on the conclusion that education must be more than a task for schools—it also depends on businesses, families, and congregations—and that young people are *assets* who can and should contribute to the city; they are not problems to be solved. That view was especially pronounced in the youth group, whose members "did not want to be viewed as broken and in constant need of fixing. They wanted to be challenged and given opportunities to make real contributions to the community."[4] Deliberation led to a desire for collaboration—a typical pattern when people are invited to true civic engagement.

The planning process ultimately created an influential Hampton Youth Commission (whose 24 commissioners are adolescents) and a new city office to work with them. The Youth Commission sits on top of a pyramid of civic opportunities for young people. Below the Commission are community service programs that involve most of the city's youth: empowered principals' advisory groups in each school, a special youth advisory group for the school superintendent, paid adolescent planners in the planning department, and youth police advisory councils whom the police chief contacts whenever a violent incident involves teenagers. Young people are encouraged to climb this pyramid from service projects toward the citywide Commission, gaining skills and knowledge along the way. Political engagement is so widespread that almost 80 percent of Hampton's young residents voted in the 2004 election, compared to 43 percent in Virginia as a whole.[5] The Hampton system for youth engagement won Harvard's Innovation in Government Award in 2007.

Engagement is not limited to young residents. When Hampton's leaders decided that race relations and racial equity were significant concerns in their southern community, which was about half white and half African American, they convened at least 250 citizens in mixed-race study circles. The participants decided that there was a need to build better skills for working together across racial lines, so they created and began to teach a set of courses—collectively known as "Diversity College"—that still trains local citizens to be speakers, board members, and organizers of discussions.[6]

Hampton's neighborhood planning process has broadened from determining the zoning map to addressing complex social issues. Planning groups include residents as well as city officials, and each may take more than a year to develop a comprehensive plan. Residents (including youth) who develop neighborhood plans emphasize their own assets and capabilities rather than their needs. There is an "attitude of 'what the neighborhood can do with support from the city' rather than 'what the city should do with the neighborhood watching and waiting for it to happen.'"[7]

The hundreds of residents involved in Hampton's shared governance have learned to regard relationships among themselves as important. Every group of citizens must have constructive relationships with all the rest. Relationships between whites and African Americans are an example, but the same principles also apply to relationships between youth and powerful adult officials. When the mayor asked the youth commissioners about his idea for a new vocational high school, they wanted to reject it for practical reasons that the mayor later fully accepted. But instead of denouncing his proposal or embarrassing him publicly, they expressed their views diplomatically and emphasized that they would welcome more dialogue. One student who was both a youth commissioner and a member of the superintendent's youth board said, "Relationship building is essential. People keep coming back because of the relationships."[8]

The police chief was converted to the proposition that youth leadership could reduce crime because one of his daughters helped design the original citywide youth engagement plan, a second daughter helped lead the city's antidrug campaign, and a son served on the school superintendent's board. In such cases, political relationships are also personal.[9]

Today, Hampton has thoroughly reinvented its government and civic culture so that thousands of people are directly involved in city planning, educational policy, police work, and economic development. Residents and officials use a whole arsenal of practical techniques for engaging citizens—from "youth philanthropy" (the Youth Commission makes $40,000 in small grants each year for youth-led projects) to *"charrettes"* (intensive, hands-on, architectural planning sessions that yield actual designs for buildings and sites). The prevailing culture of the city is deliberative; people truly listen, share ideas, and develop consensus, despite differences of interest and ideology. Young people hold positions of responsibility and leadership. Youth have made believers out of initially suspicious police officers, planners, and school administrators. These officials testify that the policies proposed by youth and other citizens are better than alternatives floated by their colleagues alone. The outcomes are impressive, as well. For example, the school system now performs well on standardized tests.[10]

Nationally, the field of deliberative democracy now includes thousands of independent citizens who organize or facilitate discussions, for pay or as volunteers, occasionally or full-time. The National Coalition for Dialogue & Deliberation has more than 2,000 members, most of whom fit this profile.

Meanwhile, a significant number of local institutions that are not defined by their work on deliberation regularly convene public discussions. That category includes community development corporations (CDCs) that hold open public meetings as well as universities that organize public deliberation in their regions.[11]

Relational community organizing. For thousands of years, people have organized political jurisdictions of all scales by creating or changing governments. For almost as long, workers and small-business owners have organized labor markets by starting guilds or unions. For hundreds of years, people have organized political parties and lobbies to try to control or influence republican governments. Between the Civil War and the Second World War, American farmers were organized through the Grange, an association based on local chapters that also advocated politically (without becoming a party).

But Saul Alinsky, the Chicago activist (1909–1972) created something at least largely new—and distinctively American—when he tried to organize a coalition of local organizations that would be independent of formal politics and centered on an urban neighborhood rather than a workplace. The original Industrial Areas Foundation (IAF) that Alinsky founded was not a party, a lobby, a union, or an urban Grange, although it drew on all those models.

Thus "community organizing" was born, but it has always been a contested term for a field full of internal controversy. Alinsky even disagreed with *himself*: his work from the 1960s is strategic and ideological, whereas in the 1930s he had advocated deep respect for local values, including religious ones. Because of the principles I defended in chapter 3, I believe that the "relational" and "broad-based" varieties of community organizing are more authentic elements of the civic renewal network than the ideological, confrontational, and strategic varieties, but our democratic ecosystem may benefit from several types.

Survey data show that most Americans have no idea what "community organizing" means,[12] but presumably the most famous example is ACORN, the large and controversial community organizing group that went bankrupt in 2010. ACORN exemplifies *strategic organizing*, which always starts with some kind of policy agenda, such as saving civilization by reducing carbon emissions or saving unborn children by ending abortion. Strategic organizers need to recruit and motivate strong supporters, find nonsupporters who might be persuadable, and mobilize people who have special assets to contribute to the cause (e.g., money, skills, serious commitment, network ties, or fame).

In contrast, relational organizing does not start with a cause, but rather with a set of people—for instance, all the residents of a neighborhood or all members of a congregation.[13] Relational organizing groups, such as the IAF in Texas, PICO, and the Gamaliel Foundation, usually recommend a long initial process of listening and discussing to decide what the common cause should be. Because their commitment is to relationships, not to predetermined outcomes, the organizers do not select which individuals to mobilize because of what they can contribute to the cause. There is an ethical commitment to the relationship itself that can survive differences of opinion or failure to contribute effectively to the cause.[14]

Relational organizing can occur within a homogeneous group, but it is related to broad-based organizing, in which there is a commitment to connect and listen to *all* sectors or perspectives within a geographical community. A broad-based organizer will want to make sure that liberals, conservatives, industries, environmentalists, and religious and secular people are all at the table.

Relational organizers may recruit participants by painting a fairly concrete picture of a better community, but then they promote open-ended discussions about both means and ends. Two classic tools are "one-on-ones" and "house parties." One-on-ones are reciprocal interviews between organizers and other citizens (or between any two citizens), designed to share underlying values, experiences, and goals as well as political preferences. House parties are small discussions that are deliberately dispersed through a community, mixing political discussions with social interaction, personal expression—and food. Romand Coles describes relational organizers as benign "tricksters" who enlist people into a genuinely democratic process by first proposing political goals and then encouraging participants to form their own opinions.[15]

Community organizers want concrete, tangible changes in local housing, industries, schools, police, or natural resources—yet they are willing to pursue goals that they had not anticipated before they began discussions with their members. They are broad-based to the extent that they welcome *diverse* views (including diverse ideologies) as assets.

Although they lie on a continuum with deliberative democracy organizations, relational organizers place less emphasis on representativeness and jury-like conversations that inform policymakers. Instead, they emphasize direct political action, leadership development and training, the strengthening of social capital, and institution building. In community organizing, deliberations are about what the participants will do, not what the government should do.

Because loyalty to communities is a fundamental value in relational organizing, the organizations devoted to it tend to be networks of religious congregations, local nonprofit agencies, and other rooted groups, rather than specialists who travel the country providing services. Important examples are the IAF, most of whose members are churches; the PICO National Network, a coalition of more than 1,000 "faith-based community organizations"; and the Gamaliel Foundation, also a network composed mainly of churches. Meanwhile, some specialized national organizations, like the Center for Community Change, advocate for community organizing and provide services to grassroots groups.

San Antonio provides one of the best documented and most impressive examples of relational organizing. Community Organized for Public Service (COPS) arose in the 1970s to represent the city's Latinos. At first inspired by Saul Alinsky, COPS used militant and confrontational tactics to win economic and political benefits for its supporters, not primarily in the workplace (like a union) nor at the ballot box (like a party) but in neighborhoods and consumer settings. For example, in 1975, COPS supporters disrupted a downtown department store and a bank (by filling these institutions all day and failing to buy anything), while their leaders negotiated with powerful businessmen over jobs for Hispanic residents.[16] Such direct actions remain part of the COPS repertoire, along with other expressions of collective power. On "accountability nights," for instance, the organization convenes large numbers of residents to ask questions of invited political candidates, who cannot fail to attend without offending those voters and potential voters (COPS has an effective voter-registration arm).

Power counts, and democracy is stronger in San Antonio because Hispanics are now politically organized. COPS has won tangible victories: more than one billion dollars in public investments, including a whole new community college, a nationally recognized comprehensive job-training program, and enough Hispanic registered voters to permit the election of Henry Cisneros as mayor.[17] COPS and Cisneros sometimes clashed, but he was publicly respectful: "I can say unequivocally, COPS has fundamentally altered the moral tone and the political and physical face of San Antonio."[18]

COPS—which is the leading Texas chapter of the national IAF—goes beyond merely flexing collective power on behalf of a segment of the population and its economic interests. It is not a standard interest group, and it has moved away from its Alinsky roots. It deliberately builds relationships among diverse people, including mutually trusting relationships that cross lines of race and class, and it promotes constant, open-ended discussions among its grassroots supporters. For these purposes, COPS uses one-on-ones, house parties, and an array of reading groups, seminars, and retreats for committed activists.[19]

Organizers place a high value on not driving these discussions toward any particular outcomes but rather encouraging participants to express their genuine values, which may be spiritual, traditionalist, or even sectarian rather than progressive and economic. To some extent, the leaders of Texas IAF are deliberately ceding their power to choose goals, because they believe in democratic procedures. But they also welcome and share their members' insights about cultural and moral discontents. The emerging shared philosophy of the organization asserts that many of our deepest problems are cultural and spiritual, although money and other resources are essential to the solutions.

COPS and other Texas IAF affiliates invest time and resources in developing civic capacity, which includes the leadership skills of poor people (often women) and their associations and networks.[20] The official members of COPS are not individuals but churches, which are powerful, organized, culturally resonant, indigenous resources in even the poorest South Texas neighborhoods. COPS offers them support in recruitment and financial management. For individuals, it offers demanding and intellectually ambitious learning opportunities. For instance, COPS leaders read and discuss advanced works of theology and politics from diverse perspectives.[21]

In short, COPS exemplifies a style of politics that mixes material interests with high moral ideals; that prizes local assets even as it demands external aid; and that combines narrowly political work (like voter registration drives) with performance and ritual, prayer, socializing, friendship, and entertainment. The network's original base in Catholic Hispanic churches meant that it was at first—in certain respects—homogeneous, but it has pushed intentionally into Protestant congregations, synagogues, and secular organizations, not only in San Antonio but across Texas.

Community-based economic development. Many thousands of not-for-profit institutions are involved in various forms of economic development in the communities where they are located. Some have used federal Community Development Block Grants and other funds to develop low-income housing and plow the proceeds from their investments into further development. They solicit public participation in their decisions, both as a matter of ethical commitment and in order to comply with funders' rules.[22] Hence these institutions overlap with the fields of community organizing and public deliberation, but their emphasis on managing tangible assets makes them different. They contribute to the civic renewal movement by promoting democratic deliberation, magnifying the voice of poor people, building civic skills, and creating assets that are subject to democratic control because they cannot be moved.

In 2005, there were 4,600 community development corporations (CDCs) in the United States, employing nearly 200,000 people, building about 86,000 residential units annually, and managing commercial property and spawning other enterprises.[23] The concept of a CDC is not defined in federal law, and in practice, CDCs resemble other nonprofit organizations that have similar missions. For example, a community development bank specializes in lending rather than developing property, but those two roles overlap. Like CDCs, community development financial institutions (such as banks and credit unions) are widespread and influential, holding more than $25 billion in assets in 2007.[24]

Churches may also build, lease, finance, or sell homes and other buildings for the good of their communities. Sometimes they create spin-offs formally known as CDCs, but often they handle the financing directly.[25] A famous example is the Greater Allen African Methodist Episcopal Cathedral in Queens, New York, which manages assets worth over $100 million, including rental properties, businesses, and a school. Meanwhile, community land trusts tend to purchase open space for preservation, but some urban land trusts operate much like CDCs, and some CDCs buy land to preserve or create open space. Community organizing groups such as the IAF have created CDCs; and some CDCs have affiliated with community organizing networks.

In the city where I write this chapter, the Somerville Community Corporation is a not-for-profit real estate developer, which invests its profits in new development; a provider of adult education; an emergency lender to low-income renters; a community organizing group affiliated with the IAF; a convener of public deliberations about matters like planning and municipal budgeting; and a lobby on behalf of employment, transportation, and welfare programs. This combination of functions is typical, and as a result the Somerville Community Corporation could be listed under several categories of civic work, as could the Allen Cathedral in Queens.

Regardless of their precise status, all these institutions are anchored legally in their physical communities. They manage assets that have market value, and they use business techniques (such as charging fees for services and lending money with interest), but they are not permitted to move. Their structure honors the civic virtue of loyalty and gives them a practical need to employ voice rather than exit to address problems. How they exercise voice varies, but typical tools include public meetings, boards that represent local residents, and public events designed to solicit public input. Meanwhile, all these organizations express—at least in theory—an ethic of trusteeship and public service. That ethic is usually codified in the organization's nonprofit status and bylaws, but there is no reason that a for-profit business cannot serve the same purposes. An example of a profitable firm that is rooted in a place, that acts as a trustee, that regularly consults empowered residents, and that invests in their education and development is Prairie Crossing, a residential and business developer in northern Illinois.[26]

CDCs have roots in Lyndon Johnson's War on Poverty, and specifically the thousands of Community Action Agencies (CAAs) that were created under federal law and asked to oversee local federal welfare programs, including Head Start, legal services, and public housing.[27] The Economic Opportunity Act of 1964 had required that all new federal welfare programs be "developed, conducted, and administered with the maximum feasible participation of the residents of the areas and the members of the groups served."[28] CAAs arose to meet that need.

They still exist; more than 1,000 belong to the Community Action Partnership, and many of those are also classified as CDCs. But the typical mechanisms for encouraging the participation of residents have evolved. In the 1960s, it was common to hold public elections for board members of CAAs. This was problematic because the United States was already covered by a smooth tessellation of local governments with their own elected leaders. Adding a new layer with different boundaries caused constant jurisdictional conflicts and struggles for power. CAAs were supposed to avoid patronage and corruption, but often turnout was poor, and elections offered new opportunities for corrupt influence. Today it is much more common for a community-based development organization to be structured as a private, not-for-profit corporation that has a board with fiduciary obligations to the public. Some or all members may be elected, but some may be representatives of local institutions, including municipal governments. Foundations and governments also exercise considerable power by deciding what to fund. CDC's and kindred organizations do not claim the kind of democratic mandate that comes from public elections, but they do welcome and promote participation.

Asset-based community development. Community development corporations and relational community organizers (two overlapping groups) widely share the principles that John L. McKnight and John P. Kretzmann have named asset-based community development (ABCD).

Just as the standard model of adolescents emphasizes their problems and threats, so the standard view of poor urban or rural communities stresses their pathologies and lack of resources. In both cases, these assumptions have an empirical basis: teenagers actually get into trouble (sometimes fatally), and poor neighborhoods really do have problems.

Just to mention one example, in the 53206 zip code of Milwaukee, Wisconsin, during the pre-recession year of 2007, 62 percent of the men in their early 30s were in or had been in state prisons. Due to premature death and incarceration, women in their 30s outnumbered men by three to two. The average income of tax filers (a small proportion of the population) was just $17,547, and 90 percent of these individuals were single parents.[29]

It is easy—and appropriate—to catalog the deficits of this place. But the net effects of a "deficit model" of urban development can be harmful. It suggests that indigenous people and their networks have little capacity, so outside agencies must provide resources. But resources that simply flow from outside tend to be misallocated or otherwise wasted. Consider, for example, that 90 percent of the people who declared any income from working within Milwaukee's 53206 zip code in 2007 lived outside it, and 56 percent of these filers were white (even though 97 percent of the zip code's residents were African American). Welfare, police, and health funds intended for this community subsidized public employees who lived elsewhere. A deficit approach also encourages authorities literally to bulldoze buildings and other assets that have value, and it may motivate residents to exit.

Hence ABCD begins with making an elaborate public inventory of the assets, both tangible and intangible, of any community. Outside resources, such as funds, experts, and volunteers, are not supposed to flow until the community has assessed and discussed its own strengths. ABCD and PYD come together in community youth development (CYD), which typically involves teenagers in assessing their communities' assets. CYD is an alternative to the kinds of programs that *remove* "at-risk" teenagers from dangerous settings to work or study apart. Instead, CYD treats their relationships with their home communities as potentially positive for both. Again, there is a strong emphasis on developing the voice and skills of participants.

Work to defend and expand the commons. A CDC is a corporation, legally similar to General Motors or Microsoft, except that it may not make a profit. However, compared to a standard firm, a CDC has a different moral and psychological relationship to the things it owns. It is a *trustee* of public or community goods. That ethic of trusteeship should be codified in its bylaws and reinforced by its regular procedures. As such, a CDC is an example of an institutional arrangement designed to preserve and enhance "the commons."

Understood more broadly, the commons includes all our shared assets: the earth's atmosphere, oceans, and water-cycle; basic scientific knowledge (which cannot be patented); the heritage of human creativity, including folklore and the whole works of Plato, Shakespeare and every other long-dead author; the

Internet, viewed as a single structure (even though its components are privately owned); public law; physical public spaces such as parks and plazas; the broadcast spectrum; the fabric of neighborhoods and other local communities; and even cultural norms and habits.

The commons is intrinsically connected to civic engagement because engaged, organized citizens are needed to produce free public goods, to protect the ones that exist, to advocate for policies favorable to the commons, and to recruit young people to defend and expand the commons for the future. As noted earlier, these citizens must contribute a combination of talk (or collective reasoning) plus work.[30]

Today, portions of the commons are under severe threat. Global fish stocks are poised to collapse due to overfishing on the unregulated high seas. Corporations that patent business practices may remove from the commons ideas that would have been free in the past. (For example, Amazon patented the idea of ordering and paying for goods online with a single mouse click.[31]) On the other hand, the growth of the Internet, of open-source software, and of various new institutional arrangements in the offline world are strengthening and expanding certain commons.

Meanwhile, the very idea of the commons has been reevaluated. Garrett Hardin's "The Tragedy of the Commons" (1968) was "one of the most frequently cited articles in the social sciences."[32] Hardin argued that a valuable resource must be owned. If it was left unowned, it would be consumed and not replenished. There appeared to be two kinds of owners: (1) private individuals or corporations, and (2) governments. A heated debate followed about the relative advantages and dangers of each, but the consensus held that one or the other type of owner ought to own everything that mattered. If you favored the government, you leaned toward the socialist side of the political spectrum; if you preferred private ownership, you were more of a libertarian. There was not much of a third way in the theoretical literature, although there were important, overlooked alternatives in practice.

Applying Hardin's theoretical framework, governments, international lenders, and experts turned forests, grazing lands, fisheries, and other resources all over the world into property: either privatizing and marketing these assets or else nationalizing them. Often the results were devastating. As Ostrom wrote, "In many settings where individuals have managed small- to medium-sized resources for centuries, drawing on local knowledge and locally crafted institutions, their disempowerment led to a worsening of environmental problems rather than their betterment."[33] This was no small matter: human famine and the extinction of natural species were sometimes the price.

As Ostrom and colleagues have shown, a *community* can own an asset.[34] That does not mean that a government that represents the community owns it. Nor does it mean that a nonprofit corporation manages the asset as the community's trustee. The community can actually own the resource. It needs rules, norms, traditions, or processes that limit the asset's use and/or cause people to replenish it.

Those rules may include large doses of individual property rights. For instance, you may own your fishing boat and nets and any fish that you catch. But the community owns the fishery if only approved people can fish there and if each can only take a certain number of fish. If those rules are local government ordinances, we may say that the community owns the fishery and uses the government as one of its instruments of control. (It will almost certainly use other tools as well, including private vigilance.) In many cases, the rules are effectively enforced *without* official government endorsement. Violence and threats of violence may never be necessary, either, if local ties are strong and outsiders are rare.

An asset can belong to a community in a meaningful sense if it is true collective property, or if it is divided among private owners who collectively regulate its use, or if it belongs to just a few official owners who depend on and are accountable to the whole community. For instance, many houses of worship all over the world belong to the state or a private party who holds title to the land and the building. Yet those religious institutions are genuinely owned by the community in the sense that they could never move or survive without the community's support.[35]

The word "commons" suggests communitarian or even communistic values—putting the group over the individual. But that is an analytical mistake. For one thing, the commons is not state centered. Some common assets are completely unowned (e.g., the ozone layer), and some are jointly owned and managed by associations. Some belong legally to states and are controlled by them: think of Yellowstone. However, it is by no means clear that states are ideal—or even adequate—owners of commons.

Further, the commons is only a part of a good society, not the whole. Some anarchists want everything to be treated as a common asset, but most of us simply value the common assets we already have and want to protect them against corporate enclosure, overuse, and other threats. We have no interest in abolishing either the state or the market; on the contrary, we think that both work better if they can draw appropriately on a range of unowned assets, from clean air to scientific knowledge.

Opening one's eyes to the possibility of community ownership that is not state *or* private ownership provides new options for managing resources, allows us to evaluate and appreciate traditional arrangements, and calls attention to the impressive skills and values that people employ all over the world to manage common assets.

New examples of commons include land-trusts and co-ops as well as cyberspace, understood as a whole structure, not as a series of privately owned components. Practical work to protect and enhance commons is underway within the American Libraries Association (ALA), because librarians see themselves as defenders of public artifacts (the books, maps, databases, and web pages in their collections); public facilities (library buildings, meeting spaces, grounds); and public ideas (including all human knowledge that is not patented or copyrighted, plus copyrighted books that people can borrow and read).[36] Librarians believe that these public goods face numerous threats, ranging from patrons' abuse of library books and budget cuts to corporations' efforts to overextend copyright law. However, the ALA fights back in the courts and legislatures.

Collaborative efforts to restore and protect natural commons (ecosystems) are often undertaken under the name of civic environmentalism. Since the keys to robust, sustainable commons include public deliberation and the wide dispersal of civic skills and attitudes, commons work must be viewed as closely related to civic renewal.

National and community service. Programs that involve citizens in community service frequently describe themselves as promoting civic engagement. Whether that claim is valid depends on a more basic question: "What is service?" That would be easy if service meant unpaid, voluntary work, but members of the Civilian Conservation Corps in the 1930s, the Peace Corps and VISTA since the 1960s, and AmeriCorps since 1993 have been paid by the federal government. Teach for America is proudly part of the service movement, yet its members receive full-time teachers' salaries from the school districts in which they work. In fact, they are paid the same salaries as their colleagues who are not Teach for America members, which invites us to ask why *all* teachers are not involved in "service." And one could go further: if we say that all teachers perform service, then why not people who provide other public goods, including people who happen to work for profitable companies?

The motives and rationales of programs that use "community service" in their mission statements differ widely. From the CCC to the modern organization called YouthBuild, some service programs aim to provide jobs for unemployed and alienated young people—jobs with a strong aspect of training and education, a public service ethic, and a sense of solidarity that comes from working in teams. On entering YouthBuild, the participants—young adults without high school diplomas—estimate their own life expectancies at 40, on average, whereas upon completing the program, they have raised the estimate to 72: evidence that they have gained a sense of opportunity, optimism, and purpose by working together, building houses.[37] One alumnus listed some of the civic skills taught in YouthBuild and depicted those skills as opening doors to rewarding engagement beyond the program itself: "I never knew what a budget plan was, I never knew how to keep minutes, I never knew how to do all that, and when I got to the policy committee and they started showing me these things, it just kept motivating me more and more to just keep doing positive and wanting to sit on not only the policy committee at YouthBuild, but what committees can I get on in my neighborhood and can I be on a neighborhood association committee.... So it definitely just opened up my mind to what else was out there."[38]

The main purpose of the Peace Corps, on the other hand, is to employ highly skilled Americans in addressing problems in the developing world, with ancillary benefits for the foreign policy of the United States. Teach for America tries to open a new pathway into the teaching profession for graduates of highly selective colleges and universities, young people who will remain involved in education policy even after they leave teaching for higher status professions. Cities of Service, a coalition of more than 100 municipalities, wants to take advantage of volunteer labor to meet urgent challenges in a time of tight budgets. Critics of that kind of program accuse it—fairly or not—of seeking to replace unionized positions with free work.

These are such different objectives that it is hard to discern a common thread or a consistent link with civic renewal. But the field as a whole is marked by several tendencies favorable to civic engagement. Most service programs show high respect for the capacity of citizens to address problems, where a citizen means anyone, not just a credentialed expert or a representative of an organization. Although some programs provide full-time, salaried positions, these jobs are alternatives to specialized careers. Participants are expected to do service for a while and then move on.

Many service programs also combine work with a significant measure of learning and discussing, including explicit civic education in programs like City Year, Public Allies, and YouthBuild (all of which enlist young people in teams to address community problems). In short, service can build participants' capacity for civic engagement and lower barriers to participation in public institutions. This is not to say, however, that either the guiding principles or the outcomes of service programs are consistent. Some simply enlist people to clean up parks or paint walls, and it is not clear why that is helpful to democracy. It could even be counterproductive if it justified laying off paid employees.

Since the 1980s, civilian service has been institutionalized with funded programs, paid professionals who lead and organize service, and rewards for the participants. Most important, the federal government launched Ameri-Corps and the Corporation for National Service (later, the Corporation for National and Community Service) in 1993. The federal programs are popular, as demonstrated on the auspicious day of September 11, 2008—just weeks before the presidential election—when both Barack Obama and John McCain traveled to New York City to endorse a bill that would triple the budget of AmeriCorps. That bill passed with bipartisan support and would have become law under a President McCain as well.

There is no single corps in AmeriCorps; instead, the Corporation funds intermediaries that include national nonprofits with diverse models and constituencies plus schools, universities, Native American nations, and local nonprofits. YouthBuild, the Peace Corps, and the Corps Network (a coalition of 143 Service and Conservation Corps) are components of the national service movement that are not within AmeriCorps. Meanwhile, some large school districts and universities and one whole state (Maryland) have enacted service requirements for all their students. Several states and major cities also have official service commissions. High school students perceive a need to volunteer in order to be competitive applicants to college.[39]

Probably as a result of these incentives, opportunities, and requirements, three-quarters of high school seniors reported volunteering at least "sometimes" by the year 2003 (up from 63 percent in the 1975), and 80 percent of incoming college freshmen reported having volunteered in high school. The Corporation for National and Community Service reports that about eight million young adults (age 16–24) volunteered in 2008.[40] The next year, AmeriCorps received congressional authorization to expand to 250,000 annual full-time service positions, although budget constraints make that goal seem increasingly optimistic.

The service field belongs within the civic renewal network, in my opinion, and it represents a powerful political asset. But service programs should be more consistently committed to deliberating about objectives and strategies, developing participants' civic skills, and collaborating with other organizations (rather than simply telling their own volunteers what to do).

Civic education. Our K–12 schools are venues for developing the skills and commitments of active citizens. They reach *all* young people (at least until the teenage years, when the dropout rate reaches epidemic levels), and they influence individuals who are still malleable and forming their identities as citizens.

Civic education is not only about preparing individuals to be effective and responsible citizens *later*. Youth are already particularly well placed to address youth issues, from violence to obesity, from bullying to low test scores. In the best cases, they help solve those problems and, as a result of their contributions, they gain motivations, skills, and values helpful in life. In adopting public roles and collaborating with adults, they soften the barriers between schools and communities and help schools to become locally anchored institutions of public value. In short, all the norms identified in chapter 3—including deliberation, work, loyalty, and a developmental ethic—are served by civic education at its best.

Civic education is more than the name of a course. In fact, my colleagues and I have assembled evidence in support of six distinct offerings of schools that help youth to develop as citizens.[41] One is a set of courses, variously named "civics," "government," or "social studies," in which politics and community engagement are explicit topics of study. The other offerings are moderated discussions of controversial issues (which may take place in any class or outside of class time), participation in extracurricular groups and clubs that require student leadership and management, student voice in the governance of schools, community service combined with academic study, and games or other simulations of adults' civic roles.

For each of these aspects of civic education, there is a body of favorable evaluations and other supportive research, but the quality of students' experiences is found to vary, and high quality is necessary for beneficial effects. Very low quality assignments can be counterproductive. For instance, if poor urban students are told that it is time to study democracy and citizenship through community service, and therefore they must clean up the school's neglected playground, they may receive a powerful message to stay clear of citizenship. A young man from Little Rock, Arkansas, recalled such an experience when we asked him about service learning in his high school. "The janitors get paid for it!" he said. "I just feel like they was using us. I mean, what's picking up trash showing us, beside being clean? . . . It didn't teach us nothing."[42]

Concerned outsiders often suggest that schools have abandoned their civic missions: that they once taught civics and must begin to do so again. In fact, all states currently require some teaching of civics and/or government.[43] Contrary to popular belief, the prevalence of civics and social studies courses is fairly high and has risen in the past 20 years at the high school level.[44] Most states have course requirements and several mandate high-stakes tests of civic knowledge.[45]

Yet outcomes are inadequate and highly unequal, even within states that have strict requirements. Schools that send most of their students to college (most of which enroll strictly middle-class children) often provide rich and effective civic experiences; schools that struggle with high rates of test failure and dropout generally do not. Within a given diverse school, students on a successful academic track usually receive civic opportunities; their less successful peers do not.[46] Public schooling was established to equalize political power by giving everyone the knowledge and skills they would need to participate. Instead, it tends to reinforce pervasive political inequalities.

Analyzing a survey of 100,000 high school students by the Knight Foundation, my colleagues and I were unable to find any state policies that had substantial impacts on what students knew about civics, despite considerable variation in the policies.[47] In sum, we know what good civic education looks like at the school and classroom level. We know that the children who need such experiences most are least likely to receive them. We do not have a tested recipe for state (let alone federal) policies that would solve those problems.

By far the most important providers of civic education are the schools themselves. In 2007–8, 15,000 teachers reported that their main assignment was high school government or civics. Many more teachers (60,000) reported teaching history at the high school level, and one could add elementary and middle school instructors with significant interests in social studies, plus administrators responsible for extracurricular groups and service programs.[48] In short, many thousands of full-time professionals are paid to participate in civic renewal. Although their levels of ability and commitment to that cause vary, they represent an asset to the movement.

Fine civic education also takes place in youth groups that are concerned primarily with healthy adolescent development. Increasingly, adults in 4-H, the Scouts, and urban youth centers believe that engaging teenagers in studying and addressing local social problems are vital ways to develop their intellects, characters, and to keep them safe. Much like proponents of asset-based community development, these people want to treat their subjects (in this case, students) as partners and assets, not as bundles of problems. They also emphasize local geographical communities as excellent subjects for youth to study and as venues for youth work. The Innovation Center for Community and Youth Development and the Forum for Youth Investment are important hubs in this movement. The Coalition for Community Schools brings a similar set of values to its work with K–12 schools.

Meanwhile, specialized nonprofit organizations provide textbooks, lesson plans, and seminars for teachers. These groups include the Center for Civic Education, the Constitutional Rights Foundation, Street Law, Public Achievement, Generation Citizen, and iCivics, among others. Their programs usually combine a focus on perennial democratic principles with investigations of immediate issues relevant to students. They also tend to combine experiential learning (e.g., debate, community service, and advocacy) with reading and writing. Because they are independent nonprofits rather than public schools or individual teachers, they can be active in national advocacy for civic education. These nonprofits advocate for civic education through the Campaign for the Civic Mission of Schools.

The engaged university. Colleges and universities have great civic potential as producers of knowledge, sites of deliberation, and powerful nonprofit economic institutions, rooted in communities. As Community Wealth notes, "Institutions of higher education have an obvious vested interest in building strong relationships with the communities that surround their campuses. They do not have the option of relocating and thus are of necessity place-based anchors. While corporations, businesses, and residents often flee from economically depressed low-income urban and suburban edge-city neighborhoods, universities remain."[49] Moreover, higher education is not just *any* sector with $136 billion in annual spending and $100 billion in real estate holdings.[50] The business of colleges and universities is the production and dissemination of knowledge and the promotion of dialogue and debate. They provide an impressive infrastructure for deliberative democracy. Lee Benson and his colleagues argue that "universities and colleges . . . *potentially* represent by far the most powerful partners, 'anchors,' and creative catalysts for change and improvement in the quality of life in American cities and communities."[51]

This does not mean that higher education is meeting its potential. The marginal place of civic themes in mainstream scholarship (analyzed in chapter 2) is one problem. Another is the profound gap in social status between those inside a university and those beyond its walls. Colleges do not just reflect class divisions; they define them. The best definition of the working class today is the people who have not attended college. It is intrinsically problematic for institutions that guard a basic social boundary to be the leaders of democratic renewal.

But higher education can contribute. For one thing, universities operate major public programs, such as hospitals and clinics, agricultural extension offices (operating in almost every county of the United States), consulting and training opportunities for adult citizens and organizations, museums, and enrichment programs for K–12 education. One example gives an indication of the scale of this work: the Industrial Extension Service at North Carolina State reports that it "hit its target of $1.0 billion" in impact on local businesses in 2010.[52] Today, many state universities coordinate such programs under the heading of civic engagement, combining their public service functions with education, research, and partnerships with communities. Many now call on specialized centers or particular senior administrators to coordinate civic engagement across their campuses.

Many colleges and universities also maintain multipurpose centers which provide specialized courses with community service components that sponsor research in and with their local communities, develop partnerships with local NGOs, and invite speakers and organize faculty fellowships and seminars. Some of these centers are large: for example, the Center for Social Concerns at Notre Dame, which conducts research, education, and outreach related to civic engagement, has about 32 full-time employees. The Center for Community Partnerships at the University of Pennsylvania provides opportunities for distinguished scholars to advance their disciplines by conducting research that benefits (and takes direction from) residents of West Philadelphia, where the university is situated. Penn has also used its economic leverage in constructive ways, collaborating with community partners.

These centers (like the Jonathan M. Tisch College of Citizenship and Public Service at Tufts University, where I work) exemplify several civic trends: a move from service to collaboration; a rediscovery of geographical communities; a reflection on colleges' power as employers, builders, and consumers; and a turn to sophisticated research that *requires* learning with and from nonacademics.

Portland State University in Oregon serves as an example. Its civic work is ambitious and pervasive, and it demonstrates how a university's distinctive offerings—such as undergraduate courses—can support other forms of civic renewal that originate outside the academy.

Portland State chose the motto "Let Knowledge Serve the City." Since the early 1990s, the university has tried to align much of its teaching, research, and outreach to address specific issues in the city. A hallmark of its approach is lengthy, ambitious, multiyear projects that involve formal partnerships between several units within the university and several community-based organizations or networks and local governmental agencies.

For example, over a five-year period, as part of one coherent effort to protect a watershed (composed of urban streams), numerous classes of PSU students collected environmental and social data, educated local children and developed high school curricula, created videos, facilitated public discussions of the watershed, and directly cleaned up wetlands and constructed facilities.[53] These classes did not work alone but in close cooperation with each other and with a large array of civic organizations.

Not coincidentally, the maintenance and restoration of watersheds is a particularly strong tradition within the emerging field of practice called civic environmentalism. Watersheds create classic wicked problems. They are vulnerable to pollution, runoff, overuse, and other abuse from many sources—not just major factories (which might be regulated effectively) but also private homes and individuals. They are not sharply delimited locations but are rather areas that overlap with human communities, ecosystems, and transportation corridors. They tend to cross political jurisdictions. Their needs compete against other legitimate needs and interest, both human and natural. Watersheds are hard to protect by command-and-control regulation alone, but they respond well when people take coordinated action on their behalf: educating one another; passing local ordinances and policies within institutions; voluntarily curtailing pollution; and contributing time and effort to understand, protect, restore, and enjoy them. Since the early 1970s, the EPA has been supporting citizens and networks that protect watersheds, by providing grants, guides, data, and training.[54]

Thus Portland State's coordinated efforts to study, discuss, and improve a local watershed belong within a larger story about civic environmentalism. But PSU brings special resources: scholars and laboratories, 17,000 students, as well as purchasing power and facilities—none of which can be picked up and moved to another location. The university and the city share a fate, and the university understands that. Its commitments extend well beyond watersheds: its partnership with city schools is equally ambitious, and there are other examples. The university has encouraged its faculty to deliberate issues that arise when an educational institution addresses a city's problems, using study circles as the format for these discussions.[55] (Study circles also played a key role in the Hampton case, discussed earlier under deliberative democracy).

One factor that works against civic engagement is a set of expectations for tenure and promotion that favor abstract, generalizable, methodologically complex research over applied or collaborative research. But some leading research institutions are reforming their expectations. For example, the tenure policy at the University of Minnesota now states, "Scholarly research must include significant publications and, as appropriate, the development and dissemination by other means of new knowledge, technology, or scientific procedures resulting in innovative products, practices, and ideas of significance and value to society."[56] That definition permits a broader range of research to be rewarded, as long as the research is done well.

Media reform. In a community of any size, people cannot directly deliberate, work, or form relationships. Their interactions must be mediated. Thus the media of communications are essential features of civil society and politics. For civic reformers, three major aspects of the media require constant attention.

First is the nature of the available media. In 1910, 110 newspapers were printed for every 100 households in the United States.[57] That meant that for most urbanites, consuming the news meant choosing one or more daily newspapers, each oriented toward a particular demographic or interest group, each filled with articles written by professional reporters. But the number of daily newspapers had already fallen in half in cities like New York City by 1940 and daily readership declined for most of the past century.[58] In 1980, 50 million Americans tuned in nightly to one of three national television networks' news broadcasts that consisted of summaries by celebrity anchors, along with short video segments from the field. But the network news audience had fallen in half by 2010.[59] In 2012, about one in 20 Americans said they regularly followed campaigns by watching videos uploaded to YouTube.[60] Some of those videos were parodies, songs, and mashups of footage from professional sources.

These shifts in the form of the media that we consume have civic implications. The amount of information, its reliability and relevance, its power to move or shock, whether we can contribute ideas, the degree to which we see people like ourselves represented, and the degree to which we share common experiences all vary.

A second topic is who controls the media and under what constraints. Traditionally, daily newspapers were privately owned. Under the Constitution, private owners can do practically anything they want with their own publications, but in a competitive market, they must be somewhat responsive to consumers' demand; that is a constraint. A publicly traded corporation, a state agency, a government-subsidized not-for-profit corporation (such as an independent public radio station), or a page on Wikipedia that anyone can edit all operate under different rules and pressures. In general, the incentives should favor the provision of reliable, substantive information, diverse opinion, and opportunities for interaction. Those principles probably do not favor one particular system of control, but rather a mix of forms.

The third topic involves the prevailing norms and self-understood purposes of the people who produce media. CNN's political director, defending his heavy use of polls, once asserted that surveys "happen to be the most authoritative way to answer the most basic question about the election, which is who is going to win?"[61] "Who is going to win?" is one definition of news. It encourages not only regular polling, but also close coverage of the mechanics and strategies of political campaigns. Around the same time, the *Wichita Eagle* asserted that its purpose was to depict the public's "struggle to find a middle ground" by giving prominent attention to civil discussions among nonaligned citizens.[62] In some cases, the *Eagle* actually convened citizens to deliberate and then covered their discussions in the news pages. That was a very different definition of news from CNN's, with significant consequences for the public.

I have been watching and occasionally participating in media reform efforts since the early 1990s. At first, relatively little attention was given to the format of media. Printed newspapers and magazines and professionally produced news programs on radio and TV seemed fairly stable and unproblematic. The main reform objective was to change the incentives operating on the owners or managers of news organizations. Reformers believed that the Federal Communications Commission (FCC) had a right and obligation to regulate certain aspects of the content of the broadcast media, because broadcast stations used the public airwaves at no cost to themselves in return for serving the "public interest, convenience, and necessity." Reformers were particularly committed to the FCC's Fairness Doctrine, which required substantive and balanced coverage of controversial current topics.[63] Newspapers could not be regulated in the same way (because of the First Amendment), but reformers wanted newspaper owners to face competition in each market so that consumers would have market power. They asked the FCC to block media mergers and prevent individuals and firms from owning newspapers and broadcast stations in the same markets. Finally, they favored government-subsidized public media as a valuable alternative source.

Those fundamental objectives remain valid today. However, courts have looked with increasing skepticism at regulation, especially now that cable news networks no longer need the public airwaves. Meanwhile, competition has largely vanished in the local news industry due to shrinking audiences and revenues. Newspaper ad revenue declined 31 percent between 2000 and 2007, while the number of reporters assigned to cover statehouses fell by almost exactly the same proportion.[64] Today, a city is lucky to have any newspaper at all, and broadcast television stations employ skeleton crews of reporters. The goal of preventing local monopolies seems quaint.

A second reform agenda gathered force during the 1990s. Called "public journalism" or "civic journalism," this was an effort to change the prevailing norms and values of professional reporters in the interest of stronger democracy. It was led by insiders, such as the *Wichita Eagle*'s W. Davis ("Buzz") Merritt and the *St. Louis Post-Dispatch*'s Cole Campbell. Generally committed to norms of deliberation, collaboration, inclusion, and community, these journalists changed daily newsroom practices in interesting ways. An important example was the decision of the *Charlotte Observer* to dispense with horse race campaign coverage, that is, stories about how the campaigns were trying to win the election. Instead, the *Observer* convened representative citizens to choose issues for reporters to investigate and to draft questions that the candidates were asked to answer on the pages of the newspaper.[65]

Public journalism produced interesting and appealing results in scattered cases, but it had lost momentum by 2000. One reason was economic tumult in the news industry. Another challenge was the intrinsic difficulty of sustaining a reform movement. But perhaps the biggest factor was the rise of the Internet, which threatened the jobs of the daily newspaper reporters who had supported public journalism in the 1990s while also promising an alternative path to reform. In the 2000s, if media professionals continued to talk about supporting democracy and civil society, their attention shifted to the nature of the media. Blogs, online news stories with comment threads, wikis, list-serves—all seemed to offer unprecedented advantages. Because they were cheap, they could break the monopoly of corporate media. Because they were interactive, they could promote dialogue and discussion more efficiently than the efforts of the *Wichita Eagle* and the *Charlotte Observer* to convene citizens and cover their deliberations. News could even be "crowdsourced," or voluntarily produced by collaborating citizens. That seemed inherently civic.

I think the new media formats have largely proved disappointing, and it has been a mistake to ignore the older issues of journalists' norms and media ownership.

Interactivity does not automatically mean civic deliberation. On the contrary, few forums are more dispiriting than the unmoderated comment field that follows a standard newspaper article.

Professional reporting continues to play a critical role. According to a study of the changing news environment in Baltimore, Maryland, conducted by the Pew Research Center, the number of news outlets in the city has proliferated to 53 "radio talk shows, . . . blogs, specialized new outlets, new media sites, TV stations, radio news programs, newspapers and their various legacy media websites." But the number of reporters has fallen. That means that there is more written and spoken text about the news, but it is highly repetitive. A search of six major news topics found that 83 percent of the articles and blog posts repeated the same material—sometimes with commentary—and more than half the original text came from paid print media such as the *Baltimore Sun*. In turn, Baltimore's remaining professional journalists are so overstretched that they cannot provide what is called "enterprise reporting" (digging to find new information not already in the public domain). The city government and other official institutions now have more, rather than less, control over the news:

> As news is posted faster, often with little enterprise reporting added, the official version of events is becoming more important. We found official press releases often appear word for word in first accounts of events, though often not noted as such.[66]

Meanwhile, even though the cost of starting a news source has fallen, media concentration remains a threat. Clear Channel Communications owns 1,200 radio stations. Rupert Murdoch's News Corporation owns the *Wall Street Journal*, Fox News, HarperCollins, and Fox News Radio, among many other news sources in the United States. The Internet may enable more voices, but if they rely on fewer enterprise reporters, and if more of those professionals work for a few media moguls, we have made no progress.

The *Charlotte Observer* story ends with an ironic but relevant coda: after the newspaper had dropped its experiments with public journalism, it acquired a citizen-produced nonprofit website, Charlotte's Web, that had been founded to promote discussion and collaboration. The *Observer* merged that site into its main commercial web portal, which retains no evident commitment to dialogue or local problem solving. Today, the *Observer* has a local monopoly, belongs to the McClatchy chain, and has shed 42 percent of its employees.

The proper role of reporters seems to draw less fruitful and constructive attention than it did a decade ago. National Public Radio recently reopened that discussion when it revised its ethics handbook so that it would no longer define "unbiased" reporting as giving equal time to opposed opinions. Instead,

> our primary consideration when presenting the news is that we are *fair to the truth*. If our sources try to mislead us or put a false spin on the information they give us, we tell our audience. If the balance of evidence in a matter of controversy weighs heavily on one side, we

acknowledge it in our reports. We strive to give our audience confidence that all [not both] sides have been considered and represented fairly.[67]

This is an example of an effort to redefine the prevailing norms of professional news producers—but as such, it is unusual today.

Overall, I think it has been a mistake to count on technical features of the new media formats—what the jargon calls their "affordances" (such as the ability to post comments)—to revive civic life. But the other paths to media reform look very difficult today, so we should certainly make the most of the new media. Since 2002, J-Lab has been funding and providing training and technical support to online citizen journalists. Some of the best local websites serve what the Knight Foundation calls the "information news of communities" without relying on the declining professional news media.[68]

For example, the Twin Cities Daily Planet in Minnesota is an impressive website that publishes numerous original stories every day while also republishing articles from more than 100 partner organizations, including the for-profit press. It is run by a nonprofit organization, the Twin Cities Media Alliance, but has achieved sustainability by selling advertising. By charter, it is "dedicated to closing the digital divide and helping citizens empower themselves with media."[69]

This is just one example; hundreds more could be cited. In taking an inventory, I would include all not-for-profit venues for news and discussion produced to a significant extent by volunteers, whose tools include not only websites but also elaborate e-mail lists and sometimes low-powered radio broadcasts. The very act of producing and sustaining such forums contributes to civic renewal, especially if the organizers promote dialogue among participants who have diverse perspectives.

The Daily Planet is unusual in its broad geographical scope (a whole metropolitan area): more commonly, citizen-generated media forums serve microcommunities, such as urban neighborhoods, specific immigrant groups within cities, or small towns. Their small scale offers civic advantages. It increases the attention paid to places and people who would otherwise be overlooked. But a small scale can also be limiting, since many important decisions are made at higher levels. The best models, therefore, are not particular forums—such as individual websites—but whole ecosystems in metropolitan areas that consist of numerous microcommunity sites along with aggregators and supportive professional news media.

The Pew study of Baltimore suggests that the ecosystem of that city is lacking: too much of the news originates in the mayor's office and is simply recycled on blogs and radio talk shows. But Lewis A. Friedland finds that Seattle has a "robust ecosystem," in which news is generated by citizens and reporters and circulates through a whole range of venues, including e-mail and Twitter lists, neighborhood blogs, and public and private professional media. The *Seattle Times* has developed formal partnerships with nonprofit sites to encourage sharing of daily content in both directions.[70]

Friedland notes that favorable public policies have strengthened Seattle's media ecosystem. The city is famous for its district council system, begun in the 1980s, which has decentralized power and enhanced citizens' civic skills. Meanwhile, Seattle has funded community groups to use new communications media. A third aspect of its strategy is a comprehensive plan to make municipal data and information available in usable formats. The city has even taken a formal inventory of citizen-generated news venues and provides them with free training. We could say that Seattle's media ecosystem meets the genuine needs of its citizens reasonably well. Enhancing other whole systems is probably the most promising strategy today.

Political reform: At the national level, at least a dozen organizations are devoted to good government in ways that Progressive Era reformers like Robert M. La Follette and Teddy Roosevelt would immediately recognize and endorse. These groups include Common Cause, the League of Women Voters, Public Citizen, the Sunlight Foundation, and Fix Congress First! A different set of organizations advances a libertarian definition of reform: small government is good government. These two networks are largely opposed, but they make strange bedfellows on certain issues.

The progressive version of reform rests on a distinction between "citizens" or "the people" (on one hand) and "special interests" and "politicians" (on the other). The people should rule, politicians should be responsible and accountable to them, and special interests should be curtailed. The government is the people's instrument and has the right and obligation to supervise the market in the public interest. The market should not influence the government.

Someone who holds these views need not assume that citizens are virtuous and wise, nor that organized political groups and elected leaders are inevitably corrupt. Rather, when people act through the channels organized for them as citizens, the odds are better that they will act well. As citizens, we talk with diverse others about common issues without coercion or bribes. As citizens, we vote, and that is basically a public-spirited act because the cost of voting is not worthwhile if one thinks of the payoff in narrowly self-ish terms. As citizens, we promote our values and interests, which, even if foolish or selfish, are at least checked by the rival interests and values of millions of peers.

In contrast to citizens, special interests expend resources to get favorable policies, and they sometimes obtain lucrative returns on their investments. (As noted in chapter 5, $15 million of lobbying on the 2010 financial reform bill bought a provision worth $10 billion.) In contrast to citizens, firms and coalitions of firms are required to maximize returns for their own share-holders are thus blocked from deliberating about what is just or best. Fighting Bob La Follette thundered against the special interests of his day: "Their re-sources are inexhaustible. Their efforts never relax. Their political methods are insidious." But, he thought, "the united power of the people expressed directly through the ballot can overthrow the enemy."[71]

In sum, the "public interest" is what the people would want if they talked, listened, learned, and voted freely. The government enacts or ensures the public interest. "Corruption" is the undue influence of special interests, whether inside or outside the government, especially if their influence can be traced to money or to special powers that they can wield. As I argued in chap-ter 5, blurring governments with markets (and lawmaking with negotiation and exchange) has not only corrupted Washington but has damaged civil so-ciety by reducing the political impact of broad popular coalitions in favor of professional lobbyists.

Today, the main elements of the progressive-style, good government reform agenda are (1) opposition to money in politics; (2) transparency in government; and (3) an accessible, equitable voting system that yields conse-quential decisions. Thus priorities for concrete, practical reforms include such measures as public funding for elections, a public right to information, and easier voting. (The last could be accomplished, for example, by allowing people to register at the same time and place that they vote.)

Good government reform in the spirit of the Progressive Era is subject to several plausible critiques. For more than a century, it has been mocked as Mugwump politics: fastidious, unrealistic, and narrowly middle class. It can be outflanked from the Left by people who believe that corporations run cap-italist societies like the United States, not just by deliberately lobbying and funding politicians but also by making discretionary (and completely legal) decisions about their own investments. In that case, democracy is basically a sham without economic reform of a type that is too radical for our actual citizens today. Charles A. Beard criticized Mugwump Progressives from this perspective in 1916.[72] He was a relatively early (non-Marxist) proponent of putting economic reform ahead of good government.

From the opposite flank, in its 2010 *Citizens United* decision, the Supreme Court defined lobbying and campaign contributions as free speech, and businesses as voluntary associations responsible to their citizen-owners. The decision legitimized and rendered fully respectable the combination of money and politics.

It is, indeed, valuable to make government responsive to citizens (as opposed to corporations and experts), especially when both representatives and citizens deliberate. But I think there is some truth to the critique of good government progressivism as fastidious. Jane Addams fought with the Chicago Democratic machine but came to respect machine politicians more than wealthy reformers. The politicians, she wrote, "are corrupt and do their work badly, but at least they avoid the mistake of a certain type of business men who are frightened by democracy, and have lost their faith in the people." Middle-class reformers were so obsessed with "the correction of political machinery" that they lost touch with the people's interests and values.[73] Decades later, in the same city, the columnist Mike Royko made fun of Lake Shore liberal "goo goos" who sneered at the necessary *business* of politics.

The solution is to see good government reform as just one part of a broader effort to renew democracy. It is equally important to strengthen the confidence, voice, and resources of working-class people and to create opportunities for people to create and manage common resources, not just vote to influence a distant government that has been insulated from corruption.

Today, transparency is the good government objective that has the most traction. Political candidates—including Barack Obama in 2008 and the Republicans who captured the House in 2010—routinely promise to open the government to more public scrutiny. Although sometimes they neglect their promises, they have the power to enhance transparency by passing fairly straightforward laws, legislative rules, or executive orders that are clearly constitutional.[74] Faith that a more transparent government will be a *better* government harmonizes with a prevailing belief in information as the basis of progress. The specific hope is that information that flows from the government to citizens will help the latter to vote and advocate better.

But it is not clear that transparency will suffice to increase public trust or engagement. In a focus group conducted by Lake Research Partners, one participant said: "I don't want to just watch it happen . . . I want to do something about it."[75] He was arguing that transparency—disclosing information about the government—is insufficient. A transparent government may still be beholden to wealthy special interests; knowing the gory details won't enhance one's trust, confidence, or willingness to participate. Lake Research Partners concluded that the public wants accountability, not transparency.

If transparency has limitations, the other aspects of political reform have been largely stymied of late. Since the 1990s, federal courts have successively overturned campaign finance laws. At the presidential level, the system of voluntary public financing (in return for accepting no private money) collapsed when Barack Obama realized that he could raise more than $650 million from individuals in the 2008 campaign.[76] Proposals to provide free broadcast time to candidates as a form of public financing now seem quaint, as candidates use numerous communications channels to reach a fractured audience. Meanwhile, the membership base for reform groups like Common Cause has shrunk.

Certain other elements of the 1970s reform agenda have dropped away completely, such as the effort to make Congress (instead of administrative agencies) responsible for lawmaking and the fight against arbitrary, anticompetitive regulations. Finally, the good government groups seem somewhat detached from the other elements of the civic renewal movement described previously. They are not closely associated, for example, with civic education groups or relational organizers. Their detachment is unfortunate, in my view, because people gain civic knowledge and motivation through action. It is unrealistic to expect citizens to play a "monitorial" role in our democracy: simply observing public information, demanding better governance, and voting their demands. Before they will seek government reforms or participate effectively in the democracy, they need to be enlisted in working together on public problems. Thus the political reform and civic renewal agendas are complementary and need to be better integrated.

Collaborative governance: The view of political reform summarized in the previous section presumes that government is fundamentally different from other institutions. It has a monopoly on the legitimate use of force and is uniquely accountable to all citizens equally. Further, it *ought* to be kept sharply distinct. Blurring the border around the government is dangerous because too much coziness between government officials and citizens encourages corruption (which is the private exploitation of governmental power), and because other institutions would be distorted if they were too closely implicated with government.

That theory supports a range of reforms and safeguards. Separation of church and state keeps the government from remaking religion in its image. Ethics rules typically prevent exchanges of goods and favors between government and private persons. The Federal Advisory Committee Act (FACA) of 1972 allows federal agencies to solicit input from groups, but only as official committees whose meetings are advertised in advance and open to the public at convenient times and locations. The FACA addresses the fear that discussions between citizens and civil servants cannot be publicly accountable unless they are fully transparent.[77] But anyone who has solicited opinions knows that naming a finite list of official advisors and letting everyone else merely observe their discussions is a recipe for annoying the individuals who are not consulted while reducing the candor of those who are. Thus the FACA is an example of a reform that separates citizens from government with some cost to dialogue and collaboration.[78]

An entirely different reform agenda shifts from *government* to *governance*.[79] We govern by shaping our common world. Law is one instrument for that, but law is not sharply different from norms and incentives. Law is never merely executed by government; without broad and active popular support, it becomes a dead letter. Besides, government is not unitary. It comes in layers and separate offices and agencies. No part of government monopolizes any kind of power. In the end, government is just a large group of people, and they are not sharply distinguishable from other people. They usually play several roles (legislator and parent, for example). Public employees appropriately act as organizers and entrepreneurs within agencies and routinely cross the line between government and nongovernment to get things done.

According to this view, a narrow theory of government is analytically unhelpful and encourages the wrong kind of reforms. Far from driving a wedge between government and society, we should encourage porous borders and collaboration. Although Saul Alinsky sharply distinguished citizens from government and treated the latter only as a target of organizing efforts, modern community organizers typically seek to organize government employees, recruiting them to discussions and projects. The Kansas City organizer Warren Adams-Leavitt says, "We are more co-creative with local government" than organizers used to be.[80] Meanwhile, AmeriCorps lets people work for a time as quasi-public employees so that they can take a private perspective into the government and vice versa. Lisa Bingham proposes a collaborative governance act to replace the FACA; it would "authorize agencies to use public participation and collaboration much differently, much more, and a lot earlier in the policy process."[81]

This book has introduced several robust and diverse examples of collaborative governance. In Bridgeport, conversations about the schools originated with civic groups but included government employees from the start and helped the public school system, local businesses, and nonprofits to coordinate their efforts. In Hampton, the city administration chose to build an elaborate structure for ongoing citizen participation in schools, policing, planning, and other aspects of governance. In San Antonio, the IAF heeded Alinsky's advice to remain formally independent of government and never took public money to run programs. But it moved away from Alinsky's basically adversarial model to a relational approach, in which public officials were seen as partners. Portland State University took advantage of two federally supported strategies for involving citizens in public work: service learning and civic environmentalism. Finally, restorative justice, problem-solving courts, and youth courts all involve collaborative governance in the judicial process.

As noted, lowering the barriers between government and civil society potentially conflicts with insulating government from improper, unequal, or hidden influence. Our fundamental goal ought to be engaging diverse citizens (including the ones who happen to work for the government) in discussion and work while developing their relationships and capacities. No single reform recipe is likely to be optimal in all situations. But in navigating this complex terrain, we should bear in mind two general ideas.

First, money is intrinsically problematic. It is very unevenly distributed, it exacerbates collective-action problems (narrow interests pay for favorable outcomes, whereas no one finances advocacy for the broad public interest), and it is uncorrelated with the most valuable civic assets: citizens of integrity whose ideas emerge from diverse experiences. Thus the relationship between civil society and the state should never be mediated by money, if that can be avoided. Individuals and groups should not be able to affect elections with private donations, and allocations of public money to specific groups (such as earmarks) should be closely scrutinized and controlled. These are problematic tools for collaborative governance.

Second, we should think in terms of citizens rather than stakeholders. To be sure, neither term is used consistently, and in some writing, the distinction dissolves. But in general, stakeholders are people with identifiable "stakes" that arise because of something specific about them, such as their employer, occupation, physical address, or demographic identity. Engaging stakeholders means identifying all the interest groups and making sure that each one is "at the table" for consequential discussions. In such practices as negotiated rulemaking, the stakeholders are almost always paid representatives of firms or lobbies who are expected to negotiate to get as much as possible for their employers. A citizen who just happened to care about the issue would not be invited to participate. Negotiation rather than deliberation is the norm, and that follows from the basic idea of "stakeholders" as people who want something for themselves or their employers. Stakeholder negotiation is better than destructive conflict, but it is not deliberative democracy.

Citizens have interests, which they are entitled to pursue. But the definition of "citizen" is more inclusive, encompassing anyone who belongs to the political community, not just individuals with identifiable stakes. The heritage and resonances of the word "citizen" suggest deliberation about what *should* happen to the community, rather than negotiation on behalf of an organized interest. The well-regarded organizer Bill Potapchuk notes, "For years, the literature on collaborative governance didn't even mention citizens."[82] But newer practices do emphasize citizens, and they tend to involve different practices from stakeholder engagement. Unaligned people are recruited to participate. Discussions are more likely to be about the choice of fundamental goals than potential agreements among organizations.

Thus, for example, in the Bridgeport and Hampton cases, all citizens were invited to participate, and traditionally marginalized people (such as low-income teenagers) were taught to engage. The organizers of these processes were paid, and citizens helped to share overall budgetary priorities, but money was far from the central concern. These were not negotiations among professional advocates; instead, citizens were at the center. Such cases should serve as models as we pursue collaborative governance.

A Case Study That Measures Our Progress: Civic Engagement in the 2008 Obama Campaign and the First Obama Administration

So far, this chapter has described a set of interconnected activities and initiatives. It invites the question: How important are these initiatives, taken together? If we want to assess the state of the whole movement, the 2008 Obama presidential campaign and the first Obama Administration provide a useful case study. I do not intend this section as a final evaluation of the Obama presidency, which has four years to go at the time of writing. I acknowledge that the political situation may change rapidly and unpredictably; civic themes may suddenly burgeon or vanish. Nevertheless, the experience of 2008–12 can be viewed as a separate story that offers broad lessons about the strength—and limitations—of civic renewal.

In his first presidential campaign, Barack Obama made the strongest case since Bobby Kennedy in 1968 for engaging Americans in changing America.

His biography and writing suggested that he knew what that would mean—concretely and practically. He had been personally involved in several of the fields of practice described in the previous section, including broad-based community organizing (as an organizer for the Gamaliel Foundation in Chicago) and civic education. He had been trained by the inventor of asset-based community development, John McKnight, who wrote his recommendation letter for Harvard Law School. He had then served on several important boards or commissions in the field, including Harvard's "Saguaro Seminar: Civic Engagement in America" (founded by Robert Putnam to study and address the decline in social capital) and Demos (a think tank that works on democratic reform). Both he and his wife, Michelle Obama, were deeply involved with one AmeriCorps program, Public Allies (he as a member of the national board; she as director of its Chicago office) and with the civilian service movement in general. Michelle Obama had also worked on engaged university issues as vice president for Community and External Affairs at the University of Chicago Medical Center.

Barack Obama's civic engagement theme was popular with voters (although largely unreported by the press), and I believe it helped him win the primaries. However, my experience on two Obama campaign policy committees and my observations since then suggest that no one who has any influence in the party or the administration—other than possibly the president and the first lady—really understood the power of civic engagement. Because Democratic party elites are ignorant of, or sometimes actually hostile to, civic engagement, it proved impossible to translate the civic themes of the campaign into new approaches to governance. On the contrary, the 2009–12 Obama administration was notably technocratic and focused on legislative tactics. The fact that someone traveled from the heart of the civic engagement movement to the Oval Office and then failed to enhance civic engagement in America suggests both strengths and limitations of the movement.

Announcing his presidential candidacy in Springfield, Illinois, on February 10, 2007, then Senator Barack Obama said, "This campaign has to be about reclaiming the meaning of citizenship, restoring our sense of common purpose, and realizing that few obstacles can withstand the power of millions of voices calling for change. [cheers] . . . That is our purpose here today. That is why I'm in this race, not just to hold an office but to gather with you to transform a nation. [cheers]"[83]

Ten months later, as he campaigned to win the Iowa caucuses, Senator Obama described his work as a community organizer

In church basements and around kitchen tables, block by block, we brought the community together, registered new voters, fought for new jobs, and helped people live lives with some measure of dignity.... I have no doubt that in the face of impossible odds people who love their country can change it. But I hold no illusions that one man or woman can do this alone. . . . That's why I'm reaching out to Democrats, and also to Independents and Republicans. And that is why I won't just ask for your vote as a candidate; I will ask for your service and your active citizenship when I am President of the United States. This will not be a call issued in one speech or program; this will be a cause of my presidency.[84]

Based on Obama's writing and experience, I would interpret his general statements about active citizenship as follows. He believed that positive change comes from organized social movements, not from the government alone. He had already reached that conclusion by 1988, when he published an article about community organizing. At that point, he had posed his main question as "how [can] black and other dispossessed people [...] forward their lot in America"? He argued that neither electoral empowerment (winning City Hall) nor economic self-sufficiency would work alone.

This is because the issues of the inner city are more complex and deeply rooted than ever before. Blatant discrimination has been replaced by institutional racism; problems like teen pregnancy, gang involvement and drug abuse cannot be solved by money alone. . . . In fact, much-needed black achievement in prominent city positions has put us in the awkward position of administering underfunded systems neither equipped nor eager to address the needs of the urban poor and being forced to compromise their interests to more powerful demands from other sectors.

Neither electoral nor purely economic strategies would work if fundamental assets (people and capital) were leaving industrial cities: a wicked problem. But community organizing could reveal and leverage the hidden assets still present in the inner city, the "internal productive capacities, both in terms of money and people, that already exist in communities." In doing so, Obama wrote, organizing "enables people to break their crippling isolation from each other, to reshape their mutual values and expectations and redis-cover the possibilities of acting collaboratively—the prerequisites of any successful self-help initiative." For organizers like Obama himself, the process "teaches as nothing else does the beauty and strength of everyday people."[85]

Obama came to believe, furthermore, that social movements should be broad based, not narrow groups of people who all agree with one another. They should promote discussion and collaboration across lines of difference—including ideological difference. Hence the need to build bridges to Republican citizens.

Obama's specific brand of faith-based organizing in Chicago was intentionally broad based—not narrowly ideological, and certainly not partisan. As he said in May 2007, "politics" usually means shouting matches on TV. But "when politics gets local, when the person talking to you is your neighbor standing on your front porch, things change." In that speech, he called for dialogues in every community on Iraq, health care, and climate change.

Further, Obama believed that social change requires work by many people. We must tap their skills, energies, networks, and local knowledge. Government programs cannot substitute for public work, nor can rights or entitlements. The "work" theme was strong and consistent in his speeches. For example, in April 2009, he said, "the answer to our problems will ultimately be found in the character of the American people. We need soldiers and diplomats, scientists, teachers, workers, entrepreneurs. We need your service. We need your active citizenship."[86]

At the root of many of our problems, Obama argued, were fractured relationships—among Americans and between Americans and major institutions. Bad policies were not the ultimate cause of our problems, and the solutions depended on repairing relationships—something that only people (not institutions) could accomplish. Finally, there was a strong moral dimension to this work. Personal moral choices were responsible for our national successes and failures; social movements could change those choices. In New Hampshire in 2006, Obama said: "We are going to reengage in our democracy in a way that we haven't done for some time.... We are going to take hold of our collective lives together and reassert our values and our ideals on our politics. And that doesn't depend on one person. That doesn't depend on me or the governor or a congressman or a speaker. It depends on you."[87]

The press, including liberal columnists and bloggers, paid virtually no attention to the civic engagement theme in the campaign. I transcribed the last quote from video because I could not find it in any print coverage of the campaign. Reporters regard a statement about "active citizenship" much like a comment about how wonderful it feels to visit New Hampshire in January. It is just throat-clearing that precedes the attack or proposal of the day. Yet the videos clearly show rising applause at the civic moments in these speeches.

Within the campaign, policy advisers did not pay much more attention to the civic themes than the press did. The campaign did endorse expanding AmeriCorps, as did John McCain. But the Democrats' proposals on matters like education and the environment included no concrete ideas for civic empowerment. On the education policy committee of the campaign, a substantial proportion of the experts were actually hostile to parental and community engagement in schools. Many Obama advisers were liberal technocrats who believed that society was divided into distinct interest groups. Progressive change would come from mobilizing the weaker interest groups to vote and then promoting their interests. They assumed that legislation is always complex and fast moving, and only insiders and the heads of interest groups can really understand it. Good government means informing, motivating, and negotiating with political leaders. All these premises were at odds with the candidate's own speeches, but the "active citizenship" theme slipped past Democratic Party elites just as it escaped the notice of the press.

If the media didn't report on active citizenship, and the candidate's policy positions didn't reflect it, how could it help him win? One reason is that voters now have direct, unmediated access to the candidate's speeches and his books. They could hear his civic rhetoric and they clapped and cheered it. More important, the campaign was structured in ways that reflected Obama's civic philosophy. Volunteers were encouraged and taught to share their stories, to discuss social problems, to listen as well as mobilize, and to develop their own plans. There was a rich discussion online as well as face-to-face. This deliberative style was particularly attractive to young, college-educated volunteers, who felt deeply empowered and who played a significant role in the election's outcomes, especially in the Iowa caucuses. (And without Iowa, Barack Obama would not have won the presidency.)

The civic theme was consistent with Barack and Michelle Obama's personal stories and so helped create a coherent narrative. Perhaps politicians' narratives rarely determine general election outcomes, but Obama told a better story than Clinton in the Democratic primary—and that mattered.

The idea of civic empowerment may not have generated major policy proposals, but it did play an important role in campaign debates. For example, candidates Hillary Clinton and Barack Obama argued over the meaning of the civil rights movement, with Obama crediting the grassroots and Clinton praising Lyndon Johnson and other national leaders. That was a legitimate disagreement, but Obama's position was consistent with his whole campaign.

A related argument arose between Obama and Paul Krugman of the *New York Times*; Krugman said that America's problem was the Republicans, and Obama replied (although not directly to Krugman) that the problem was our civic fabric.

On his first day of office, the president issued a strong memorandum to the heads of all executive departments and agencies, entitled "Transparency and Open Government." This memorandum said (in part): "Government should be participatory. Public engagement enhances the Government's effectiveness and improves the quality of its decisions. . . . Executive departments and agencies should offer Americans increased opportunities to participate in policymaking and to provide their Government with the benefits of their collective expertise and information. . . . Government should be collaborative. Collaboration actively engages Americans in the work of their Government. Executive departments and agencies should use innovative tools, methods, and systems to cooperate among themselves, across all levels of Government, and with nonprofit organizations, businesses, and individuals in the private sector."[88]

After that announcement, the actual agenda was strong on service and transparency but almost entirely missing were participation and collaboration. The president signed the Kennedy Serve America Act, which authorized tripling AmeriCorps. But service does not necessarily build civic skills or address fundamental problems; besides, even an expanded AmeriCorps offers no role to most people. "Transparency" meant providing information that, in practice, has been used by organized interest groups, reporters, and a few independent citizens who have deep interests and skills in particular areas.

The Democrats passed a stimulus package that could have been described— justly—as public work. Thanks to the stimulus, some Americans built roads, bridges, and schools. Some monitored federal spending on websites. Some advocated for priorities. Some volunteered time in the same schools and hospitals where the federal funds went. Some could have deliberated about where the money *should be* spent at the local level. All this could have been called active citizenship and described as a common project. Instead, it turned into a service of the federal government to citizens—inadequate for the task and deeply distrusted. According to the CBS/*New York Times* poll conducted in February 2010, just 6 percent of Americans believed that the stimulus bill had created *any* jobs so far (although almost half thought it ultimately would).[89] And according to Gallup, Americans believed that 50 cents of each dollar of federal spending was wasted.[90] Since the federal government spends $3.7 trillion per year, that implied $1.85 trillion in total annual waste, or more than $6,000 of waste per person.

The White House chose to make health care the next major focus and included no aspects of civic engagement in the deliberations about the bill, in their advocacy for the legislation, or in the design of the statute. There could have been real public discussions, instead of sham town meetings held in the summer of 2009 that were really speeches by politicians with time for Q&A. Progressive volunteers could have been encouraged to conduct face-to-face dialogues in their communities and to form relationships with one another (instead of merely finding themselves on the receiving end of an e-mail list). The legislation could have included health co-ops as an experiment in engaging citizens in policy.

In other words, a range of civic engagement strategies was available to the administration, including a deliberative approach (bringing liberals and conservatives together at the grassroots level to develop policy options), a more partisan and ideological strategy (empowering progressive citizen-activists to build relationships and persuade neighbors), and/or incorporating community panels or local insurance co-ops into the bill itself. The White House chose none of these strategies but opted instead for an inside game, trying to negotiate their way to a bill.

The Affordable Health Care Act ultimately passed early in 2010, after several near-death experiences. The bill was strikingly fragile because no passionate, organized, credible group of citizens supported it. It had the endorsement of some smart, independent policy experts but no enthusiastic popular backing. Lincoln was right: "Public sentiment is everything. With public sentiment, nothing can fail; without it nothing can succeed."[91] Instead of building momentum for other social reform, the Affordable Health Care Act apparently exhausted the political system and tolerance of Americans, who voted for a Republican House majority in 2010.

Meanwhile, the president's rhetoric was subtly shifting from civic empowerment to a focus on his own personal leadership—from we to I. Seeking the nomination in Iowa, Barack Obama had said, "I hold no illusions that one man or woman can do this alone." More than two years later, responding to the election of a Republican senator in Massachusetts that appeared to doom health reform, he said:

> So long as I have some breath in me, so long as I have the privilege of serving as your president, I will not stop fighting for you. I will take my lumps, but I won't stop fighting to bring back jobs here. [applause] I won't stop fighting for an economy where hard work is rewarded. I won't stop fighting to make sure there's accountability in our financial

system. [applause] I'm not going to stop fighting until we have jobs for everybody.

Civic engagement was certainly not a risk-free alternative for President Obama. Empowering grassroots volunteers to advocate for health care might have yielded a peaceful army in favor of a single payer system (with the government as the sole insurer), which would have died in Congress. Public discussions of health care, even if moderated and appropriately structured, could have been ruined by angry opponents. No one knows for sure how to involve citizens in the administration of health plans over time. Yet the lack of innovation and experimentation in these areas was striking after the impressive record of the campaign.

Sometimes, the administration even reduced opportunities for active citizenship that had existed under George W. Bush. For example, Community Action for a Renewed Environment (CARE) is a program within the EPA that makes grants to communities that have formed local partnerships to address environmental issues and determined their local needs. CARE also provides training and technical assistance and puts an interdisciplinary EPA team in partnership with each community. Environmentalists supported CARE under Republican administrations, believing that grassroots activity could make progress while regulatory solutions were frozen in Washington. But once they had a Democratic president, they advocated regulation to the exclusion of local collaboration and problem solving. CARE's funding was cut by the Obama administration. Similarly, in 2011, as a last-minute compromise with House Republicans, the administration eliminated federal support for service learning and civic education.

It was hard to identify anyone inside the administration who even wanted to try a civic strategy. But prominent liberal critics of the Obama campaign took the administration's political struggles as evidence that a civic strategy had been tried and had failed. In a *New Republic* piece headlined, "Live By the Movement, Die By the Movement: Obama's Doomed Theory of Politics," the Princeton historian Sean Wilentz wrote: "Clearly, the hopes and dreams that propelled Obama to the White House are in disarray. The social movement politics that some of his most fervent followers ascribed to him—the idea of electing a 'post-partisan' president as the leader not of a nation or even of a political party but of a personalized social movement—has failed."[92] The two aspects of Obama's philosophy that Wilentz believed had been repudiated were an alleged distaste for partisan politics and a belief that change derived from social movements instead of national leaders. Wilentz wrote,

Fundamental to the social movement model is a conception of American political history in which movements, and not presidents, are the true instigators for change. Presidents are merely reactive. They are not the main protagonists. Obama himself endorsed this conception constantly on the campaign trail, and has repeated it often as president, proclaiming that "real change comes from the bottom up."

Just a few days later, in the *New York Times*, Krugman concurred. "In retrospect, the roots of current Democratic despond go all the way back to the way Mr. Obama ran for president. Again and again, he defined America's problem as one of process, not substance—we were in trouble not because we had been governed by people with the wrong ideas, but because partisan divisions and politics as usual had prevented men and women of good will from coming together to solve our problems. And he promised to transcend those partisan divisions." Instead, Krugman argued, the president should have explained why Republicans were "people with the wrong ideas" and liberal Democrats were right about economic policy. Communication was everything: "Mr. Obama could and should be hammering Republicans . . . There were no catchy slogans, no clear statements of principle . . . The president 'has the bully pulpit.'"[93]

My diagnosis is just the opposite. Although candidate Barack Obama rightly depicted our problems as ones of process and culture and wisely unleashed a grassroots social movement to solve them, President Barack Obama tried to govern from the Oval Office, negotiating with—and sometimes angrily denouncing—conservative politicians. It is not that a social movement strategy failed but that it was never tried.

The missing ingredients were policies, political strategies, and personnel. Appropriate policies would have been ones that supported and invited public participation, such as an expanded (rather than a contracted) office of grassroots environmentalism in the EPA and similar offices in other agencies. The administration's political strategies should have empowered activists to discuss, define, and press for new policies. And personnel appointments should have included people from the fields of practice described earlier in this chapter: community organizing, community economic development, youth engagement, and the like. No cabinet secretary came from any of those fields. The first director of the White House Office of Social Innovation and Civic Participation House was a very talented and dedicated person, Sonal Shah, who came not from community organizing but from Goldman Sachs and Google.

Stepping back, we might ask why policies, political strategies, and personnel were not favorable to civic renewal (even though a community organizer and acute student of civic renewal was the president). I would blame three factors: the resistance of elites in the Democratic Party and progressive circles to decentralization and public participation; the failure of the movement to come forward with concrete policy proposals even when there were opportunities to lobby; and the weakness of grassroots support for such reforms. When Sonal Shah, Christina Tchen (the White House director for Public Engagement), and their colleagues met with civic renewal leaders in 2009, they encountered an overwhelmingly white group of experts and non-profit executives who were enthusiastic about projects and reforms that had little public currency. I believe Shah, Tchen, and others reasonably read the group as a middle class good government coalition rather than a broad social movement. How to change that situation is the theme of chapter 7.

7

Strategies

HOW TO ACCOMPLISH CIVIC RENEWAL

THIS BOOK BEGAN with a litany of wicked problems: high school drop-out rates, crime, and global warming. If more Americans were involved in constructive and empowered ways, we could make progress on these problems. Put more positively, as active citizens, we could help build a better commonwealth, with a better national culture, economy, and polity and more opportunities for deeply satisfying public work. Nor would the benefits of engagement stop at our borders: America's active citizens would collaborate with peers in other countries to address international problems and improve the earth.

Those predictions cannot be proved with existing data, because the strategy of engaging Americans has not been tried in our era. But I have argued (on the basis of theoretical considerations and concrete, local experiments) that more and better civic engagement is a path to social reform.

This is not an argument for revolutionary change or participatory democracy as an alternative to our constitutional order of markets and representative institutions. If we could only recover the level and impact of civic engagement that America witnessed in the mid-twentieth century (along with greater equity and integration), we would make enormous progress. That evocation of the past suggests that the project of civic renewal is in some respects conservative, but the strategies and means required today must be new, and entrenched interests will have to be checked and curtailed.

In the struggle for civic renewal, we have powerful assets, starting with the experimental projects and organizations identified in chapter 6. They provide a base of committed activists, tested strategies, and network ties. But we also face serious obstacles or deficits:

- Our political system is organized to favor professionally led, well-funded interests instead of deliberating communities and grassroots movements.

- Our major social policies are hostile to active civic participation. (For example, education is driven by standardized tests that experts write; public health depends on insurance companies and state bureaucracies rather than co-ops and community-based organizations.)
- Our voluntary associations no longer have the means to recruit millions of Americans and develop the skills and motivations to participate as active citizens.
- Our companies, because of their ability to withdraw investment, are virtually ungovernable by local authorities and communities.
- Our culture lacks positive and plausible descriptions of collective agency, although it provides many depictions of lone heroes and of apolitical groups of friends.
- Our news media generally overlook examples of deliberation and public work but relentlessly cover competition among professional politicians.
- Despite their commitments to political rights and their heritage of experiments with participatory democracy, liberals and progressives are enamored of expertise, command-and-control regulation, and redistributive politics to the exclusion of active citizenship.
- Despite their resistance to technocratic elites and their heritage of experiments with decentralization, conservatives are enamored of markets and negative liberties to the exclusion of active citizenship.
- Our schools and colleges offer inadequate civic education, distributed unjustly to favor the most advantaged students, with an emphasis on factual knowledge instead of civic skills.
- Our scholars in the social sciences and humanities produce an inadequate supply of knowledge relevant to active citizens (people who make moral and strategic judgments about how to improve the world directly).
- Our funders—in both the state and philanthropic sectors—provide negligible streams of money for participatory processes, as compared to the funds available for concrete services.

What is to be done? That classic question is the wrong one, because its gerundive verb form hides the subject and thus suppresses accountability. It is too easy to say what should be done (a start would be government funding for civic engagement) without explaining how to get there.

What should we do? is a better question, but the "we" must be concrete. It is no use saying that we Americans should prize active citizenship. That is true, but saying it achieves nothing. Instead, I mean to take the "we" quite seriously. What should *we* do—I who writes these words and you who reads them—along with anyone whom we can enlist for our cause? That seems to be the correct question, but not if the answer stops with changes in our personal behavior and immediate circumstances. National and global needs are too great for us only to "*be* the change" that we want in the world. We must also *change* the world. Our own actions (yours and mine) must be plausibly connected to grand reforms in society and policy. That is a matter of civic strategy.

In an essay entitled "Why Last Chapters Disappoint," David Greenberg lists American books about politics and culture that are famous for their provocative diagnoses of serious problems but that conclude with strangely weak recommendations. These works include, in his opinion, Upton Sinclair's *The Jungle* (1906), Walter Lippmann's *Public Opinion* (1922), Daniel Boorstin's *The Image* (1961), Allan Bloom's *Closing of the American Mind* (1987), Robert Shiller's *Irrational Exuberance* (2000), Robert Putnam's *Bowling Alone* (2001), Eric Schlosser's *Fast Food Nation* (2001), and Al Gore's *The Assault on Reason* (2007). Greenberg asserts that practically every book on this list, "no matter how shrewd or rich its survey of the question at hand, finishes with an obligatory prescription that is utopian, banal, unhelpful or out of tune with the rest of the book." The partial exceptions are works like Schlosser's *Fast Food Nation* that provide fully satisfactory legislative agendas while acknowledging that the most important reforms have no chance of passing in Congress.[1]

The gap between diagnosis and prescription is no accident. Many serious social problems could be solved if everyone chose to behave better: eat less fast food, invest more wisely, use less carbon, or study the classics. But the readers of a given treatise are too few to make a difference, and even before they begin to read they are better motivated than the rest of the population. Therefore, books that conclude with personal exhortations seem inadequate. Likewise, some serious social problems could be ameliorated by better legislation. But the readers of any given book are too few to apply sufficient political pressure to obtain the necessary laws. Therefore, books that end with legislative agendas disappoint just as badly.

The failure of books to change the world is not a problem that any single book can solve. But it is a problem that can be addressed, just as we address complex challenges of description, analysis, diagnosis, and interpretation that arise in the social sciences and humanities. Every work of empirical scholarship should contribute to a cumulative research enterprise and a robust debate. Every worthy *political* book should also contribute to our understanding of how ideas influence the world. That means asking questions such as: "Who will read this book, and what can they do?"

Who reads a book depends, in part, on the structure of the publishing industry and news media and the degree to which the public is already interested in the book's topic. What readers can do depends, in part, on which organizations and networks are available for them to join and how responsive other institutions are to their groups.

These matters change over time. Consider, for example, a book that did affect democracy, John W. Gardner's *In Common Cause: Citizen Action and How It Works* (1972). After diagnosing America's social problems as the result of corrupt and undemocratic political processes and proposing a series of reforms, such as open-government laws and public financing for campaigns, Gardner encouraged his readers to join the organization Common Cause. He had founded this organization two years earlier by taking out advertisements in leading national newspapers, promising "to build a true 'citizens' lobby—a lobby concerned not with the advancement of special interests but with the well-being of the nation. . . . We want public officials to have literally millions of American citizens looking over their shoulders at every move they make." More than 100,000 readers quickly responded by joining Gardner's organization and sending money. Common Cause was soon involved in passing the Twenty-Sixth Amendment (which lowered the voting age to 18), the Federal Election Campaign Act, the Freedom of Information Act, and the Ethics in Government Act of 1978.[2] The book *In Common Cause* was an early part of the organization's successful outreach efforts.

It helped that Gardner was personally famous and respected before he founded Common Cause. It also helped that a series of election-related scandals, culminating with Watergate, dominated the news between 1972 and 1976, making procedural reforms a high public priority. As a book, *In Common Cause* was well written, carefully researched, and clear about which laws were needed.

But the broader context also helped. Watergate dominated the news because the news business was still monopolized by relatively few television networks, agenda-setting newspapers, and wire services whose professional reporters believed that a campaign-finance story involving the president was important. Everyone who followed the news at all had to follow the Watergate story, regardless of their ideological or partisan backgrounds. In contrast, in 2010, some Americans were appalled by the false but prevalent charge that President Obama's visit to Indonesia was costing taxpayers $200 million per day. Many other Americans had no idea that this accusation had even been made, so fractured was the news market.[3]

John Gardner was able to reach a generation of joiners who were setting records for organizational membership.[4] Newspaper reading and joining groups were strongly correlated, and presumably people who read the news *and* joined groups also displayed relatively deep concern about public issues.[5] Thus it was not surprising that more than 100,000 people should respond to Gardner's newspaper advertisements about national political reform by joining his new group. By the 2000s, the rate of newspaper reading had dropped in half, and the rate of group membership was also down significantly. The original membership of Common Cause aged and was never replaced in similar numbers after the 1970s. John Gardner's strategy fit his time but did not outlive him.[6]

Any analysis of social issues should take account of contextual changes like these. Considering how one's thought relates to the world means making one's scholarship "reflexive," in the particular sense advocated by the Danish political theorist Bent Flyvbjerg. He notes that modern writers frequently distinguish between rationality and power. "The [modern scholarly] ideal prescribes that first we must know about a problem, then we can decide about it. . . . Power is brought to bear on the problem only after we have made ourselves knowledgeable about it."[7] With this ideal in mind, authors write many chapters about social problems, followed by unsatisfactory codas about what should be done. As documents, their books evidently lack the capacity to improve the world. Their rationality is disconnected from power. And, in my experience, the more critical and radical the author is, the more disempowered he or she feels.

Truly reflexive writing and politics recognizes that even the facts used in the analytical sections of a scholarly work come from institutions that have been shaped by power. For example, I have been able to cite historical data about voting and volunteering in the United States. The federal government tracks these indicators by fielding the Census Current Population Surveys and funding the American National Election Studies. Various influential individuals and groups have persuaded the government to measure these variables, for the same (somewhat diverse) reasons that they have pressed for changes in voting rules and investments in volunteer service. On the other hand, there are no reliable historical data on the prevalence of public engagement by government agencies. One cannot track the rate at which the police have consulted residents about crime-fighting strategies or the importance of parental voice in schools. That is because no influential groups and networks have successfully advocated for these variables to be measured. Thus the empirical basis of this book is affected by the main problem that I have identified in the book: the lack of official support for deliberative public work.

Reflexive scholarship also acknowledges that values motivate all empirical research. Our values—our beliefs about goals and principles—should be influenced and constrained by what we think can work in the world; "*ought* implies *can*." I have not argued from basic philosophical principles alone but have also considered salient and troubling trends in American civil society along with successful experiments that aim to reverse those trends. An experiment can be a strong argument for doing more of the same: in those cases, "*can* implies *ought*." If there were no recent successful experiments in civic engagement, I would have advocated more modest and pessimistic values. If recent experiments were more robust and radical, I might have adopted more ambitious positions. In short, my values rested on other people's practical work, even as my goal was to support their work.

Finally, as I have already suggested, reflexive scholarship should address the question of what readers ought to do. A book is fully satisfactory only if it helps persuade readers to do what it recommends *and* if their efforts actually improve the world. In that sense, the book offers a hypothesis that can be proved or disproved by its consequences. No author will be able to foresee clearly what readers will do, because they will contribute their own intelligence—and the situation will change. Nevertheless, the book and its readers can contribute to a cumulative intellectual enterprise that others will then take up and improve.

Two Inadequate Strategies: Messaging and Social Networking

The central problem under consideration in this chapter is how to obtain broader, better, and more influential civic engagement in the United States. Before proposing a strategy that we (you and I) might use for that purpose, I will note the limitations of two strategies that are frequently proposed. They may be helpful, but neither is adequate on its own.

The first is to develop more potent messages about the need for active citizenship and then use those messages to motivate American citizens to participate and to demand reforms in institutions.

"If three Americans were dropped from an airplane at 10,000 feet, by the time they had reached the ground they would probably have formed an association and elected themselves president, vice president, and secretary-treasurer," wrote E. Digby Baltzell years ago.[8] Today, the plummeting Americans would turn themselves into a communications committee and brainstorm "messages" to "get the word out" or "raise awareness" of their plight before they hit the ground.

Messaging is now second nature. If you ask students to pick an issue that concerns them and do something about it, very often they will choose a bad behavior and develop a communications plan against it. They have learned that style of engagement from their elders. In almost all meetings and conferences about civic engagement that I have attended since the 1980s, the participants advocate for better messages and communications.

Strategic communication (trying to get other people to do something by sending them some kind of message) has its own folklore. We assume that effective messages are short, simple, and memorable. They stress benefits and never complicate matters by mentioning any drawbacks. If a message mentions opponents, it disparages them. Ideally, the message comes from famous supporters. The more repetition, the better.

We borrow these techniques from commercial advertising, the medium in which we all swim. But commercial advertisers want people to do things that are (1) conceptually simple, (2) available, (3) free of organized enemies, and (4) of tangible value. Tropicana, for example, wants us to pay for an available good that affords some pleasure and health benefits and that may have competitors, but that no one is advertising against. The Tropicana brand costs more than generic orange juice of the same quality; the company appeals to emotions to generate demand for the brand.

Political campaigns face a similar situation and borrow most of the same techniques. Like buying orange juice, voting is conceptually simple and available. To be sure, most candidates are in zero-sum struggles for votes, a situation that encourages far more negative advertising than we see in the commercial world. Also, the benefits of voting are intangible, which is why candidates either resort to nebulous sentiments or try to make their impact appear more concrete than it is. But in general, the principles of commercial advertising apply.

These principles apply, too, if you want people to buckle their seatbelts or not to drink and drive. Those are concrete choices, available to all who have cars in the first place. But the normal forms of strategic communication *cannot* work if:

- What you want people to do is unavailable. Individuals cannot join labor unions if there aren't any, for example.
- What you want them to do is complex and requires experience to grasp and to value. For example: "Understand American history" means nothing unless one understands something about history already.
- What you want to communicate is complex, ambiguous, or sensitive to context, and a simple message is worse than none.

- People don't trust your motives and judgment.
- You can only afford to purchase a tiny slice of the public's attention and competing or even contrary messages occupy much more time.

Unfortunately, civic engagement, deliberation, reforming public institutions, and promoting social justice face all the challenges listed above, which is why I am generally skeptical about the advantages of a communications strategy, except as an element of a broader plan.

A second tempting idea is to take advantage of information technology to bypass organizations and create a loose, self-organized, completely voluntary *network* for civic renewal. "Crowdsourcing" means issuing an open call to collaborate on some common task, such as improving open-source software, contributing entries to Wikipedia, or detecting fraud and abuse in a government's budget. The question arises whether we could crowdsource civic renewal by asking anyone who wants to participate to join a movement online.

Clay Shirky's book *Here Comes Everybody: The Power of Organizing Without Organizations* is a sophisticated statement of the crowdsourcing idea, albeit without a specific focus on civic renewal. Helpfully, Shirky invokes Ronald Coase's "theory of the firm," first proposed in 1937.[9] Coase set out to explain why firms existed, since one might expect that in a market, individuals would simply come together to produce and sell goods. In fact, that occasionally happens: some independent movies are made by ad hoc teams that hold together only for the duration of the production. But independent films are unusual examples; much more important in the global marketplace are relatively durable companies that have administrative hierarchies, clear boundaries, fairly stable personnel, and offices that serve regular functions, such as payroll, legal counsel, and sales.

Coase explained that the transaction costs necessary to put together ad hoc teams were usually too high; firms were more efficient, even though their bureaucracies introduced costs. One could say the same thing about not-for-profit associations in Coase's era. Like firms, the NAACP, the Knights of Columbus, and the League of Women Voters saved transaction costs for individuals who were interested in working together.

However, as Shirky argues, information technology has now reduced transaction costs to the point that it is often no longer necessary to create firms or other organizations. He offers a compelling example: the "extravagant and weird" Mermaid Parade in Coney Island, New York. This annual event is evidently worth documenting and describing in detail. Decades ago, it wouldn't have been covered unless media companies had sent reporters or someone had organized a newsletter just for the parade. They would have needed funding, personnel, and an audience. But now, anyone who takes a picture or writes a blog post about the Mermaid Parade can cheaply give it away online. Moreover, if people use common phrases to identify (tag) all descriptions of the parade, then anyone who searches for those tags will find a whole anthology of descriptions and photos. The most popular material will rise to the top in the search results. Thus many of the traditional functions of a magazine are rendered superfluous by technology.[10]

So we should consider whether we could avoid the challenges of creating or strengthening civic organizations by issuing an open call to crowdsource civic renewal. In past eras of reform, organizations were certainly essential. The League of Women Voters was founded by women's suffragists in 1920, on the eve of their winning the right to vote, as a durable mechanism for improving the quality of American democracy. In the same era, the great reform senator Robert M. La Follette tried to spark civic renewal with the People's Legislative Service, the Progressive Party, and the NAACP, all groups that he founded or played a role in starting. Almost 50 years later, Ralph Nader launched Public Citizen and John Gardner founded Common Cause with similar methods and motivations. In each of these cases, leaders recruited members to contribute dues that paid for professional staff and overhead.

But in January 2010, a documentary filmmaker and political theorist named Annabel Park simply wrote a short manifesto on her Facebook page against the Tea Party, the conservative grassroots movement that had sprung up soon before. She defined her opposition not to conservatism but to divisiveness and negativity. Many thousands of people joined her on Facebook and began to form the alternative network that she recommended, called the Coffee Party. In less than a month, Park also had a video on YouTube (Google's service for sharing free videos) that called for a movement, and within weeks, more than 400 face-to-face meetings of the Coffee Party had been held. By voting online, members of the free and open movement chose financial reform and campaign finance reform as their priorities and began to lobby Congress.[11]

At the first national meeting of the Coffee Party, in Louisville, Kentucky, the legal scholar and activist Lawrence Lessig electrified the audience with a proposal to crowdsource campaign finance reform. In contrast (although not in opposition) to the traditional campaign finance reform organizations, such as Common Cause and the League of Women Voters, Lessig had created a loose, online network called Fix Congress First to lobby for reform. Visitors to his website were asked to organize local house parties, "spread the word," pledge not to contribute financially to any federal candidates who refused to back reform, and contact members of Congress. Because of a combination of its goal (nonpartisan political reform) and its format (loose, voluntary, and viral) Fix Congress First was a perfect match for the Coffee Party.

By the winter of 2011–12, the energy and attention of democratic reformers seemed to have shifted, in large measure, from the Coffee Party to a series of protests known collectively as Occupy Wall Street. Although many of the occupiers defined their cause in egalitarian, economic terms, they were also eager to use deliberative democratic methods inside their occupations and avidly debated political reforms that would make formal institutions more deliberative. For example, some of them spun off a group called the Community Democracy Project that promoted participatory budgeting, but others opposed this strategy as too institutional.[12] Like the Coffee Party, the occupy movement is decentralized, without a formal leadership structure or even a membership list.

It would be risky to make any predictions about these developments so early in their history. I certainly hope they succeed and believe that they will contribute to the goals defended in this book. Yet I doubt it is fully possible to crowdsource civic renewal. Jay Rosen, a journalism professor who has a deep understanding of democratic theory and civic themes, has been experimenting with crowdsourced journalism projects: efforts to generate valuable news and information by issuing open calls to volunteers. He has observed three preconditions for success. First, in a crowdsourced project, because people no longer sit together to discuss assignments, you need "extreme clarity about tasks and goals."[13] Lawrence Lessig, for example, asks volunteers to call specific members of Congress to ask them to support particular legislation. Rosen has had comparable success posting lists of people who need to be interviewed and asking volunteers to conduct the interviews and post their notes online. But asking people to construct a whole news article, design legislation, or govern a local asset would require too much discussion and deliberation to succeed by crowdsourcing.

Second, an open call for assistance must go to a preexisting group with a "shared background narrative." In Rosen's example, participants in the liberal blog *Talking Points Memo* were able to collaborate online very quickly to review a ream of leaked Justice Department documents to find embarrassing evidence about the attorney general. They were successful because they already agreed on that goal, its importance, and what would count as relevant evidence. Most of the prominent examples of successful crowd-sourcing come from domains such as software design, in which the goals are fairly self-evident. But politics is laden with values and is profoundly contentious, so that virtually no two people have exactly the same political objectives and beliefs. If they hold divergent values and ideas, they need to talk before they collaborate. They can certainly talk online instead of face-to-face, but their conversation needs structure and moderation. They can only crowdsource a problem once it has become a discrete element of some larger political project that they already share.

Finally, the example of *Talking Points Memo* points to a condition that is somewhat less explicit in Rosen's presentation. The people who receive an open call must know and trust the person who sent it. As Rosen says, "If people have been following you, then you can enlist them." For example, when the British newspaper the *Guardian* asked its readers to examine former Prime Minister Tony Blair's financial documents to determine the sources of his income, they did so because they had expertise to contribute, they had received a clear request, they shared distaste for Blair, and they trusted the *Guardian*. If I issued a call to help with some aspect of civic renewal, my friends might help. But my friends are not very numerous, and other people would have no reason to trust me or even to notice my call. The examples of successful viral messages, like Annabel Park's manifesto for the Coffee Party, are vastly outnumbered by messages that no one reads outside the authors' narrow circles of friends.

For civic renewal, these requirements create serious challenges. We do not have many people or organizations that are capable of issuing calls for help to large numbers of loyal followers. Instead, we have organizations and leaders that need subtle and complex assistance, such as developing legislation rather than simply calling members of Congress to vote for it. And even within the nascent civic renewal movement that I described in chapter 6, differences of values, priorities, and tactics are profound. Participants will need to debate before they act, and then deliberate to review their actions, and then act and talk some more.

In short, I think crowdsourcing techniques will be valuable once we have moved to the point where we agree that we need information, money, calls to Congress, or products to boycott. Those do not seem our most pressing needs at this point, except in areas like campaign finance reform where appropriate legislation is already before Congress. (But note that even a large number of phone calls will probably not get such legislation passed against the interests of major industries and incumbent politicians.)

A Base for Civic Renewal

Having argued that messaging and crowdsourcing strategies cannot work, I now propose a different approach. In chapter 5, I showed that millions of people used to belong to associations that developed civic skills, managed and created public goods, promoted discussions, and connected people to their government. Americans typically entered such associations *not* because they had strong, preexisting civic commitments, but because of economic needs, religious beliefs, social ties, and personal identities. The unions, fraternal associations, churches, and synagogues that they joined then turned them into active citizens.

These organizations have since shed most of their members and have also lost impact because of the corruption of our formal political institutions, which increasingly respond to narrow special interests, money, and expertise. Now we need a broad base of active citizens to promote the types of associations that recruit people into political life *and* demand political reforms that make government more responsive and fair. But since people are not organized into civic groups, we lack the scale of support we seem to need. This is a conundrum.

The solution begins with recognizing that a significant minority of Americans have recently participated in meaningful civic work that includes aspects of open-ended discussion, problem solving, education, and collaboration with diverse peers. We still have civic organizations, albeit smaller and less visible than their predecessors 50 years ago. As in the past, these groups do not rely solely on recruits who have remarkable civic motivations from the start. Instead, they offer various concrete and sometimes even materialistic benefits, such as jobs, educational credentials, or solutions to local problems. But often the people they recruit have rewarding experiences when they are invited to act as deliberative, constructive citizens. They enjoy themselves, they feel that they have solved problems, and they gain satisfaction. These Americans represent a base for civic renewal. We need them to develop a greater self-awareness as active citizens, stronger network ties, and an agenda for renewing democracy together.

How many Americans have participated recently in worthy democratic activities? One way to answer that question is to ask representative samples about their own experiences. Eighteen percent of survey respondents in 2007 said that they had participated within the past year in a meeting with people of diverse views "to determine ideas and solutions for problems in their community."[14] That 18 percent was diverse in terms of race, ethnicity, and educational background. A different source is Census data collected annually from 2005–7, which suggest that 11.8 percent of adult Americans have either attended community meetings or worked on community problems. That group is somewhat skewed toward older, richer, better educated, native-born, white people.[15]

In 2003, a team of political scientists surveyed 1,001 Americans about various deliberative experiences and found that 25 percent had "attended a formal or informal meeting . . . to specifically discuss a local, national, or international issue—for example, neighborhood crime, housing, schools, social security, election reform, terrorism, global warming, or any other public issue that affects people."[16] In this study, African Americans and young people (ages 18–29) were as numerous or even slightly more numerous among the deliberators as in the whole sample.

It is no surprise that these estimates of the proportions of active citizens differ, given the diverse survey questions and sampling methods. But a fairly consistent pattern emerges: somewhere between 10 percent and 20 percent of adult Americans claim that they have engaged in deliberative politics, with the number falling as we add conditions. Although voting and volunteering are stratified by social class, talking and working together on local problems draw a more diverse and representative segment of the population. Talk alone is more common than talk combined with action, as might be expected. If the lower range of these estimates is correct, 10 percent of adult Americans participate annually. That is a base of 25 million people: plenty to build a movement.

The problem with surveys about obviously desirable activities (such as collaborating with one's diverse neighbors) is the tendency for respondents to exaggerate their own participation. Less than 2 percent of adults seem to lie about their voting in the biannual Census survey.[17] However, the problem of overreporting may be worse when we try to measure an activity less concrete and discrete than voting. For example, in some surveys of news consumption, some subsamples are *eight times* more likely to say that they regularly watch the news as actually watch the news.[18] Similarly, if you are asked whether you talked with your neighbors about community issues within the last year, you can probably persuade yourself that you did so, even if a close observer would say that you did not.

Another way to build an estimate of the number of already engaged citizens is to aggregate counts of the actual participants in particular initiatives. For example:

- Public Allies is an AmeriCorps-funded program that recruits mostly disadvantaged young people and places them in leadership roles in nonprofits, developing their ability to invent solutions in collaboration with peers. Public Allies has 2,800 alumni.

- The American Democracy Project (ADP) of the American Association of State Colleges and Universities is one of several national networks of campuses that enhance the civic engagement of their own students and build partnerships with local civil society. ADP is distinctive because its member campuses are mostly nonselective, local, state colleges and universities that serve demographically diverse students. I estimate that ADP directly involves at least 11,000 people.[19]
- The National Coalition for Dialogue & Deliberation (NCDD) has more than 2,000 members and 27,000 email subscribers who are interested in organizing and facilitating public discussions, often linked to local action.
- Community Development Corporations (CDC) employ almost 200,000 people, but I estimate that about 13,800 CDC employees are directly involved with deliberation, community organizing, civic education, or public work.[20]
- The River Network is a movement that empowers residents to understand, enjoy, and protect their local watersheds. Its focus is local collaboration and problem solving rather than centralized regulation. It has formal partnerships with 600 nonprofit organizations across the country. If we assume that each nonprofit involves an average of 30 people (staff and volunteers), that implies a movement of about 18,000 active participants.
- In 2008, the Case Foundation announced a grant competition called "Make It Your Own," seeking projects that they defined as "citizen-centered." The foundation expected all applicants to promote deliberation about goals, to move from talk to action, and to build capacity for future projects. I estimate that the competition drew about 1,840 applicants who truly understood and practiced citizen-centered work, representing roughly 36,800 people.[21]
- Everyday Democracy has been promoting study circles and other forms of deliberative community organizing since 1989. It has worked on more than 450 separate dialogue projects in 600 communities. Since each project by definition involves a substantial group, I cautiously estimate the number of alumni of study circles at 60,000.
- The Coffee Party, a movement for civility and political reform, has attracted almost 500,000 "likes" on Facebook, but a safer estimate of its active membership in March 2011 would be its e-mail list, which numbers 65,000 people.
- YouthBuild USA recruits young people who have dropped out of high school by offering them both hourly pay and training opportunities. Once in YouthBuild, participants find themselves governing their own work

sites through deliberative democracy, and some members progress through a set of civic education experiences to become highly effective leaders.[22] YouthBuild USA claims 100,000 alumni.

- Community, Migrant, Homeless, and Public Housing Health Centers are not-for-profit corporations that provide health care, that are rooted in poor communities and unable to move, and that are governed in part by their own clients. Those that qualify as Federally Qualified Health Centers must have governing boards of which more than half are current clients of the center who demographically represent the population that the center serves. "The governing board ensures that the center is community based and responsive to the community's health care needs."[23] Overall, community health centers employ 123,000 full-time workers or the equivalent. There are 12,000 centers, and if the average board numbers ten, that implies 120,000 board members.[24]

- More than 165,000 people are employed full-time in our public schools to teach social studies or civics.[25] Part of their job is to encourage and moderate informed, civil discussions of issues. Most say that they do so. Ninety-four percent of high school civics teachers say they use "controversies as teaching opportunities to get students engaged and to model civil debate and discussion."[26] That response suggests that about 150,000 adults promote deliberation with democratic goals and a developmental ethic.

- The League of Women Voters claims 150,000 members and active supporters, organized in chapters, states, and a national network.[27] Typical League activities include holding and facilitating local discussions, advocating for political reforms, and educating the public.

- America*Speaks* organizes large, day-long deliberations called Twenty-First Century Town Meetings, that are assigned significant influence over governmental decisions. At least 160,000 people have participated in these events since 1995.

- Members of the IAF are religious congregations and other institutions, not individual people. No census of participants is available, but there are 47 regional IAF organizations, each a hub for scores of local congregations. The Greater Boston Interfaith Organization (by no means the largest or oldest IAF affiliate) drew 4,000 individuals to its founding assembly in 1998. If similar numbers of people are active participants at the average IAF site, then the total count would be almost 200,000 Americans.

- Between its launch in December 2011 and the spring of 2012, 450,000 Americans joined an organization called No Labels. One message of this organization was centrism and opposition to ideological polarization. I have not endorsed that view in this book; on the contrary, I have argued that the national political debate is too narrow. However, No Labels also emphasizes political reform (including limiting the filibuster in the Senate), new deliberative forums (such as Question Time for both the president and Congress), and the active participation of its own members in their home districts. One of its founders, William Galston, says that members are drawn to it for a variety of reasons: some to resist polarization, but others "to enhance the efficacy of citizens' voices in national politics."[28] For that reason, I would count at least some of its members as supporters of civic renewal.

Aggregated, these organizations and professions number more than one million members, even if one presumes that they overlap a bit. (Some social studies teachers belong to the League of Women Voters; some CDC workers are active in IAF). The list is illustrative, not exhaustive, and it could easily be extended, even doubled. I anticipate that most readers already belong to some of these groups or similar ones. If you do not, an important first step is to join or create one and experience its concrete work.

Strengthening the Network

It is safe to say that the base for civic renewal numbers at least one million people. But how tight and effective a network do they form? My casual observations over 20 years in the domains of service learning, civic education, political reform, public journalism, and deliberative democracy suggest that frequently the leaders and the most committed activists know one another and have histories of collaboration. Many organizations involved in civic work have bilateral relationships: for example, CIRCLE (which I direct) has been a formal evaluator of YouthBuild USA. But to track all such relationships would be an ambitious undertaking, and it would reveal networks whose political power is latent, not actual.

A network gains political power when it forms coalitions that can advocate for reforms. In 2010, I identified seven activist coalitions whose goals are congruent with the argument of this book.[29] One hundred and seventeen organizations belonged to at least one of these seven coalitions. They were fairly diverse. A simple Left–Right spectrum seems crude for understanding how these groups differed, but it is interesting that the 117 member organizations included both ACORN (since defunct) and Teach for

America. I would classify both organizations as having a strategy for civic renewal—but each had a very different strategy. The demographic diversity of the organizations' leaders was not as impressive: almost all were college educated and most were white.

These 117 organizations and their coalitions formed a reasonably tight network. Any group could theoretically communicate with any other by going through a maximum of two intermediaries. But the robustness of the network depended heavily on the existence of a few bridging coalitions, notably the Campaign for a Stronger Democracy and the Campaign for the Civic Mission of Schools. Removing those two nodes from the network would cut its density by 60 percent, turning it into a set of scattered nodes.[30] Unfortunately, these two campaigns were very small organizations, each with one or two full-time workers and a very limited budget. Many of their member organizations could not reach their own grassroots participants and allies because they did not have the resources to maintain mailing lists. There was certainly nothing that resembled one list of all the citizens who had been touched by the 117 groups. This analysis points to the need for much stronger bridging organizations.[31]

It is tempting to propose the creation of one powerful, well-funded, broadly representative political organization for civic renewal. But studies of several successful political movements emphasize that they were not led by a single organization, which could have made poor strategic choices, alienated some potential supporters, or even become corrupt for lack of competition. Instead, the successful political movements were led by sets of fractious and competing organizations that collectively represented the whole field.

At its moment of greatest glory, the American civil rights movement was led by the Southern Christian Leadership Conference, the Student Nonviolent Coordinating Committee, the NAACP, the Congress on Racial Equality, and the Urban League, with the Nation of Islam operating somewhat to the side. These groups were strikingly different in ideology and theology, structure, demographics, strategy, and regional base. They sometimes competed for the same members and funds.[32] Nevertheless, their network ties were dense and they were capable of highly effective collective action at moments of crisis and opportunity.

Similarly, the conservative legal movement that has succeeded in remaking the federal judiciary encompasses libertarians, social conservatives, constitutional originalists, neoconservatives, and others whose views are not mutually consistent. The donors who built this movement practiced "spread-betting," investing in a wide range of philosophies and strategies to maximize the chance of success. They also invested in the Federalist Society, which has played several complementary roles. It helps young legal conservatives to form networks and support one another's careers. It takes formal positions on judicial nominations. And it organizes an annual conference that has been genuinely diverse ideologically, regularly drawing influential liberal and leftist thinkers along with all stripes of conservatives. The ideological diversity of the Federalist Society makes it interesting, keeps its participants sharp, and broadens the conservative coalition.[33]

With these examples and others in mind, I would argue for the formation or strengthening of several partially overlapping civic renewal coalitions, each having a distinct philosophy and strategy. Our responsibility (yours and mine) is to join one or more of these coalitions, to advocate for other groups to join these coalitions, or—if necessary—to work with peers to create new coalitions.

In turn, the coalitions should have three major functions.

Debate: Civic renewal is not a fully elaborated theory. It incorporates difficult, unsettled questions. Its core commitments to deliberation, public work, relational politics and the other values defended in chapters 3–4 may conflict with one another in practice. Just as twentieth-century liberalism drew on diverse philosophical traditions, interest groups, and bodies of experimentation to produce a complex and balanced ideology—along with much heated debate and competition—so too should civic renewal encompass a range of ideals and strategies in fruitful dialogue.

I would expect one persistent debate within the movement to concern the relationship between civic renewal, on one hand, and partisanship, polarization, or ideological conflict, on the other. Some proponents of civic renewal regard it as ideologically neutral and scrupulously nonpartisan, an effort to improve our democratic processes that should be welcomed by well-meaning political activists across the spectrum. For instance, Martín Carcasson and his colleagues see "passionate impartiality" as one of the "Key Aspects of the Deliberative Democracy Movement" (which, while not identical to a civic renewal movement, bears a close resemblance to it).[34] Others view civic renewal as ideologically centrist, filling a gap between the hostile major political parties and appealing to moderate voters.[35] Yet another group holds that civic renewal is the heir to participatory democracy in the 1960s—the decentralizing and populist impulses of the New Left—and is thus the best strategy to revive the political Left, including Greens, democratic socialists, and left-liberals.[36] A few thinkers have argued that civic renewal is authentically conservative in its embrace of small, voluntary groups and local traditions.[37]

These disagreements are by no means an embarrassment but represent an opportunity. Many different kinds of Americans can find a place in discussions of civic renewal and contribute their own insights. It would be a victory if the major political parties began to incorporate insights from their respective allies who are working on various flavors of civic renewal. We need to have a debate about what democracy means and how to promote it, much like the debates we already have about what prosperity means and how to attain that. The result is not consensus but appropriate competition. Within the democracy field itself, we should expect the internal ideological debates to be heated and divisive because the underlying disagreements are genuine and important. For instance, the Coffee Party—introduced earlier as an example of a civic renewal organization—split in 2011 when a faction committed to liberal economic and social reforms created Coffee Party Progressives as a left counterforce to the Tea Party.[38] On behalf of the original Coffee Party, Eric Byler responded that, although he welcomed "an energetic, populist left" to participate, his vision was a broader, more ideologically diverse movement that would reduce political polarization.[39] This kind of disagreement is to be expected, possibly even welcomed, but it will not always be pleasant.

A related question is the relationship between civic renewal and civility. Some proponents of deliberative democracy and civic education are motivated by a belief that public discourse has become far too harsh and uncivil, driving away ordinary people who expect conversations to be friendly and polite.[40] In May 2010, President Barack Obama told graduates at the University of Michigan, "The . . . way to keep our democracy healthy is to maintain a basic level of civility in our public debate."[41] He was responding to widespread public concern. According to a 2010 Allegheny College national survey, 95 percent of Americans believe that civility is important in politics. Most perceive that civility has declined, especially if they listen to the radio and/or pay close attention to politics, and 50 percent believe that there has been a decline in the tone of politics since Obama was elected.[42]

On the other hand, some proponents of civic renewal are themselves angry about corruption and inequality and believe that stirring up anger (in themselves and others) is an appropriate response. Calls for civility can be efforts to silence marginalized and legitimately resentful citizens. For example, the civil rights historian William Chafe describes the situation in Greensboro, North Carolina, in the 1960s, "From a black point of view, of course, the ground rules, or 'civilities,' were often just a way of delaying action."[43] Like the question of ideology, the issue of civility will provoke ongoing discussion that may be fruitful but may also be uncomfortable.

A third contested issue concerns the relationships among political reform, economic reform, and civic empowerment (i.e., building ordinary people's skills, networks, and sense of confidence). Many alternative theories about these three factors are plausible. For example, one can assert that economic equality is a precondition for citizens to act effectively in their own political interests. I argued against this thesis in chapter 4, but reasonable people hold it. One can argue instead that political reform must precede civic empowerment, because individuals will be discouraged from acting as citizens until political institutions are fair and responsive. Or one can assert that the first step is civic empowerment, without which elites will never concede a fair political system. Each theory suggests a different starting point but looks naive from the perspective of the other two. Thus this debate will be as heated and divisive as the ones previously mentioned. Meanwhile, there will be many routine debates about which concrete strategies, reforms, and organizations to support. Readers of this book should develop positions on these issues and join or even provoke the debate.

Communications: If a first task for the coalitions and organizations involved in civic renewal is to debate unresolved issues, a second is to generate and disseminate public messages. But their messages should not be introductory slogans about the importance of civic engagement, directed at a mass public, with vague objectives, competing with countless other media campaigns in the public sphere.

Instead, the primary audience should be roughly one million Americans who have already had meaningful experiences doing civic work. They should not all receive the same message from the same source; instead, there should be much communication from various organizations to their own members and allies. Each communication should be tailored to its particular context. Still, these messages should share a common theme, which I would briefly paraphrase thus: "You have done important political work that improved the world and fulfilled you personally. (Specifics about the nature of the work would be helpful here.) Your work is deliberative, educational, experiential, loyal, hopeful, democratic, and open to a wide range of fellow citizens. Such work is very rare in our society. Please join with peers to evaluate why it is so rare and take action together to strengthen it."

An important purpose of these communications is to help people feel part of a larger movement for civic renewal or stronger democracy. A hallmark of any successful movement is such a shared sense of belonging and identity. Today, people who define themselves as leaders of public deliberation, political reform, engaged scholarship, citizen journalism, community organizing, or civic engagement have ways of interacting with peers within their own fields at the national level: journals, associations, meetings, and e-mail lists. But rarely do the organizers of one strand of civic renewal feel connected to the leaders of the other strands. For example, a professor who organizes local citizens to conduct health research is very unlikely to feel that she is part of the same movement as an entrepreneur who has started a website for civic journalism in a different city. Even less do ordinary citizens recruited into one form of civic engagement recognize a common cause with citizens involved in a different type of engagement in a different place.

Thus, if the elaborate public deliberations known as Clear Vision Eau Claire (under way in Eau Claire, Wisconsin) were suddenly canceled, it is very unlikely that the citizen-journalists involved in writing articles for the Honolulu *Civil Beat* would know what had happened, let alone feel that their own work had been attacked. Similarly, if the *Civil Beat* folded, the deliberating citizens in Eau Claire would have no way of knowing or any reason to care. In contrast, at the height of the civil rights movement, if peaceful protesters were arrested in Chicago, people from Atlanta might send bail money or even get on a bus to support them. We will have a real movement for civic renewal once the citizens involved in such disparate efforts as Clear Vision Eau Claire and the Honolulu *Civil Beat* are communicating about common issues and supporting one another's efforts.

Advocacy: The communications sent by organizations and coalitions in the field of civic renewal should certainly ask for resources—money and time—as well as ideas. Armed with these resources, organizations can conduct political advocacy at the local, state, national, and global levels. In short, they can lobby and litigate.

Exactly what to advocate will be controversial and will vary by location and year. Many factors enter into wise decisions about political priorities, including the potential impact of any given reform, its costs and trade-offs, its chance of passage, its popularity, its potential to divide a coalition, and its likelihood of surviving once originally passed. Some reforms begin helpful feedback loops. A funding stream for youth service, for example, might support organizations that then become advocates of further democratic reform while generating useful lessons about what works.[44] Other policies are dead ends. An annual $30 million federal earmark for the Center for Civic Education during the 1990s and 2000s proved to be stable (because the Center developed a national network that lobbied for the annual congressional appropriation), but it failed to generate excellent civic education or to strengthen the broader movement.[45] Annual funding competitions might have worked better.

Considering all the factors that one must weigh to develop a policy agenda—and the rapidly changing political environment—I hesitate to use the static medium of a book to list policy priorities. However, as illustrative examples, I would suggest the following ten priorities for *national* efforts at the time of writing:

1. Choose one grave national issue and use federal policy to support participatory, deliberative solutions. The issue could be, for example, the high school dropout rate, constantly rising costs of medical care, the loss of jobs and population in our postindustrial cities, childhood obesity, or the failure of policing and sentencing to deter crime. Regardless of the issue, the response would involve a substantial amount of decentralized decision-making and direct work by empowered local bodies that are supported with funds and education and held accountable for results. Youth would be recruited, trained, and rewarded to play important roles in both the discussions and the work.

To be sure, each social or environmental issue connects to others; people do not live within particular institutions such as high schools or clinics. However, the momentum for civic renewal is too weak to permit the federal government to use civic strategies broadly right away. Too few citizens and leaders are now demanding such strategies and are equipped to help implement them. A deep investment in one issue area would provide a high-profile model. At the same time, it would train and empower hundreds of thousands of active citizens, some of whom would later create or demand civic opportunities in other issue domains. For example, if the US Department of Education (reversing 20 years of momentum in the opposite direction) were to delegate important decisions to empowered bodies of parents, teachers, students, and other residents, some members of those bodies would become active at the local level in related topics, such as crime and obesity. Many historical case studies indicate that the strongest impact of particular projects comes later, when participants start unanticipated initiatives of their own.[46]

2. Pass the Fair Elections Now Act or a close equivalent. This legislation would provide clean public funding for candidates who were able to raise sufficient numbers of small private contributions to demonstrate a base of support. It would not only reduce corruption—in the broad (ethical, not legal) sense of that word—by making wealthy donors less influential; it would also articulate a public philosophy that money is problematic in politics. Money is not equivalent to speech and participation. What should count is the best argument, not the most cash.

3. Make voluntary national service a means to develop civic capacities. Early in the Obama administration, Congress voted on a bipartisan basis to authorize the tripling of federal voluntary service programs (Ameri-Corps, Senior Corps, Peace Corps, and others). That was an important step that only became controversial after the Republican congressional victories of 2010. Maintaining or expanding the size of national and community service is valuable, but at least as important is to make service programs into opportunities for civic discussion and learning. Every participant should have opportunities to discuss and influence the strategies used in his or her service program and should be expected to obtain skills for deliberating, facilitating meetings, recruiting citizens, analyzing issues, and advocating publicly. To achieve that objective would require setting standards for learning across all the federal service programs.

4. Prepare a new generation of active and responsible citizens. People form attitudes and habits related to civil society when they are young and tend to keep them for the rest of their lives. But many school systems have reduced their commitment to civic education; state standards for civics emphasize factual knowledge rather than skills for collaboration and deliberation; and the federal government has withdrawn completely from the field. (In 2011, Congress eliminated the Learn & Serve America program that provided competitive grants for service learning and withdrew all funding for the Center for Civic Education. The federal Office of Civic Education is buried within the Office of Safe and Drug-Free Schools.) High priorities include new state standards that emphasize civic engagement, new curricula and tests that align with those standards, and federal investment in innovative civic education.[47] The federal government should also bring together a range of agencies, including the Department of Education, the Corporation for National and Community Service, the National Park Service, the National Endowments for the Humanities and the Arts, the Corporation for Public Broadcasting, and the Defense Department, to promote civic education in a coordinated way.

5. Put citizenship back in the civil service. Because of the looming retirement of baby boomers in public service, the federal and state governments face an enormous challenge in recruiting and hiring adequate numbers of highly skilled workers, even if they cut their payrolls because of budget cuts and efficiencies. The Partnership for National Service estimates that the federal government alone needs about 91,000 new employees every fiscal year for positions defined as "mission-critical."[48] Governments' need to attract and retain qualified civil servants creates an

opportunity for civic renewal. Public sector jobs would become more attractive if they were more creative, collaborative, and rewarding. Encouraging public employees to work in partnership with communities and civic groups would help. At the same time, the federal government should declare that it is looking for employees who have demonstrated experience and skills in deliberation, collaboration, and public work. By setting specific criteria for new employees that include civic skills, the government could change curricula in colleges and universities.

6. Support charter schools, Community Development Corporations, watershed councils, and Federally Qualified Health Centers: These are examples of public institutions that have expanded opportunities for civic engagement. Citizens may found such organizations or help guide them by serving on their boards. Their structures vary in ways that matter for civic renewal. For example, a charter school that has a board composed of parents and community members promotes active citizenship more than a charter school dominated by its charismatic founder. A school that must accept students from a lottery promotes equity better than one that can select its student body. Thus, the government should sustain or expand support for these innovative institutions while also moving them in maximally civic directions.

7. Give the public a voice in policymaking. When members of Congress meet the public in open sessions misleadingly called town meetings, they encounter polarized and mobilized members of advocacy groups, acting strategically.[49] But when citizens are convened to discuss complex and divisive issues, majorities usually choose reasonable policies and almost all the participants report satisfaction with the process. A model is the national deliberation called "AmericaSpeaks: Our Budget, Our Economy," which convened 3,500 participants to develop budget outlines for the federal government in 2010. Participants, although highly diverse, shifted toward a mixed package of revenue increases and budget cuts. Ninety-seven percent agreed, "People at this meeting listened to one another respectfully and courteously," and 81 percent thought, "Decision makers should incorporate the conclusions of this town meeting into federal budget policy."[50]

To make such processes common and enhance their influence on policies and on the broader political culture, Congress should take two major steps. One would be to fund a high-profile deliberation on a divisive and important topic. The participants' favored policy would come back to Congress as a bill requiring an up-or-down vote. The other important step would be to create an infrastructure that is ready to organize this and other public deliberations when needed. The infrastructure would consist of standards for fair and open public deliberations, a federal office that could coordinate many simultaneous forums and collect all their findings, and a list of vetted contractors that would be eligible to convene public deliberations with federal grants.

8. Use the Internet to make the regulatory process more deliberative. As shown in chapter 5, regulation by administrative agencies has become a dominant mode of lawmaking, but it is problematic. Appointed officials lack the legitimacy to make explicit value judgments, so rule making degenerates into a combination of bargaining and cost-benefit analysis that is not morally justifiable. Citizens' voices can help, and administrative agencies have long been required to receive and formally consider public comments. But the influential comments tend to come from well-placed experts and stakeholders. In October 2002, the federal government launched eRule-making, an initiative to allow the public to comment electronically on pending rules and to search and read others' comments. The resulting system has won awards for technical excellence and for making government more accessible and transparent, but it still does not favor deliberative norms. Each comment is a separate communication to the government; participants do not exchange reasons, judgments, and evidence with one another. One important exception is the Peer-to-Patent website of the US Patent and Trademark Office, which encourages a community of volunteer reviewers to assess pending patent applications collaboratively.[51] Assessing the merits of a patent claim is a relatively technical and nonideological matter. The next step is to build similar websites that encourage users to discuss controversies that have come before federal agencies. The goal would not be consensus—which could suppress the right of individuals to petition the government in their own voice—but rather an illuminating public dialogue.

9. Launch a Civic Communications Corps: The metropolitan daily newspaper and its professional roster of reporters was a pillar of civil society for more than a century, complementing voluntary civic associations. Newspapers and traditional journalism are in dire condition. Without government's help, citizens are creating diverse and interactive new forms of media—mostly online—to counteract the decline of the commercial news and entertainment businesses. But many Americans cannot participate in or benefit from these new media because they lack equipment and broadband access or the necessary skills to be creative online. Meanwhile, thousands of young adults (including many without college educations)

have relevant skills, from highly technical expertise with computers and networks, to human relationships in their communities, to creativity with videos and music.

To take advantage of their potential, the government should launch a small new Civic Communications Corps within AmeriCorps.[52] Full-time volunteers would be placed in community organizations to serve their communications needs and would also meet at the municipal level to work on citywide or countywide strategies for enhancing the flow of information and discussion. They would generate software, examples, training videos, and other resources for the rest of the national and community service world to use in serving public communications needs. College and universities would also be encouraged to use these tools to become communications hubs for their neighboring communities.

10. Incorporate immigrants into civic life. As a result of the great modern migration into the United States, more than one-quarter of young Americans could be classified broadly as "immigrants" (having at least one parent born abroad). Despite variation among immigrant groups—and changes over the course of most immigrants' lives—their levels of active civic engagement are lower than average, even once education and income are taken into consideration.[53] Our goal should not be to wash out the distinctive aspects of immigrants' political and civic cultures. On the contrary, communities that value immigrants' distinctive contributions see much higher levels of immigrant civic engagement.[54] But it will take investment and reform to raise their rates of civic participation. Two important steps would be to make the naturalization process a supportive education in civic engagement rather than a hurdle to be jumped and to pass the DREAM Act (Development, Relief and Education for Alien Minors), which would make undocumented young people eligible for financial aid.[55]

The theory behind this Ten Point Plan is not that federal policy reforms can cause a renewal of civic life in America. Well-chosen reforms may provide some support for civic renewal in the form of financial incentives, legitimacy, publicity, relevant jobs, and training. Just as important, the successful pursuit of policy reforms may turn disparate and politically weak organizations into a movement.

The Voting Rights Act offers an analogy. Its passage did not (by itself) change the balance of political power in the United States. Separate from the law, the civil rights movement had to educate, motivate, and register voters; recruit and develop political candidates; change the consciousness of African

Americans and whites; reform the inner workings of the Democratic Party; and litigate for reforms in district maps, ballots, election dates, and many other areas of the electoral system: a struggle that continues today. Nevertheless, the Voting Rights Act was a powerful tool for activists, and the struggle to pass it was a unifying and inspiring goal for the civil rights movement. The same could be said today of policy reforms for civic renewal.

I have emphasized federal reforms here for the sake of brevity, but states and localities could be equally important if one or more jurisdictions became genuine laboratories for democracy. There should also be crucial struggles for civic engagement in universities, nonprofit service agencies, professional associations, unions, religious congregations, and newsrooms, to mention only some of the important venues outside government.

Some of the most promising steps may seem rather far removed from you and from me. For example, the first item on the Ten Point Plan was to drive civic renewal strategies deep into the work of at least one federal agency. That would take a committed, skillful, and experienced cabinet-level official. Unless you are the president of the United States, you cannot nominate individuals for the cabinet. Unless you are nominated (and confirmed by the Senate), you cannot lead a federal agency. Few of us will ever play either of those roles.

Nevertheless, if you work at the local level on a particular issue—say, education—in ways that combine deliberation and work and that develop your own and others' civic capacities, you are building the foundations for strategies at the federal level. A successful federal initiative would not be possible without persuasive examples and evidence, local organizations and individuals capable of handling grants and power, and active supporters who defend civic strategies. By working at the local level, you can help provide those conditions for success at the federal level. You can do more if you recruit new people to such work, build networks connecting your projects to other similar ones, view yourself as part of a nascent movement for civic renewal, encourage peers to think of themselves in similar ways, and provoke conversations about the broad topic of civic engagement.

Those conversations should encompass facts, values, and strategies. The factual questions to pose (regardless of the scale of one's civic work) include: Who is engaging, and who is left out? What are the consequences of our civic activities, both positive and negative?

The values questions include: Are our goals consistent with justice? Are our discussions and processes ethical and fair? What are the consequences of our work for the virtues and dispositions of the people involved?

The strategic questions include: What resources and opportunities (including funds, skilled people, legal rights, and responsive institutions) do we possess for our civic work? What resources and opportunities do we lack? What would it take to get what we need? That last question moves us to consider reforms in institutions and policies as well as changes in our own behavior.

Overall, the goal is to replace a vicious cycle of citizens' disempowerment and public corruption with a virtuous cycle of reengagement and reform. The obstacles to changing our national direction in such a profound way are serious. They include a disempowered and divided citizenry, a shattered civic infrastructure, and a set of interest groups that will fight to defend the status quo. But the opportunities are also significant: they include a substantial base of skillful, motivated, and increasingly experienced and interconnected civic reformers.

Cynicism and pessimism are obstacles to reform that we (you and I) should strive to counter. After all, cynicism and pessimism are belied every day by the many organizations already working on civic renewal in America. Although success is hardly guaranteed, the consequences of failure are dire. In the words of the Port Huron Statement, "If we appear to seek the unattainable, it has been said, then let it be known that we do so to avoid the unimaginable."[56]

A Note on the Title of This Book

DURING HIS 2008 presidential campaign, then Senator Barack Obama often said, "We are the ones we have been waiting for." He did not coin this phrase and never said that he did. David Mathews, president of the Kettering Foundation, calls it "an old song from the civil rights movement."[1] He may have heard it sung by the gospel ensemble Sweet Honey in the Rock; Alice Walker explains, "It was the poet June Jordan who wrote, 'We are the ones we have been waiting for.' Sweet Honey in the Rock turned those words into a song. Hearing that song, I have witnessed thousands of people rise to their feet in joyful recognition and affirmation."[2]

The words do appear in Jordan's "Poem for South African Women," which she presented at the United Nations on August 9, 1978, in "commemoration of the 40,000 women and children who, August 9, 1956, presented themselves in bodily protest against the 'dompass' in the capital of apartheid."[3] So Jordan may have invented this phrase in (or not long before) 1978. That would make it a product of the *late* civil rights movement.

But the sentence is italicized and typeset as its own stanza, as if it were an epigraph. Maybe Jordan quoted it from known or anonymous predecessors. Both Senator John Edwards and Sojourners founder Jim Wallis quote the late activist Lisa Sullivan (1961–2001) as their source for the phrase.[4] Sullivan may have quoted Jordan, or both could have had older sources.

In any case, the 2008 Obama Campaign did not own the phrase or have a right to monopolize its resonances, although Obama deserves credit for understanding and using it. Ultimately, it is *our* phrase and we have the obligation and opportunity to develop its meaning through our talk, our work, and our civic relationships.

Notes

CHAPTER 1: OVERVIEW: THE PUBLIC AND OUR PROBLEMS

1. Gallup Organization polls from 1979 to 2013, http://www.gallup.com/poll/1669/general-mood-country.aspx.

2. Horst W. J. Rittel and Melvin M. Webber, "Dilemmas in a General Theory of Planning," *Policy Sciences* 4 (1973): 155–69, quoting p. 165. This is a classic paper whose major points apply as accurately today as in 1973.

3. Thomas Shepherd, "The Parable of the Ten Virgins Unfolded," in Shepherd's *Works*, vol. 2 (Boston: Doctrinal Tract and Book Society, 1853), pp. 375–76.

4. The Sentencing Project, http://www.sentencingproject.org/template/page.cfm?id=107 (2010 data).

5. Rebecca Ruiz, "Eyes on the Prize: Our Moral and Ethical Duty to End Mass Incarceration," *American Prospect*, January–February 2011, p. A3.

6. Spending: OECD, *Education at a Glance 2008: OECD Indicators*, table B1.1a, Annual Expenditure on Educational Institutions Per Student for All Services (2005), www.oecd.org. Dropouts and incarceration: Sam Dillon, "Study Finds High Rate of Imprisonment Among Dropouts," *New York Times*, October 8, 2009. Spending: OECD, *Education at a Glance 2004*, chart, Annual Secondary Education Expenditures Per Student, at US Dept. of Education, http://www.ed.gov/about/overview/fed/10facts/edlite-chart.html#1.

7. Spending: The Organisation for Economic Co-operation and Development (OECD), *OECD Health Data 2012: How Does the United States Compare?*, http://www.oecd.org/unitedstates/BriefingNoteUSA2012.pdf. Mortality: Andrew P. Wilper et al., "Health Insurance and Mortality in US Adults," *American Journal of Public Health* 99, no. 12 (December 2009): 2292.

8. Citizens' Research Council of Michigan, *Growth in Michigan's Corrections System: Historical and Comparative Perspectives*, report 350 (June 2008), p. v.

9. Office of Management and the Budget, Historical Tables: Table 1.2—Summary of Receipts, Outlays, and Surpluses or Deficits (-) as Percentages of GDP: 1930–2017, http://www.whitehouse.gov/omb/budget/Historicals. The lowest levels of taxation in relation to GDP were reached in 1949, 1950, 2009, and 2010; the peak years included 1970, 1981, and 2000.

10. Peter Levine, *The New Progressive Era: Toward a Fair and Deliberative Democracy* (Lanham, MD: Rowman & Littlefield, 2000).

11. Thomas Philippon, "Has the U.S. Finance Industry Become Less Efficient? On the Theory and Measurement of Financial Intermediation," National Bureau of Economic Research Working Paper 18077, http://www.nber.org/papers/w18077.

12. Elizabeth Gudrais, "Flocking to Finance," *Harvard*, May–June 2008, http://harvardmagazine.com/2008/05/flocking-to-finance.html.

13. District of Columbia, State Center for Health Statistics, "The 2007 Infant Morality Rate for the District of Columbia," May 13, 2009, dchealth.dc.gov; statehealthfacts.org.

14. Lonnae O'Neal Parker, "For Jonathan Lewis, It's Fourth and Goal," *Washington Post*, November 12, 2007.

15. US Census Bureau, *Census of Population*, 1950, District of Columbia, vol. 2, part 9, tables 64, 73, http://www.census.gov/prod/www/decennial.html.

16. US Census Bureau, 2007–11 American Community Survey, "Selected Economic Characteristics" for the District of Columbia, http://factfinder2.census.gov/faces/tableservices/jsf/pages/productview.xhtml?pid=ACS_11_5YR_DP03.

17. US Dept. of Labor, Bureau of Labor Statistics, "Employed Persons by Occupation, Race, Hispanic or Latino Ethnicity, and Sex," 2011–12, http://www.bls.gov/cps/cpsaat10.pdf.

18. An ambitious study of the way that young African Americans see the social contract, their own obligations, and the limits on their agency is Cathy J. Cohen, *Democracy Remixed* (New York: Oxford University Press, 2010).

19. Greg J. Duncan and Richard J. Murnane, "Introduction: The American Dream, Then and Now," in Duncan and Murnane, eds., *Whither Opportunity? Rising Inequality, Schools, and Children's Life Chances* (New York: Russell Sage, 2011), pp. 11–12.

20. Annette Lareau, *Unequal Childhoods: Class, Race, and Family Life* (Berkeley: University of California Press, 2003). For application to samples outside of Lareau's study city of Philadelphia, see Katerina Budovski and George Farkas, "'Concerted Cultivation' and Unequal Achievement in Elementary School," *Social Science Research* 37, no. 3 (September 2008): 903–19. They test Lareau's thesis on a national sample and find that parental socioeconomic status is very strongly associated with "concerted cultivation."

21. Jennifer Comey, "Performance of Students Attending District of Columbia Public Schools (DCPS), District of Columbia Public Charter School Board (PCSB) Schools, and District of Columbia Board of Education (BOE) Schools"

(statement submitted to the Agency Performance Oversight Hearings Committee of the Whole, Council of the District of Columbia, February 22, 2008), http://www.urban.org/UploadedPDF/901148_Comey_dcps.pdf.

22. A strong and recent study with good data and a sophisticated method is Eric A. Hanushek et al., "Charter School Quality and Parental Decision Making with School Choice," *Journal of Public Economics* 91, nos. 5–6 (2007): 823–48. Charters appear to add slightly less value than regular schools do, but the key finding is the tremendous diversity of impact in both sectors, which suggests that the important goal is not to move students from regular schools into charters, nor vice versa, but rather to improve schools in both categories.

23. Bill Turque, "Education Reform Long Troubled in the District," *Washington Post*, October 31, 2009.

24. William L. Sanders and June C. Rivers, "Cumulative and Residual Effects of Teachers on Future Student Academic Achievement" (University of Tennessee Value-Added Research and Assessment Center, November 1996); Raj Chetty et al., "How Does Your Kindergarten Classroom Affect Your Earnings? Evidence from Project STAR" (presentation outline, February 2011), http://obs.rc.fas.harvard.edu/chetty/STAR_slides.pdf.

25. Ben Smith, "Teachers Union Helped Unseat Fenty," *Politico*, September 15, 2010, http://www.politico.com/blogs/bensmith/0910/Teachers_union_helped_unseat_Fenty.html.

26. Vote counts from the DC Board of Elections, "City-Wide Registration and Turnout," last updated, September 29, 2010, http://www.dcboee.org/election_info/election_results/results_2010.asp?electionid=4&prev=0&;result_type=1. Population estimates from US Commerce Dept., *Estimates of the Voting Age Population for 2009*, 75 Fed. Reg. 4343, Jan. 27, 2010, http://www.federalregister.gov/articles/2010/01/27/2010-1522/estimates-of-the-voting-age-population-for-2009.

27. Dakarai I. Aarons, "Rhee Reflects on Her Stormy Tenure in D.C.," *Education Week*, September 17, 2010, http://www.edweek.org.

28. Robert D. Putnam, "Community-Based Social Capital and Educational Performance," in Diane Ravitch and Joseph P. Viteritti, eds., *Making Good Citizens: Education and Civil Society* (New Haven, CT: Yale University Press, 2001), pp. 69–72.

29. Thomas L. Friedman, "Advice from Grandma," *New York Times*, November 21, 2009.

30. Jeff Holtz, "Bridgeport Mayor's Office, and Race for It, Drawing Spotlight as Usual," *New York Times*, June 10, 2007; Fred Musante, "Teachers' Strike Stirs Bitter Memories," *New York Times*, February 1, 1998.

31. These organizations were the Public Agenda Foundation and the Connecticut Community Conversations Project (which, in turn, was a project of the Connecticut League of Women Voters and some partners).

32. American Institute of Architects (AIA), *Sustainable Design Assessment Team Report for Bridgeport, CT*, 2010, p. 73, http://www.aia.org. The same report, however,

finds that city officials in 2010 were not aware of the community conversations. "The recent transition from one mayoral administration to another may be a factor here; another may be that the Community Conversations have focused mainly on school issues, and participants have not seen the applicability of the process to other local concerns" (p. 73).

33. Will Friedman, Alison Kadlec, and Lara Birnback, "Transforming Public Life: A Decade of Citizen Engagement in Bridgeport, CT," *Case Studies in Public Engagement* 1 (2007), Public Agenda Foundation, http://www.publicagenda.org/files/pdf/cape_bridgeport.pdf, p. 9.

34. Ibid. The case is also mentioned in Elena Fagotto and Archon Fung, *Sustaining Public Engagement: Embedded Deliberation in Local Communities* (research paper, Everyday Democracy and the Kettering Foundation, 2009), http://www.everyday-democracy.org/en/Resource.136.aspx.

35. Harry C. Boyte and Nancy N. Kari, *Building America: The Democratic Promise of Public Work* (Philadelphia: Temple University Press, 1996).

36. E.g., by Cynthia Gibson in *Citizens at the Center: A New Approach to Civic Engagement* (Washington, DC: Case Foundation, 2006), http://www.casefoundation.org/spotlight/civic_engagement/summary.

37. National Conference on Citizenship, "How to Talk About Civic Engagement," in *America's Civic Health Index 2008*, www.ncoc.net.

38. Kei Kawashima-Ginsberg, Chaeyoon Lim, and Peter Levine, "Civic Health and Unemployment II: The Case Builds" (Washington, DC: National Conference on Citizenship, 2012).

39. On skills, see JoAnn Jastrzab et al. "Serving Country and Community: A Longitudinal Study of Service in AmeriCorps" (Washington, DC: Corporation for National and Community Service, 2004), http://www.abtassociates.com/reports/COMSRVS.pdf. On trust, see K. M. Sønderskov, "Does Generalized Social Trust Lead to Associational Membership? Unravelling a Bowl of Well-Tossed Spaghetti," *European Sociological Review* (2001), doi:10.1093/esr/jcq017; and Francis Fukuyama, *Trust: Social Virtues and the Creation of Prosperity* (New York: Free Press, 1995). On the impact of civic engagement on governance see Putnam, "Community-Based Social Capital," in Ravitch and Viteritti, *Making Good Citizens*; and Putnam, *Making Democracy Work: Civic Traditions in Modern Italy* (Princeton, NJ: Princeton University Press, 1993); Jeffrey M. Berry, Kent E. Portney, and Kenneth Thomson, *The Rebirth of Urban Democracy* (Washington, DC: Brookings Institution, 1993); Kent E. Portney and Jeffrey M. Berry, "Participation and the Pursuit of Sustainability in U.S. Cities," *Urban Affairs Review* 46, no. 1 (2010): 119–39. On affection for communities and its connection to civic engagement and economic growth, see Gallup, *Knight Soul of the Community* (Knight Foundation, 2010), p. 5, http://www.soulofthecommunity.org.

40. Sean Safford, *Why the Garden Club Couldn't Save Youngstown* (Cambridge, MA: Harvard University Press, 2009).

41. Median household income and median home prices 2007–11 from U.S. Census Bureau, "State & County QuickFacts" for Allentown (city) and Youngstown (city), quickfacts.census.gov. Homicide rate for the cities calculated by the author using FBI Uniform Crime Reports as prepared by the National Archive of Criminal Justice Data (http://bjs.gov/ucrdata) for 2000–10. Life expectancies for the counties (2009) are from the University of Washington's Institute for Health Metrics and Evaluation, http://www.healthmetricsandevaluation.org.

42. Safford, *Why the Garden Club Couldn't Save Youngstown*, p. 75.

43. Ibid., p. 131.

44. Ibid., p. 125.

45. See also Vaughn L. Grisham, *Tupelo: The Evolution of a Community* (Dayton, OH; Kettering Foundation Press, 1999), which associates the remarkable economic success of Tupelo, MS, with its civic infrastructure, and Berry, Portney, and Thomson, *Rebirth of Urban Democracy*, which shows that cities with stronger associational participation are able to make difficult decisions better.

46. Robert J. Sampson, *Great American City: Chicago and the Enduring Neighborhood Effect* (Chicago: University of Chicago Press, 2012), p. 372.

47. Corey L. M. Keyes, "Promoting and Protecting Mental Health as Flourishing," *American Psychologist* 62, no. 2 (2007), pp. 95–108; Keyes, "The Mental Health Continuum: From Languishing to Flourishing in Life," *Journal of Health and Social Behavior* 43, no. 2 (2002): 207–22; conversations with Keyes. See also Jacquelynne J. Eccles, Jennifer Gootman, and Jennifer J. Appleton eds., *Community Programs to Promote Youth Development: A Report of the National Research Council and Institute of Medicine, Board on Children, Youth, and Families, Committee on Community-Level Programs for Youth* (Washington, DC: National Academies Press, 2002). For positive effects on retirees, see Terry Y. Lum and Elizabeth Lightfoot, "The Effects of Volunteering on the Physical and Mental Health of Older People," *Research on Aging* 27 (January 2005): 31–55. On the other hand, it is important to note that helping the participants is not always the main purpose of a civic engagement effort, nor do they always benefit psychosocially. Based on rigorous research with a control group, Doug McAdam finds that participating in Freedom Summer, the voter registration effort in Mississippi in 1964, made the participants more politically active but also less well off. Compared to the control group, they were more likely to be unhappily divorced and had lower incomes 20 years later. The point of their activism, of course, was not to be happy but to help end Jim Crow. Doug McAdam, *Freedom Summer* (New York: Oxford University Press, 1988), pp. 199–232.

48. YouthBuild graduate interview, conducted by CIRCLE, fall 2011. Tufts University Internal Review Board study #1104001. This quotation was not used in our published report, but the report provides general context and findings: see CIRCLE, *Pathways into Leadership: A Study of YouthBuild Graduates* (Medford, MA: CIRCLE, 2012), www.civicyouth.org.

49. This section is indebted to Albert Dzur, *Punishment, Participatory Democracy, and the Jury* (New York: Oxford University Press, 2012).

50. Arie Freiberg and Karen Gelb, eds., *Penal Populism, Sentencing Councils, and Sentencing Policy* (Sydney, Australia: Hawkins Press, 2008), provides an overview.

51. The seminal study is Harry Kalven Jr. and Hans Zeisel, *The American Jury* (Boston: Little, Brown, 1966), but confirmation comes from Theodore Eisenberg et al., "Judge-Jury Agreement in Criminal Cases: A Partial Replication of Kalven & Zeisel's *The American Jury*" (research paper no. 04–025, Cornell Law School, 2004).

52. Dzur, *Punishment, Participatory Democracy, and the Jury*, p. 60.

53. James S. Fishkin, *The Voice of the People: Public Opinion & Democracy* (New Haven, CT: Yale University Press, 1995), pp. 215–16.

54. Richard A. Oppel Jr., "Sentencing Shift Gives New Leverage to Prosecutors," *New York Times*, September 25, 2011, http://www.nytimes.com/2011/09/26/us/tough-sentences-help-prosecutors-push-for-plea-bargains.html?pagewanted=all.

55. Syllabus of *Missouri v. Freye*, Supreme Court, no. 10–444 (2011), p. 2.

56. American National Election Studies data, analyzed by the author using the Survey Documentation and Analysis tool from the University of California, Berkeley, http://sda.berkeley.edu/.

57. See Dzur, *Punishment, Participatory Democracy, and the Jury*, pp. 85–104.

58. Matt Leighninger, *The Next Form of Democracy: How Expert Rule Is Giving Way to Shared Governance . . . and Why Politics Will Never Be the Same* (Nashville, TN: Vanderbilt University Press, 2006), pp. 127–34.

59. Jim Campbell, "Oklahoma Prison Sentencing Reform Has Factious History," *Tulsa World*, February 14, 2011.

60. *Oklahoma Department of Corrections Annual Report*, 2009, http://www.doc.state.ok.us; National Institute on Money in State Politics, "Industry Influence," tables at http://www.followthemoney.org/database/IndustryTotals.phtml?f=0&s=OK&b[]=G7000.

61. Becky Lawmaster and Sharon Neumann, "Community Sentencing: The Department's '¢ents-able' Alternative to Incarceration," *Inside Corrections*, January 2009, pp. 9–12, http://www.doc.state.ok.us/.

62. Greg Berman and John Feinblatt, *Good Courts: The Case for Problem-Solving Justice* (New York: New Press, 2005), p. 5.

63. Ibid., pp. 84, 122. In one impressive example, a housing court judge worked with a neighborhood association to fight urban blight and abandonment in Buffalo, NY. The judge used his power to fine landlords who violated the housing code, but he would also accept improvements satisfactory to the neighborhood activists. The activists would observe and report housing violations and, when properties were seized by the court, would take them over and rehabilitate them. The court and the neighborhood group chose their targets selectively to redevelop the community block by block and were able to raise the value of privately owned homes tenfold,

essentially creating wealth for long-term residents. Ronald J. Oakerson and Jeremy D. W. Clifton, "Neighborhood Decline as a Tragedy of the Commons: Conditions of Neighborhood Turnaround on Buffalo's West Side" (under review, manuscript cited by permission, 2011). I recognize the significant danger of corruption (not reflected in this case), so oversight would be important.

64. See National Association of Youth Courts website, www.youthcourt.net; Robert A Wolf, *Principles of Problem-Solving Justice* (Bureau of Justice Assistance, Center for Court Innovation, 2007), www.courtinnovation.org/.

65. Albert W. Dzur, *Democratic Professionalism: Citizen Participation and the Reconstruction of Professional Ethics, Identity, and Practice* (University Park: Pennsylvania State University Press, 2008), pp. 175–79.

66. Ibid., pp. 205, 252.

67. Michael O'Hear, "Rethinking Drug Courts: Restorative Justice as Response to Racial Injustice," *Stanford Law and Policy Review* 20, no. 9 (2009): 128. O'Hear argues that problem-solving drug courts do not reduce racial disparities but that restorative justice would build "constructive citizen-police interactions," "stronger relationships among community members," and "the sort of social capital that permits communities to address their own problems more effectively" (p. 137).

68. John Gastil et al., *The Jury and Democracy: How Jury Deliberation Promotes Civic Engagement and Political Participation* (New York: Oxford University Press, 2010).

69. "Overview: Community Development Corporations," Community Wealth.org, citing a 2005 survey of national CDCs, http://community-wealth.org/strategies/panel/cdcs/index.html.

70. Young Voter Strategies and CIRCLE, *Young Voter Mobilization Tactics* (2006), http://www.civicyouth.org/PopUps/Young_Voters_Guide.pdf.

CHAPTER 2: HOW TO THINK ABOUT POLITICS: VALUES, FACTS, AND STRATEGIES

1. Nancy C. Lutkehaus, *Margaret Mead: The Making of an American Icon* (Princeton, NJ: Princeton University Press, 2008), p. 261.

2. For an ambitious statement of that view, see Larry M. Bartels and John Zaller, "Presidential Vote Models: A Recount," *Political Science & Politics* 34 (2001): 9–20. The idea that presidential elections can be predicted by macroeconomic trends has become a prominent topic of debate since that article, and critics have scored some points. See, for example, Nate Silver, "What Do Economic Models Really Tell Us About Elections?" *New York Times*, June 3, 2011, http://fivethirtyeight. blogs.nytimes.com/2011/06/03/what-do-economic-models-really-tell-us-about-elections/. I still think the correlation is much more significant than one would expect if "small groups of thoughtful, committed citizens"—such as presidential candidates and their handlers—were the main force in changing society.

3. Peter Ackerman, "Skills or Conditions: What Key Factors Shape the Success or Failure of Civil Resistance?" (paper, Conference on Civil Resistance & Power Politics, St Antony's College, University of Oxford, March 15–18, 2007), available at http://www.nonviolent-conflict.org/PDF/AckermanSkillsOrConditions. pdf; Marshall Ganz, "Why David Sometimes Wins: Strategic Capacity in Social Movements," in David M. Messick and Roderick M. Kramer, eds., *The Psychology of Leadership: New Perspectives and Research* (Mahwah, NJ: Lawrence Erlbaum, 2005); Steven M. Teles, *The Rise of the Conservative Legal Movement* (Princeton, NJ: Princeton University Press, 2008).

4. For a general review (without specific application to South Africa) see Seymour Martin Lipset, "The Social Requisites of Democracy Revisited: 1993 Presidential Address," *American Sociological Review* 59, no. 1 (February 1994): 1–22.

5. Ibid., p. 17.

6. See, for example, Richard Wolin, *The Wind from the East: French Intellectuals, the Cultural Revolution, and the Legacy of the 1960s* (Princeton, NJ: Princeton University Press, 2010), pp. 118–22; 193–94.

7. In December 2010, I searched the catalog of the University of Washington for course titles including the words "strategy" or "strategies." I chose this sample because Washington is a large, multipurpose, public university, and its catalog's search function is particularly well designed. The search yielded 50 total courses. Approximately 26 courses were about strategies for teaching or learning. Eighteen courses were in business. There was one course in history (on the evolution of strategy) and one in political science about "alternative methods of social choice." (It was decision-making from the point of view of the sovereign, not the citizen.) A course in public health was about community organizing and other strategies for social change that might include citizens.

8. John Rawls, *A Theory of Justice*, rev. ed. (1971; repr., Cambridge, MA: Harvard University Press, 1999), p. 3.

9. Plato, *Seventh Letter* (the authenticity of which has been questioned).

10. Amartya Sen, *The Idea of Justice* (Cambridge, MA: Harvard University Press, 2009), p. 409.

CHAPTER 3: VALUES: COLLABORATION, DELIBERATION, AND CIVIC RELATIONSHIPS

1. Harold D. Laswell, *Politics: Who Gets What, When, How*, 1st ed. (New York, London: Whittlesey House, McGraw-Hill, 1936); influential 2nd ed., 1958.

2. Cathy Davidson, "Why Technology Innovation Needs Critical Thinking," March 7, 2011, HASTAC, http://www.hastac.org/blogs/cathy-davidson/why-technology-innovation-needs-critical-thinking.

3. Amy Gutmann and Dennis Thompson, *Democracy and Disagreement* (Cambridge, MA: Harvard University Press, 1996), pp. 69–73.

4. A sophisticated defense of self-interest in deliberation is Jane Mansbridge et al., "The Place of Self-Interest and the Role of Power in Deliberative Democracy," *Journal of Political Philosophy* 18, no. 1 (2010): 64–100.

5. Michael J. Sandel, *Liberalism and the Limits of Justice*, 2nd. ed. (Cambridge: Cambridge University Press, 1998), p. 183.

6. Alexander Hamilton, "The Federalist No. 1," in Hamilton, James Madison, and John Jay, *The Federalist Papers* (New York: Bantam Books, 1982), p. 2.

7. See Levine, *The New Progressive Era: Toward a Fair and Deliberative Democracy* (Lanham, MD: Rowman & Littlefield, 2000).

8. Hamilton, "The Federalist No. 1," p. 2.

9. Vijayendra Rao and Paromita Sanyal, "Dignity Through Discourse: Poverty and the Culture of Deliberation in Indian Village Democracies," World Bank Policy Research Working Paper Series, 4924 (May 2009), http://ssrn.com/abstract=1401229, p. 2.

10. Peter Levine and Rose Marie Nierras, "Activists' Views of Deliberation," *Journal of Public Deliberation* 3, no. 1 (2007), art. 4, http://services.bepress.com/jpd/vol3/iss1/art4.

11. Lynn M. Sanders, "Against Deliberation," *Political Theory* 25, no. 3 (June 1997): 347–76.

12. Cited in ibid., p. 361.

13. See Diana C. Mutz, *Hearing the Other Side: Deliberative Versus Participatory Democracy* (Cambridge: Cambridge University Press, 2006).

14. Doug McAdam, John D. McCarthy, and Mayer N. Zald, "Introduction: Opportunities, Mobilizing Structures, and Framing Processes—Toward a Synthetic, Comparative Perspective on Social Movements," in McAdam, McCarthy, and Zald, eds., *Comparative Perspectives on Social Movements: Political Opportunities, Mobilizing Structures, and Cultural Framings* (Cambridge: Cambridge University Press, 1996), p. 9.

15. Iris Marion Young, "Activist Challenges to Deliberative Democracy," in James S. Fishkin and Peter Laslett, eds., *Debating Deliberative Democracy* (Malden, MA: Blackwell, 2003).

16. For evidence that people do learn when they deliberate, see, e.g., Fishkin, *The Voice of the People* (New Haven, CT: Yale University Press, 1997), pp. 161–68.

17. Cf. Harry C. Boyte, "Constructive Politics as Public Work: Organizing the Literature," *Political Theory* 39, no. 5 (2011): 630–60.

18. National Conference on Citizenship, *America's Civic Health Index 2007*, www.ncoc.net.

19. Carolyn J. Lukensmeyer, *Bringing Citizen Voices to the Table: A Guide for Public Managers* (San Francisco: Jossey-Bass, 2012), pp. 117–24.

20. In 2012, Fenty's successor, Mayor Vincent C. Gray, revived the summits. That demonstrates their enduring popularity and political value to incumbent politicians, but they remain dependent on politicians' judgment.

21. James Fishkin, "Town Halls by Invitation," *New York Times*, August 15, 2009.

22. John Gaventa distinguishes among political processes that are closed, invited, and claimed. When powerful people simply make decisions, the process is "closed." When leaders randomly or purposively select representatives of the community to advise them or to share in decision-making, the process is "invited." That is a step forward, but more democratic are "spaces claimed by less powerful actors from or against the power holders, or created more autonomously by them." John Gaventa, "Exploring Power for Change" (presentation, November 2007), via /www.power-cube.net.

23. In this paragraph, I draw heavily on Anthony Simon Laden, *Reasoning: A Social Picture* (New York: Oxford University Press, 2012).

24. Marshall Ganz and Ruth Wageman, *Sierra Club Leadership Development Project: Pilot Project Report and Recommendations* (2008), p. 24.

25. Nina S. Eliasoph, *Avoiding Politics: How Americans Produce Apathy in Everyday Life* (Cambridge: Cambridge University Press, 1998); and Mutz, *Hearing the Other Side*. I am using a framework here that derives (with important modifications) from Jürgen Habermas's threefold distinction: lifeworld, system, and public sphere. The "lifeworld," reflected in ordinary conversation among friends and family, is natural and authentic but does not necessarily connect to broad public issues. The "system" refers to strategic communications by organizations that have fixed interests and goals, especially corporations and government agencies. The "public sphere" is the metaphorical space in which citizens emerge from their diverse lifeworlds to discuss public issues, creating reasoned public opinion that is a counterforce to the system. I hold that this theory is too cognitive: the public sphere should not be understood primarily as a place for talking and forming public opinion, because most people lack motivation for mere talk, and talk alone is not adequately informed by experience. The public sphere should rather be a place of talk and work. Cf. a somewhat similar critique in Albert W. Dzur, *Democratic Professionalism: Citizen Participation and the Reconstruction of Professional Ethics, Identity, and Practice* (University Park: Pennsylvania State University Press, 2008), pp. 35–36.

26. Laden, p. 30.

27. I draw here on Xavier de Souza Briggs, *Democracy as Problem Solving: Civic Capacity in Communities across the Globe* (Cambridge, MA: MIT Press, 2008).

28. Hannah Arendt, *On Revolution* (London: Penguin Books, 1990), p. 119.

29. Cf. Thomas Dietz et al., "The Drama of the Commons," in Elinor Ostrom et al., eds., *Drama of the Commons*, National Research Council, Division of Behavioral and Social Sciences and Education (Washington, DC: National Academies Press, 2002), p. 18.

30. Elinor Ostrom, "Beyond Markets and States: Polycentric Governance of Complex Economic Systems," Nobel Prize Lecture (2009), http://nobelprize.org/nobel_prizes/economics/laureates/2009/ostrom-lecture.html.

31. David Lazer et al., *Online Town Meetings: Exploring Democracy in the 21st Century* (Washington, DC: Congressional Management Foundation, 2009); and see also Michael Neblo et al., "Who Wants to Deliberate—and Why?" (HKS faculty research working paper series RWP09-027, September 2009).

32. See John Gastil and Peter Levine, eds., *The Deliberative Democracy Handbook: Strategies for Effective Civic Engagement in the Twenty-First Century* (San Francisco: Jossey-Bass, 2005), for many other cases.

33. Reed W. Larson, "Toward a Psychology of Positive Youth Development," *American Psychologist* 55, no. 1 (January 2000): 17–83.

34. Richard F. Catalano et al., "Positive Youth Development in the United States: Research Findings on Evaluations of Positive Youth Development Programs," *Annals of the American Academy of Political and Social Science* 591 (January 2004): 98–124 (see p. 115 for the fact that 88% of the validated cases, or 22 programs, included "opportunities for prosocial involvement").

35. Eva L. Baker et al., *Problems with the Use of Student Test Scores to Evaluate Teachers* (Washington, DC: Economic Policy Institute, 2010), http://www.epi.org/publication/bp278/.

36. E.g., Melvin J. Dubnick and H. George Frederickson, *Public Accountability: Performance Measurement, The Extended State, and the Search for Trust* (Washington, DC: National Academy of Public Administration, and Dayton, OH: Kettering Foundation, 2011); and Christopher Pollitt, "Performance Blight and the Tyranny of Light: Accountability in Advanced Performance Measurement Regimes," in Melvin J. Dubnick and H. George Frederickson, eds., *Accountable Governance: Problems and Promises* (Armonk, NY: M.E. Sharpe, 2011), pp. 81–97.

37. Robert D. Behn advocates "360-degree performance feedback" (evaluation of everyone, by everyone) for similar reasons in his *Rethinking Democratic Accountability* (Washington, DC: Brookings Institution Press, 2001). For an example in practice, see Carmen Sirianni, "Neighborhood Planning as Collaborative Democratic Design: The Case of Seattle," *Journal of the American Planning Association* 73, no. 4 (2007): 373–87.

38. Marcia W. Baron, Philip Pettit, and Michael Slote, *Three Methods of Ethics: A Debate* (Oxford: Blackwell, 1997).

39. US Dept. of Justice, Office of Legal Counsel, *Memorandum for John A. Rizzo Senior Deputy General Counsel, CIA* (Washington, DC: Office of the Principal Deputy Assistant Attorney General, May 10, 2005), p. 15, http://www.fas.org/irp/agency/doj/olc/techniques.pdf.

40. The research on how people actually talk when they deliberate is relatively sparse, but I draw on Laura W. Black, "How People Communicate During Deliberative Events," in Tina Nabatchi, John Gastil, G. Michael Weiksner, and Matt Leighninger, eds., *Democracy in Motion: Evaluating the Practice and Impact of Deliberative Civic Engagement* (New York; Oxford Univesrity Press), pp. 59–81; Brian E. Adams, "Conversational Dynamics in Deliberative Forums: The Use of Evidence

and Logic," American Political Science Association Annual Meeting Paper, 2012, via http://papers.ssrn.com; and especially David M. Ryfe, "Narrative and Deliberation in Small Group Forums," *Journal of Applied Communication Research* 34, no. 1 (February 2006): 72–93.

41. Readers with some background in modern Anglophone moral philosophy may recognize John Rawls's concept of reflective equilibrium here. But I am expanding that idea dramatically. Rawls (*Theory of Justice*, p. 18) envisions a binary dialog between fundamental principles and concrete situations. I think there can be a reflective equilibrium between any two concrete or abstract moral ideas in a person's brain.

42. I address this issue in more technical detail in Peter Levine, *Reforming the Humanities: Literature and Ethics from Dante Through Modern Times* (New York: Palgrave Macmillan, 2009), pp. 73–83.

43. Albert-Laszlo Barabasi, *Linked: How Everything Is Connected to Everything Else and What It Means* (New York: Plume, 2003).

44. Laden, p. 20.

45. Danielle S. Allen, *Talking to Strangers: Anxieties of Citizenship since Brown v. Board of Education* (Chicago: University of Chicago Press, 2004), pp. xxi–xxii.

46. Jefferson, "Letter to Samuel Kercheval," June 12, 1816, http://teachingamericanhistory.org/library/index.asp?document=459.

47. Jean Johnson, Jonathan Rochkind, and Samantha DuPont, *Don't Count Us Out: How an Overreliance on Accountability Could Undermine the Public's Confidence in Schools, Business, Government, and More* (Public Agenda and the Kettering Foundation 2011), http://www.publicagenda.org/pages/dont-count-us-out.

48. Robert D. Putnam, *Bowling Alone: The Collapse and Revival of American Community* (New York: Simon & Shuster, 2000), p. 19.

49. James S. Coleman, "Social Capital in the Creation of Human Capital," *American Journal of Sociology* 94 supp. (1988): S. 98, S. 113.

50. Mark R. Warren, Karen L. Mapp, and the Community Engagement and School Reform Project, *A Match on Dry Grass: Community Organizing as a Catalyst for School Reform* (New York: Oxford University Press, 2011), pp. 26–30.

51. Celina Su, *Streetwise for Book Smarts: Grassroots Organizing and Education Reform in the Bronx* (Ithaca, NY: Cornell University Press, 2009), p. 16.

52. Carmen Sirianni and Lewis Friedland, *Civic Innovation in America: Community Empowerment, Public Policy, and the Movement for Civic Renewal* (Berkeley: University of California Press, 2001), p. 51.

53. Mark R. Warren, *Dry Bones Rattling: Community Building to Revitalize American Democracy* (Princeton, NJ: Princeton University Press, 2001), p. 68; Warren, "Power and Conflict in Social Capital: Community Organizing and Urban Policy," in Bob Edwards, Michael W. Foley, and Mario Diani, eds., *Beyond Tocqueville: Civic Society and the Social Capital Debate in Comparative Perspective* (Hanover, NH: Tufts University Press, 2001), pp. 177–78.

54. Warren and Mapp, *A Match on Dry Grass*, p. 139.

55. Kristin Layng Szakos and Joe Szakos, eds., *We Make Change: Community Organizers Talk About What They Do—And Why* (Nashville, TN: Vanderbilt University Press, 2007), pp. xvii (from the introduction by Harry C. Boyte), 97, 107.

56. Su, *Streetwise for Book Smarts*, p. 85.

57. Bo Kinney, "Deliberation's Contribution to Community Capacity Building," in Nabatchi et al., *Democracy in Motion*, pp. 163–80.

58. Harold H. Saunders, *Politics Is about Relationships: A Blueprint for the Citizens' Century* (New York: Palgrave, 2005), p. 150.

59. Allen, *Talking to Strangers*, pp. 157–58.

60. Albert O. Hirschman, *Exit, Voice, and Loyalty: Responses to Decline in Firms, Organizations, and States* (Cambridge, MA: Harvard University Press, 1970).

61. Bill Bishop with Robert G. Cushing, *The Big Sort: Why the Clustering of Like-Minded America Is Tearing Us Apart* (Boston: Houghton Mifflin, 2008).

62. Theda Skocpol, *Diminished Democracy: From Membership to Management in American Civic Life* (Norman: University of Oklahoma Press, 2003).

63. Hannah Arendt, *The Human Condition* (Chicago: University of Chicago Press, 1958), p. 9.

64. Ibid., p. 247.

65. Important stage theories have been presented by Sigmund Freud, Jean Piaget, Erik Erikson, Lawrence Kohlberg, and others. These theories offer important insights, but I am persuaded by a general critique. The idea of stages makes the developmental process seem internally regulated and automatic except under exceptional circumstances. That is plausible for language acquisition but not for civic or moral identity after early childhood. Development is a complex and variable interaction between the organism, its own norms, prevailing external norms, and other aspects of the environment.

66. Harry G. Frankfurt, "Freedom of the Will and the Concept of a Person," *Journal of Philosophy* 68, no. 1 (January 14, 1971): 5–20.

67. Ibid., p. 17.

68. *Port Huron Statement of the Students for a Democratic Society*, 1962, courtesy of the Office of California State Senator Tom Hayden, http://www.h-net.org/~hst306/documents/huron.html.

69. Jon Elster, "The Market and the Forum: Three Varieties of Political Theory," in Jon Elster and Aanund Hyland, eds., *Foundations of Social Choice Theory* (New York: Cambridge University Press, 1986).

CHAPTER 4: VALUES: THE LIMITS OF EXPERTISE,
IDEOLOGY, AND MARKETS

1. Donna E. Shalala, "Mandate for a New Century: Reshaping the Research University's Role in Social Policy" (Eleventh David Henry Dodds Lecture, University of Illinois at Urbana-Champaign, October 31, 1989), quoting pp. 6, 9, 12.

2. For a strong statement, see Bent Flyvbjerg, "Social Science That Matters," *Foresight Europe* 2 (October 2005– March 2006): 38–42. "No predictive theories have been arrived at in social science, despite centuries of trying. This is a wasteful dead end."

3. George Bernard Shaw, *The Doctor's Dilemma: A Tragedy* (London: Penguin Books, 1913), pp. 15–16.

4. Albert W. Dzur, *Democratic Professionalism: Citizen Participation and the Reconstruction of Professional Ethics, Identity, and Practice* (University Park: Pennsylvania State University Press, 2008), p. 45.

5. Ibid., pp. 49, 59. Dzur discusses the "particularism" of professions, but he uses the word to capture the narrow focus of professionals on certain problems and goals across all cases. By particularism, I mean a focus on the whole, particular case. In fact, "particularism" and "holism" are sometimes equated in moral philosophy.

6. See Levine, *Reforming the Humanities*, and Peter Levine, *Living Without Philosophy: On Narrative, Rhetoric, and Morality* (Albany: SUNY Press, 1998).

7. J. Cohen, in *Statistical Power for the Behavioral Sciences* (Hillsdale, NJ: Erlbaum, 1988), suggested as a rule of thumb that a standardized mean difference of .8 or a correlation coefficient of .5 would be a "strong" effect in the social sciences. In fields like education and welfare, findings of such strength are very rare. Even when they are found, they almost never settle practical questions. For example, there is a relationship between class size and test scores in the early grades. (Smaller classes are better.) See Frederick Mosteller, "The Tennessee Study of Class Size in the Early School Grades," *Future of Children* 5, no. 2 (Summer–Autumn, 1995): 113–27 for a summary with a cogent explanation of the effect of class sizes. But this finding does not prove that one should use scarce resources to employ more teachers, especially if average levels of skill, preparation, and enthusiasm would fall. The best judgment incorporates this finding but does not exaggerate its importance.

8. Dzur, *Democratic Professionalism*, p. 99, emphasis added.

9. On medical ethics, see ibid., pp. 207–43. Community-based participatory research is well introduced by Meredith Minkler and Nina Wallerstein, "Introduction to Community Based Participatory Research," in Minkler and Wallerstein, eds, *Community Based Participatory Research for Health* (San Francisco: Jossey-Bass, 2002), pp. 3–26. For a flavor of civic professionalism in public management, see Tina Nabatchi, *A Manager's Guide to Evaluating Citizen Participation* (Washington, DC: IBM Center for the Business of Government, 2012).

10. Greg Berman and John Feinblatt, *Good Courts: The Case for Problem-Solving Justice* (New York: New Press, 2005), p. 27.

11. Harry C. Boyte, *Everyday Politics: Reconnecting Citizens and Public Life* (Philadelphia: University of Pennsylvania Press, 2005), p. 119.

12. US Senate Judiciary Committee, *Hearings on the Nomination of John Roberts to Be Chief Justice of the United States*, 109th Congress, 1st Session, September 12, 2005.

13. Alan I. Abramowitz, *The Disappearing Center: Engaged Citizens, Polarization, and American Democracy* (New Haven, CT: Yale, 2010) shows that this correlation is

strong and has increased since the 1950s. Its variation over time suggests that it is not an iron law but a tendency, subject to influence by other factors such as the behavior of parties and the media.

14. Levine, *New Progressive Era: Toward a Fair and Deliberative Democracy* (Lanham, MD: Rowman & Littlefield, 2000), p. 19. See also Michael Schudson, *The Good Citizen: A History of American Civic Life* (Cambridge, MA: Harvard University Press, 1999), p. 192; Matthew A. Crenson and Benjamin Ginsberg, *Downsizing Democracy: How America Sidelined Its Citizens and Privatized Its Public* (Baltimore, MD: Johns Hopkins University Press, 2002), pp. 56–57.

15. Sara Margaret Evans and Harry C. Boyte, *Free Spaces: The Sources of Democratic Change in America* (Chicago: University of Chicago Press, 1992).

16. Vaclav Havel, address (Wroclaw University, Poland, December 21, 1992), http://old.hrad.cz/president/Havel/speeches/1992/2112_uk.html.

17. Ibid.

18. Libertarian Party platform, section 2.0, http://www.lp.org/platform.

19. John Dewey, *The Public and Its Problems* (New York: Henry Holt, 1927), pp. 74, 202.

20. Johnson's 1964 State of the Union message is anthologized in Marvin E. Gettleman and David Marmelstein, eds., *The Great Society Reader: The Failure of American Liberalism* (New York: Vintage Books, 1967), p. 184. For context, see Levine, *The New Progressive Era*, pp. 48–53.

21. Rawls, *Theory of Justice*, sections 12, 46, 77.

22. Unger, *Democracy Realized: The Progressive Alternative* (London and New York: Verso, 1998), p. 187.

23. Cf. Vijayendra Rao, "Symbolic Public Goods and the Coordination of Collective Action: A Comparison of Local Development in India and Indonesia" (World Bank policy research working paper 3685, August 2005), p. 17: "Old style development is technocratic: predicated on an excessive reliance on a 'model'—either based on a 'best-practice' framework (a project design that worked wonders in one place would have the same impact in another), or on methodologically individualist rational-choice modeling that is totally ignorant of symbolic, social and cultural logic. . . . Dealing with these challenges, which have always been present but rarely confronted, requires a way of doing development that is more decentralized, more difficult, more honest, and—arguably—more sustainable."

24. See Robert J. Sampson, *Great American City: Chicago and the Enduring Neighborhood Effect* (Chicago: University of Chicago Press, 2012), for a sustained argument against viewing communities like interventions that can be assigned to individuals.

25. For a careful summary of the diverse views of charter supporters, see Jeffrey Henig, *Spin Cycle—How Research Is Used in Policy Debates: The Case of Charter Schools* (New York: Russell Sage, 2008).

26. See, for example, the concluding paragraphs of Robert Nozick, *Anarchy, State, and Utopia* (New York: Basic Books, 1974), pp. 333–34.

27. Brandeis definitely held that the concentrated power of management in an industrial conglomerate was incompatible with democracy. See Brandeis' testimony on "Industrial Relations," anthologized in Osmond K. Fraenkel, ed., *The Curse of Bigness: Miscellaneous Papers of Louis D. Brandeis* (Port Washington, NY: Kennikat Press, 1965), p. 78; and for context, Michael J. Sandel, *Democracy's Discontent: America in Search of a Public Philosophy* (Cambridge, MA: Harvard University Press, 1996), pp. 211–16.

28. Edward N. Wolff, "Recent Trends in Household Wealth in the United States: Rising Debt and the Middle-Class Squeeze—an Update to 2007" (Levy Economics Institute of Bard College working paper, March 2010), www.levyinstitute.org.

29. David A. Shultz, "The Phenomenology of Democracy: Putnam, Pluralism, and Voluntary Associations," in Scott L. McLean, David Andrew Schultz, and Manfred B. Steger, eds., *Social Capital: Critical Perspectives on Community and "Bowling Alone"* (New York: New York University Press, 2002), p. 92.

30. General Social Survey, 1978–2008, analyzed by the author using the Survey Documentation and Analysis tool from the University of California, Berkeley, http://sda.berkeley.edu. In 2008, when asked whether "people who make more money should pay a larger percent of their income in taxes to the government than people who make less money," 60 percent of respondents agreed, but fully 40 percent did not. In the same poll (conducted in the depths of the recession), 45 percent said "the government should provide more services than it does now," but a clear majority favored either fewer services or maintaining the current level. American National Election Study 2008, analyzed by the author.

31. Poverty rate (1999–2000) from Ira N. Gang, Myeong-Su Yun, and Kunal Sen, "Caste, Ethnicity and Poverty in Rural India," Departmental Working Papers 200225, Rutgers University, Department of Economics, 2002, p. 3. Turnout: Pushpendra, "Dalit Assertion Through Electoral Politics," *Economic and Political Weekly* 34, no. 36 (September 4–10, 1999): 2611.

32. US Census Bureau, *Current Population Survey*, November 2008 and earlier reports, http://www.census.gov/hhes/www/socdemo/voting/publications/historical/index.html.

33. Peter Levine, "Social Accountability as Public Work," in Sina Odugbemi and Taeku Lee, eds., *Accountability through Public Opinion: From Inertia to Public Action* (Washington, DC: The World Bank, 2011), p. 295.

34. John Gaventa and Gregory Barrett, *So What Difference Does It Make? Mapping the Outcomes of Citizen Engagement* (IDS), Working Paper 347 (Institute of Development Studies: Brighton, England, 2010).

35. John Foster-Bey, "Do Race, Ethnicity, Citizenship and Socio-economic Status Determine Civic-Engagement?" (CIRCLE working paper 62, 2008), www.civicyouth.org.

36. Sampson, p. 168.

37. Gaventa, interview with the author April 14, 2011, as quoted in "Professor John Gaventa receives Tisch Civic Engagement Research Prize," May 2011, Tufts University,

http://activecitizen.tufts.edu/?pid=1154 and approved by Gaventa. The classic book is *Power and Powerlessness: Quiescence and Rebellion in an Appalachian Valley* (Urbana: University of Illinois Press, 1982).

38. Vaclav Havel at Wroclaw University, Wroclaw, Poland, December 21, 1992 http:// old.hrad.cz/president/Havel/speeches/1992/2112_uk.html.

CHAPTER 5: FACTS: THE STATE OF AMERICAN DEMOCRACY

1. Theda Skocpol, *Diminished Democracy: From Membership to Management in American Civic Life* (Norman: University of Oklahoma Press, 2003).

2. As in chapter 3, I employ Habermas's basic conceptual and normative scheme. See Habermas, "The Public Sphere: An Encyclopedia Article," *New German Critique* 3 (1974): 49–55 for a short introduction.

3. "And if it has been correctly advanced that associations will increase in number as the conditions of men become more equal, it is not less certain that the number of newspapers increases in proportion to that of associations. Thus it is in America that we find at the same time the greatest number of associations and of newspapers." Tocqueville, *Democracy in America*, trans. Henry Reeve and Phillips Bradley (New York: Vintage Books, 1954), vol. 2, book 2, ch. vi, p. 120.

4. Timothy Hurley, Loc Cheng, and Michael McGrath, "The 2007 All-America City Awards," *National Civic Review*, Winter 2007, pp. 25–26.

5. "The Harward Center: What We Stand For," http://www.bates.edu/x171616.xml.

6. The GSS has been conducted regularly since 1972; data are available from NORC, formerly the National Opinion Research Center, at the University of Chicago. Selected DDB data can be downloaded from the Bowling Alone website at bowlingalone.com.

7. General Social Survey for member of groups and DDB Needham Life Style Survey for attend meetings.

8. Burton Bledstein, *The Culture of Professionalism* (New York: W. W. Norton & Co., 1976), pp. 84–86.

9. Robert L. Buroker, "From Voluntary Association to Welfare State: The Illinois Immigrants' Protective League, 1908–1926," *Journal of American History* 58, no. 3 (December 1971): 652.

10. APSA Committee of Seven, 1914, p. 263, quoted in Stephen T. Leonard, "'Pure Futility and Waste': Academic Political Science and Civic Education," *PSOnline* (December 1999).

11. Steven Brint, *In an Age of Experts: The Changing Role of Professionals in Politics and Public Life* (Princeton, NJ: Princeton University Press, 1994), p. 3.

12. American National Election Studies data, analyzed by the author using the Survey Documentation and Analysis tool from the University of California, Berkeley, http://sda.berkeley.edu/.

13. Thomas Webler and Seth Tuler, "Fairness and Competence in Citizen Participation: Theoretical Reflections from a Case Study," *Administration & Society* 32 (2000): 584.

14. Skocpol, *Diminished Democracy*, pp. 186–87.

15. Nansook Park and Christopher Peterson, "Does It Matter Where We Live?: The Urban Psychology of Character Strengths," *American Psychologist* 65, no. 6 (September 2010): 535–47.

16. Bill Bishop with Robert G. Cushing, *The Big Sort: Why the Clustering of Like-Minded America Is Tearing Us Apart* (Boston: Houghton Mifflin, 2008), pp. 9–11.

17. Ibid., p. 14.

18. Corporation for National and Community Service, Volunteering and Civic Life in America website, http://www.volunteeringinamerica.gov/, pages on Miami and Minneapolis/St. Paul.

19. Bill Bishop with Robert G. Cushing, *The Big Sort*, p. 3.

20. James G. Gimpel, J. Celeste Lay, and Jason E. Schuknecht, *Cultivating Democracy: Civic Environments and Political Socialization in America* (Washington, DC: Brookings Institution Press, 2003) find that politically diverse jurisdictions produce young adults more interested in politics.

21. American National Election Study 2008, analyzed by the author using the Survey Documentation and Analysis tool from the University of California, Berkeley, http://sda.berkeley.edu. The United States scores 7.5 on Transparency International's index of perceived corruption, better than most countries in the world but worse than the Nordic and Antipodean democracies, Canada, and Germany.

22. Alexander Hamilton, "The Federalist No. 27," in Hamilton, James Madison, and John Jay, *The Federalist Papers* (New York: Bantam Books, 1982), p. 131.

23. In the same two-year period, the US Supreme Court found a right to free legal counsel (*Gideon v. Wainwright*), redefined freedom of the press and libel law (*New York Times v. Sullivan*), required state electoral districts to be of roughly equal size (*Reynolds v. Sims*), and resolved more than 2,000 other cases. In a contemporary law review summary, Paul C. Bartholomew wrote, "With a consistency that seems to know no bounds, the Supreme Court during the recent term continued the history-making course it has been following for some time." Bartholomew, "The Supreme Court of the United States, 1963–64," *Western Political Quarterly* 17, no. 4 (December 1964): 595.

24. J. Tobin Grant and Nathan J. Kelly, "Legislative Productivity of the U.S. Congress, 1789–2004," *Political Analysis* 16, no. 3 (2008): 303–23. According to their Major Legislation index, the period 1989–90 rivaled the Johnson years for landmark acts of Congress. But I think that illustrates the limitations of a quantitative measure of "important" legislation, since the Americans with Disabilities Act, the Immigration Act of 1990, and other reforms of 1989–90 clearly pale in significance compared to the enactments of 1963–64.

25. Sarah A. Binder, *Stalemate: Causes and Consequences of Legislative Gridlock* (Washington, DC: Brookings Institution Press, 2003), pp. 50–52.

26. Theodore Lowi, *The End of Liberalism: The Second Republic of the United States*, 2nd ed. (New York: W. W. Norton, 1979), p. 55.

27. Data from the Office of the Federal Register, "Annual Federal Register Pages Published," compiled by the Law Librarians' Society of Washington, DC, http://www. llsdc.org/sourcebook/docs/fed-reg-pages.pdf. The Society notes, "Proposed rules were not required before 1947. Explanatory material did not begin until the mid-1960's and extensive preambles were not required before 1973." Those changes would cause the number of rules to swell, and yet the upward trend appears smooth, not discontinuous at 1947 or 1973.

28. Lowi, *End of Liberalism*, p. 86.

29. Peter Levine, "Lessons from the Brooklyn Museum Controversy," *Report from the Institute for Philosophy and Public Policy* 20, nos. 2–3 (Summer 2000): 19–27.

30. Clean Air Act Amendments of 1970, 42 USC § 7409 (1970).

31. Compare a similar critique in Michael J. Sandel, *Democracy's Discontent: America in Search of a Public Philosophy* (Cambridge, MA: Harvard University Press, 1996), especially ch. 9 ("The Triumph and Travail of the Procedural Republic"), pp. 275–315.

32. Skocpol, *Diminished Democracy*, pp. 204–5.

33. Matthew A. Crenson and Benjamin Ginsberg, *Downsizing Democracy: How America Sidelined Its Citizens and Privatized Its Public* (Baltimore, MD: The Johns Hopkins University Press, 2002), pp. 16, 144. See also Skocpol, *Diminished Democracy*, pp. 7, 174, 200–211.

34. Robert B. Reich, "Policy Making in a Democracy," in Reich, ed., *The Power of Public Ideas* (Cambridge, MA: Harvard University Press), pp. 123–37.

35. Lowi, *End of Liberalism*, p. 63.

36. For example, Frank Sorauf wrote in a book-length study that campaign money "is not a simple case of paying the piper and calling the tune. American campaigns are funded by a series of varied and complex exchanges in which different actors seek different goals in different modes of rationality. One cannot easily identify aggressors or exploiters in such a marketplace, for the relationships between contributors and candidates are bilateral and unstable, dependent always on very specific but shifting calculations of cost and benefit." Note the easy equation of democracy with a "marketplace" in this passage. So long as no player in the market dominates, the system is legitimate. This is exactly the standard that Lowi ascribed to interest-group liberalism. Frank Sorauf, *Inside Campaign Finance: Myths and Realities* (New Haven, CT: Yale University Press, 1992), p. 96. Cf.

37. *New Realities, New Thinking: Report of the Task Force on Campaign Finance Reform* (Citizens' Research Foundation, University of Southern California, 1996).

38. American National Election Study data, analyzed by the author.

39. Ward Just, *Jack Gance*, first published in 1980 (Boston and New York: Houghton Mifflin, 1997), pp. 141–42. References are to the 1997 edition.

40. See Michael C. Dorf and Charles F. Sabel, "A Constitution of Democratic Experimentalism," *Columbia Law Review* 98, no. 2 (March 1998): 267–473.

41. Arnold F. Fege, "Getting Ruby a Quality Public Education: Forty-Two Years of Building the Demand for Quality Public Schools through Parental and Public Involvement," *Harvard Educational Review* 76 no. 4 (Winter 2006): 576.

42. Ronald Reagan, First Inaugural Address, en.wikiquote.org/wiki/Ronald_Reagan.

43. Andrew S. McFarland, "Why Creative Participation Today?" in Michele Micheletti and Andrew S. McFarland, eds., *Creative Participation: Responsibility-Taking in the Political World* (Boulder, CO: Paradigm, 2011), p. 28.

44. Steven Brill, "Government for Sale: How Lobbyists Shaped the Financial Reform Bill," *Time*, July 1, 2010, http://www.time.com/time/politics/article/0,8599,2000880,00.html#ixzz0sXxPUAa3.

45. Binyamin Appelbaum, "On Finance Bill, Lobbying Shifts to Regulations," *New York Times*, June 26, 2010, p. A1.

46. Alexander Hamilton, "The Federalist No. 62," in Hamilton, Madison, and Jay, *The Federalist Papers*, p. 317.

47. *Citizens United v. Federal Election Commission*, 558 U.S. 50 (2010), 40, 55.

48. Michael Luo, "Money Talks Louder than Ever in Midterms," *New York Times*, October 7, 2010.

49. James Madison, "The Federalist No. 10," in Hamilton, Madison, and Jay, *The Federalist Papers*, p. 43.

50. César E. Chávez, "The Plan of Delano," archived by the California Department of Education, chavez.cde.ca.gov/ModelCurriculum/Public/Justice.aspx, p. 67.

51. See Jane Mansbridge et al., "The Place of Self-Interest and the Role of Power in Deliberative Democracy," *Journal of Political Philosophy* 18, no. 1 (2010): 73.

52. "Relationship Between MDs, ODs Changing as Integrated Eye Care Gains in Popularity," *Ocular Surgery News*, US ed., January 10, 2009, http://www.healio.com/.

53. M. Soroka and B. J. Barresi, "Predicted and Observed Effects of the Medicare Optometry Parity Amendment," *Journal of the American Optometric Association* 62, no. 7 (1991): 525–28.

54. "Relationship Between MDs, ODs Changing as Integrated Eye Care Gains in Popularity."

55. Milton Friedman, *Capitalism and Freedom* (Chicago: University of Chicago Press, 1962), pp. 137–60, quotation at p. 159.

56. An insightful critique of this option can be found in Mark Sagoff, "The View from Quincy Library or Civic Engagement in Environmental Problem Solving," in Sagoff, *Price, Principle and the Environment* (Cambridge: Cambridge University Press, 2004), pp. 201–32.

57. PBS, "John Gardner: Uncommon American," http://www.pbs.org/johngardner/sections/writings.html.

58. "Real Estate," http://www.opensecrets.org/industries/indus.php?ind=F10.

59. E. E. Schattschneider, *The Semi-Sovereign People* (New York: Holt, Rinehart and Winston, 1960), p. 35.

60. Chávez, "The Plan of Delano," p. 65.

CHAPTER 6: FACTS: A CIVIC RENEWAL MOVEMENT EMERGES

1. See John Gastil and Peter Levine, eds., *The Deliberative Democracy Handbook: Strategies for Effective Civic Engagement in the Twenty-First Century* (San Francisco: Jossey-Bass, 2005) for diverse responses to that question.

2. The Center for Deliberative Polling at Stanford University and the Jefferson Center are two organizations strongly committed to random selection. The National Issues Forum Institute and Everyday Democracy are two that see themselves more as deliberative community organizers: diversity and not statistical representativeness is the goal. America*Speaks* aims for representativeness but does not rely on random selection as its main tool.

3. Keystone Center, *Public Engagement Project on the H1N1 Pandemic Influenza Vaccination Program* (Keystone, CO: Keystone Center, 2009).

4. Carmen Sirianni and Diana Marginean Schor, "City Government as an Enabler of Youth Civic Engagement: Policy Design and Implications," in James Youniss and Peter Levine, eds., *Engaging Young People in Civic Life* (Nashville, TN: Vanderbilt University Press, 1999), pp. 125, 126.

5. Andrea Batista Schlesinger, "The Power of 'Why?': Students in Hampton, Virginia, and Brooklyn, New York, Learn That Asking Questions Is More Powerful than Memorizing Answers," *YES!*, September 9, 2009, www.yesmagazine.org.

6. William R. Potapchuk, Cindy Carlson, and Joan Kennedy, "Growing Governance Deliberatively: Lessons and Inspiration from Hampton, Virginia," in Gastil and Levine, *The Deliberative Democracy Handbook*, p. 261.

7. Ibid., p. 264.

8. Tamara Whitaker, quoted in Sirianni and Schor, "City Government as an Enabler of Youth Civic Engagement," p. 132. See Sirianni and Schor, pp. 131–32 and Schlesinger, "The Power of 'Why?' for the vocational school example.

9. Carmen Sirianni, "Youth Civic Engagement: Systems Change and Culture Change in Hampton, Virginia" (CIRCLE working paper 31, April 2005), www. civicyouth.org.

10. Hampton lags behind the Virginia average in passing rates for the state math and English tests by 6 to 8 percentage points (Virginia Department of Education, Hampton Public Schools report card, 2011, https://p1pe.doe.virginia.gov/reportcard/), but 23% of its public school students come from families in poverty, versus 14% for Virginia as a whole (U.S. Census Bureau, Small Area Income and Poverty Estimates, https://www.census.gov/did/www/saipe/data/interactive/#view=SchoolDistricts) and the city spends a relatively modest $10,637 per student (U.S. Census Bureau, Public School Finance Data, http://www.census.gov/govs/school/). I acknowledge a critical assessment of the Hampton strategy that I received from a Hampton citizen, Joan Charles, who argues that "open debate" is actually discouraged there. A Brandeis University PhD student, Diana Schor, is investigating the city's civic engagement record in considerably more detail.

11. Caroline W. Lee describes the practitioners of deliberative democracy in "Five Assumptions Academics Make about Public Deliberation, and Why They Deserve Rethinking," *Journal of Public Deliberation* 7, no. 1, art. 7 (2011), http://services. bepress.com/jpd/vol7/iss1/art7. She finds that practitioners are not actually divided by methodology and do not focus exclusively on deliberation. Instead, they share underlying values, such as "appreciative inquiry" and a positive attitude toward existing communities, that attract them to deliberation and to other practices described in this chapter.

12. National Conference on Citizenship with CIRCLE and the Saguaro Seminar, *America's Civic Health Index 2008*, www.ncoc.net.

13. Selina Su, *Streetwise for Book Smarts: Grassroots Organizing and Education Reform in the Bronx* (Ithaca, NY: Cornell University Press, 2009), p. 16.

14. Mark R. Warren, *Dry Bones Rattling: Community Building to Revitalize American Democracy* (Princeton, NJ: Princeton University Press, 2001), pp. 31–32.

15. Romand Coles, "Of Tensions and Tricksters: Grassroots Democracy Between Theory and Practice," *Perspectives on Politics* 4, no. 3 (2006): 547–61.

16. Warren, *Dry Bones Rattling*, pp. 40–41.

17. Ibid., pp. 53, 55; Carmen Sirianni and Lewis A. Friedland, *The Civic Renewal Movement: Community-Building and Democracy in the United States* (Dayton, OH: Kettering Foundation Press, 2005), pp. 19–21.

18. Roberto Vazquez, "The San Antonio COPS Revolution," LaRed Latina News Network, March 14, 2005, http://www.lared-latina.com/cops.htm.

19. See also Coles, "Of Tensions and Tricksters."

20. For a moving story of the leadership trajectory of one particular IAF activist in San Antonio (Virginia Ramirez), see Paul Rogat Loeb, *Soul of a Citizen: Living with Conviction in Challenging Times* (New York: St. Martin's, 2010), pp. 22–29.

21. Warren, *Dry Bones Rattling*, pp. 63–64, 223.

22. See Thad Williamson, David Imbroscio, and Gar Alperovitz, *Making a Place for Community: Local Democracy in a Global Era* (New York: Routledge, 2002), pp. 112–14 on public participation in Community Development Block Grants, and p. 117 on Empowerment Zones.

23. "Community Development Corporations: Basic Statistics," Community-Wealth. org, http://community-wealth.org/strategies/panel/cdcs/index.html.

24. Ibid.

25. T. David Reese and Christina A. Clamp, *Faith-Based Community Economic Development: Principles & Practices* (Boston: Federal Reserve Bank of Boston, n.d.) http://www.bos.frb.org/commdev/faith/ced.pdf.

26. John S. Watson, "Capitalist Housing Developers as Green Activists," in Michele Micheletti and Andrew S. McFarland, eds., *Creative Participation: Responsibility-Taking in the Political World* (Boulder, CO: Paradigm Publishers, 2011), pp. 82–102.

27. Peter Levine, *The New Progressive Era: Toward a Fair and Deliberative Democracy* (Lanham, MD: Rowman & Littlefield, 2000), pp. 48–53.

28. The Economic Opportunity Act of 1964, 47 U.S.C. § 2782 (1964).

29. Lois M. Quinn, *New Indicators of Neighborhood Need in Zip Code 53206* (Employment and Training Institute, University of Wisconsin-Milwaukee, 2007), www.eti.uwm.edu.

30. See Peter Levine, "Collective Action, Civic Engagement, and the Knowledge Commons," in Charlotte Hess and Elinor Ostrom, eds., *Understanding Knowledge as a Commons: From Theory to Practice* (Cambridge, MA: MIT Press, 2006).

31. Lawrence Lessig, *The Future of Ideas: The Fate of the Commons in a Connected World* (New York: Random House, 2001), p. 209. This patent was litigated and reviewed in several countries but was substantially upheld by the US Patent and Trademark Office in 2010: see Eric Engleman, "Amazon.com's 1-Click Patent Confirmed Following Re-exam," TechFlash.com, March 10, 2010.

32. See Mark van Vugt, "Averting the Tragedy of the Commons: Using Social Psychological Science to Protect the Environment," *Current Directions in Psychological Science* 18, no. 3 (June 2009): 169. See Garrett Hardin, "The Tragedy of the Commons," *Science*, December 13, 1968, Garret Hardin Society, www.garretthardinsociety.org.

33. Elinor Ostrom, "Crowding Out Citizenship" *Scandinavian Political Studies* 23, no. 1 (2000).

34. See Thomas Dietz et al., "The Drama of the Commons," in Elinor Ostrom et al., *Drama of the Commons* (Washington, DC: National Academies Press, 2002), pp. 3–26, and Ostrom, "Covenants, Collective Action and Common Pool Resources," in Karol Soltan and Stephen L. Elkin, eds., *The Constitution of Good Societies* (University Park: Penn State University Press, 1996), pp. 23–38.

35. Vijayendra Rao, "Symbolic Public Goods and the Coordination of Collective Action" World Bank Policy Research Working Paper 3685 (Washington, DC: The World Bank, 2005), http://elibrary.worldbank.org/content/workingpaper/10.1596/1813-9450-3685.

36. For this theoretical analysis, see Charlotte Hess and Elinor Ostrom, "A Framework for Analyzing the Knowledge Commons" (pp. 41–82), and for the role of librarians, see Nancy Kranich, "Countering Enclosure: Reclaiming the Knowledge Commons" (pp. 85–122), both in Hess and Ostrom, *Understanding Knowledge as a Commons*.

37. Andrew Hahn et al., *Life after YouthBuild* (Somerville, MA: YouthBuild USA, 2004), www.youthbuild.org.

38. CIRCLE, *Pathways into Leadership: A Study of YouthBuild Graduates* (Medford, MA: Center for Information and Research on Civic Learning and Engagement, 2012)," p. 28, http://www.civicyouth.org/released-today-at-the-white-house-circle-study-shows-youthbuild-builds-leaders/.

39. Lewis A. Friedland and Shauna Morimoto, "The Changing Lifeworld of Young People: Risk, Resume-Padding, and Civic Engagement" (CIRCLE working paper 40, September 2005), www.civicyouth.org.

40. Data from Monitoring the Future and the Higher Education Research Institute, analyzed by CIRCLE. Also, *Volunteering in America: Research Highlights*, July 2009, http://www.volunteeringinamerica.gov/assets/resources/VolunteeringIn AmericaResearchHighlights.pdf.

41. Carnegie Corporation of New York and CIRCLE, *The Civic Mission of Schools*, February 2003, www.civicmissionofschools.org. A "successor" to this report (with the same six practices) is *Guardian of Democracy: The Civic Mission of Schools*, produced in 2011 by the Campaign for the Civic Mission of Schools; the Leonore Annenberg Institute of Civics of the Annenberg Center for Public Policy at the University of Pennsylvania; the National Conference on Citizenship; the Center for Information and Research on Civic Learning & Engagement at Tufts University; and the Public Education Division of the American Bar Association. Available via http://civicmissionofschools.org/site/guardianofdemocracy. See also Peter Levine, *The Future of Democracy: Developing the Next Generation of American Citizens* (Medford, MA: Tufts University Press, 2007), pp. 119–55.

42. Surbhi Godsay et al., *That's Not Democracy: How Out-of-School Youth Engage in Civic Life and What Stands in Their Way* (Medford, MA: CIRCLE, 2012), p. 38, www.civicyouth.org.

43. The Education Commission of the States (ECS) National Center for Learning and Citizenship (NCLC), *ECS Policy Brief: Civics Education*, July 2006, http://www. civicyouth.org/quick-facts/quick-facts-civic-education/.

44. Peter Levine, Mark Hugo Lopez, and Karlo Barrios Marcelo, *Getting Narrower at the Base: The American Curriculum After NCLB* (CIRCLE special report, 2008), http://www.civicyouth.org/? p=325.

45. Surbhi Godsay et al., *State Civic Education Requirements* (Medford, MA: CIRCLE, 2012), www.civicyouth.org.

46. Joseph Kahne and Ellen Middaugh, "Democracy for Some: The Civic Opportunity Gap in High School," in Youniss and Levine, *Engaging Young People in Civic Life*, pp. 29–58; and Meira Levinson, *No Citizen Left Behind* (Cambridge, MA: Harvard University Press, 2012).

47. Mark Hugo Lopez et al., "Schools, Education Policy and the Future of the First Amendment," *Political Communication* 26, no. 1 (January–March 2009): 84–101.

48. US Dept. of Education, National Center for Education Statistics, Schools and Staffing Survey (SASS), "Public School Teacher Data File," 2007–08, http://nces. ed.gov/surveys/sass/tables/sass0708_006_t1n.asp.

49. "University & Community Partnerships," Community-Wealth.org, http:// community-wealth.org/strategies/panel/universities/index.html.

50. Ibid.

51. Lee Benson, Ira Harkavy, and John Puckett, *Dewey's Dream: Universities and Democracies in an Age of Education Reform* (Philadelphia: Temple University Press, 2007), p. 84.

52. "A Year in Review," by Jim Zuiches, vice chancellor, North Carolina State University, http://www.ncsu.edu/extension/news/vcupdate03.02.07.php.

53. Dilafruz R. Williams and Daniel O. Bernstine, "Building Capacity for Civic Engagement at Portland State University: A Comprehensive Approach," in Maureen Kenny, ed., *Learning to Serve: Promoting Civil Society through Service Learning*, International Series in Outreach Scholarship, vol. 7 (New York: Springer, 2002), pp. 261–62.

54. Carmen Sirianni, *Investing in Democracy: Engaging Citizens in Collaborative Governance* (Washington, DC: Brookings Institution Press, 2009), pp. 158–75.

55. Williams and Bernstine, "Building Capacity for Civic Engagement at Portland State University," pp. 270–74.

56. University of Minnesota, Office of Academic Affairs & Provost, "Promotion and Tenure: Key Changes to the Faculty Tenure Policy," 2007, http://www.academic.umn.edu/provost/faculty/tenure/changes.html.

57. Bruce M. Owen, *Economics and Freedom of Expression: Media Structure and the First Amendment* (Cambridge, MA: Ballinger, 1975), pp. 64–69.

58. Mitchell Stephens, "History of Newspapers," from *Collier's Encyclopedia*, 1994, http://www.nyu.edu/classes/stephens/Collier%27s%20page.htm.

59. Pew Research Center Project for Excellence in Journalism, "2011 State of the News Media," http://www.stateofthemedia.org.

60. Pew Research Center for the People and the Press, "Cable Leads the Pack as Campaign News Source: Twitter, Facebook Play Very Modest Roles," February 7, 2012.

61. Quoted in James Bennet, "Polling Provoking Debate in News Media on Its Use," *New York Times*, October 4, 1996, p. A24.

62. Documents provided by the *Wichita Eagle* for a meeting at the American Press Institute (April 1995) that I attended.

63. Since the doctrine was not statutory but emerged from evolving FCC decisions, the canonical summary is in the Supreme Court decision that upheld it: *Red Lion Broadcasting Co., Inc. v. Federal Communications Commission*, 395 U.S. 367 (1969).

64. Statistics cited in the Knight Commission on the Information Needs of Communities in a Democracy, *Informing Communities: Sustaining Democracy in a Digital Age* (Washington, DC: Aspen Institute, 2009), pp. 4, 15.

65. I describe this case in *The New Progressive Era*, pp. 156–57. See also Albert W. Dzur, *Democratic Professionalism: Citizen Participation and the Reconstruction of Professional Ethics, Identity, and Practice* (University Park: Pennsylvania State University Press, 2008), pp. 146–47.

66. Pew Research Center, "How News Happens: A Study of the News Ecosystem of One American City" January 11, 2010, http://www.journalism.org/analysis_report/how_news_happens.

67. National Public Radio's 2012 ethics handbook, discussed by Jay Rosen in "NPR Tries to Get Its Pressthink Right," Pressthink.org, February 26, 2012.

68. Knight Commission on the Information Needs of Communities in a Democracy.

69. "About the Twin Cities Daily Planet," http://www.tcdailyplanet.net/about.

70. Lewis A. Friedland, "Civic Communication in a Networked Society," in Carmen Sirianni and Jennifer Girouard, eds., *Varieties of Civic Innovation: Deliberative, Collaborative, Network, and Narrative Approaches* (Nashville, TN: Vanderbilt University Press, forthcoming).

71. Robert M. La Follette in *La Follette's Magazine*, October 17, 1914, quoted in Ellen Torrelle, ed., *The Political Philosophy of Robert M. La Follette* (Madison, WI, The Robert M. La Follette Company, 1920), p. 173.

72. Charles A. Beard, *The Economic Basis of Politics* (New York: Alfred A. Knopf, 1922), a published version of lectures delivered at Amherst College in 1916.

73. Jane Addams, *Democracy and Social Ethics, 1902* (New York: Macmillan, 1905), pp. 222, 224.

74. For a summary of transparency politics at the federal level, see Cary Coglianese, "The Transparency President? The Obama Administration and Open Government," *Governance: An International Journal of Policy, Administration, and Institutions* 22, no. 4 (October 2009), pp. 529–44. For the state level, see Beth Fouhy, "AP 50-State Survey: There's Some Progress Toward Open Government, but Many Obstacles Remain," *Washington Post*, March 13, 2012.

75. Lake Research Partners focus groups, cited in Lake Research Partners, "Public Opinion on Key Measures of Democracy: A Review of Recent Literature," September 26, 2011, p. 7.

76. Federal Election Commission, Presidential Campaign Finance, Contributions to Barack Obama, www.fec.gov.

77. US General Service Administration, "Federal Advisory Committee Act (FACA) Brochure," http://www.gsa.gov/portal/content/101010.

78. Matt Leighninger, *The Next Form of Democracy: How Expert Rule Is Giving Way to Shared Governance . . . and Why Politics Will Never Be the Same* (Nashville, TN: Vanderbilt University Press, 2006), p. 14, sees the FACA as part of a general pattern.

79. See, for example, Susan A. Ostrander, *Citizenship and Governance in a Changing City: Somerville, MA* (Philadelphia: Temple University Press, 2013), p. 6.

80. Leighninger, *The Next Form of Democracy*, pp. 161–62, Adams-Leavitt quote at 162.

81. Lisa Blomgren Bingham, "The Next Generation of Administrative Law: Building the Legal Infrastructure for Collaborative Governance," *Wisconsin Law Review* 10, no. 2 (2010): 297–356, p. 344.

82. Leighninger, *The Next Form of Democracy*, p. 67.

83. "Remarks by Senator Barack Obama (D-IL) Announcing His Candidacy for President of the United States," Springfield, Illinois, February 10, 2007, archived by Project Vote Smart and collected by the author at http://peterlevine.ws/?p=5704.

84. "Obama Issues Call to Serve, Vows to Make National Service Important Cause of His Presidency," Mt. Vernon, Iowa, December 5, 2007, archived by Project Vote Smart and collected by the author at http://peterlevine.ws/?p=5704.

85. Barack Obama, "Why Organize? Problems and Promise in the Inner City," 1988. Originally published in the August–September 1988 edition of *Illinois Issues*, www.gatherthepeople.org/Downloads/WHY_ORGANIZE.pdf.

86. Town Hall Meeting, Arnold, Missouri, April 29, 2009, as archived by Project Vote Smart and collected by the author at http://peterlevine.ws/?p=5704.

87. Transcribed by the author from a video posted by WMUR channel 9 in New Hampshire on December 10, 2006, http://www.wmur.com/video/10505167/detail.html.

88. Barack Obama, "Memorandum for the Heads of Executive Departments and Agencies" on "Transparency and Open Government," January 21, 2009, http://www.whitehouse.gov/the_press_office/TransparencyandOpenGovernment/.

89. CBS/*New York Times* poll, February 11, 2010, http://www.cbsnews.com/htdocs/pdf/poll_Obama_Congress_021110.pdf.

90. Lydia Saad, "Americans: Uncle Sam Wastes 50 Cents on the Dollar," Gallup, September 15, 2009, http://www.gallup.com/poll/122951/americans-uncle-sam-wastes-50-cents-dollar.aspx.

91. Paul M. Angle, ed., *The Complete Lincoln-Douglas Debates of 1858* (Chicago: University of Chicago Press, 1991), p. 128.

92. Sean Wilentz, "Live By the Movement, Die By the Movement: Obama's Doomed Theory of Politics," *New Republic*, November 9, 2010, http://www.tnr.com/article/politics/79004/you-said-you-wanted-revolution-midterm-elections-obama.

93. Paul Krugman, "The World as He Finds It," *New York Times*, November 14, 2010, http://www.nytimes.com/2010/11/15/opinion/15krugman.html?_r=2&src=ISMR_HP_LO_MST_FB.

1. David Greenberg, "Why Last Chapters Disappoint," *New York Times*, March 18, 2011.

2. Common Cause, "History and Accomplishments," http://www.commoncause.org/.

3. CNN Wire Staff, "Debunking the Myth: The Cost of Obama's Trip to Asia," November 5, 2010, http://articles.cnn.com/2010-11-05/politics/obama.asia.cost_1_hotel-rooms-trip-amy-brundage?_s=PM:POLITICS.

4. In 1974, 80 percent of the Greatest Generation (people born between 1925 and 1944) said that they were members of at least one club or organization. Among baby boomers at the same time, the rate of group membership was 66.8 percent. The Greatest Generation continued to belong at similar rates into the 1990s. The boomers never caught up with them, their best year being 1994, when three-quarters reported belonging to some kind of group. In 1974, 6.3 percent of the Greatest Generation said they were in political clubs. The boomers have never reached that level: their highest rate of belonging to political clubs was 4.9 percent in 1989. General Social Survey data analyzed by the author.

5. In the General Social Survey during the 1970s, reading the newspaper and the number of group memberships correlated at the 0.4 level.

6. A valuable study is Andrew S. McFarland, *Common Cause: Lobbying in the Public Interest* (Chatham, NJ: Chatham House, 1984).

7. Bent Flyvbjerg, *Making Social Science Matter* (Cambridge: Cambridge University Press, 2001), p. 143.

8. E. Digby Baltzell, "Five Contemporary Ben Franklins," in Baltzell with Howard G. Schneiderman, *Judgment and Sensibility: Religion and Stratification* (New Brunswick, NJ: Transaction, 1994), p. 113.

9. R. H. Coase, "The Nature of the Firm," *Economica* 4, no. 16 (1937): 386–405. Discussed in Clay Shirky, *Here Comes Everybody: The Power of Organizing Without Organizations* (New York: Penguin, 2008), pp. 30 and later.

10. Shirky, *Here Comes Everybody*, pp. 31–33.

11. Coffee Party Time Line, http://www.coffeepartyusa.com/content/coffee-party-time-line.

12. Gabriel Hetland and Abigail N. Martin, "A New Way to Occupy City Hall: Participatory Budgeting," *Nation*, March 15, 2010.

13. Jay Rosen, "TEDxNYED talk," March 6, 2010, YouTube.

14. National Conference on Citizenship, *America's Civic Health Index 2007*, www.ncoc.net.

15. J. Foster-Bey, "Do Race, Ethnicity, Citizenship and Socio-economic Status Determine Civic-Engagement?" (CIRCLE working paper 62, 2008), www.civicyouth.org.

16. Lawrence R. Jacobs, Fay Lomax Cook, and Michael X. Delli Carpini, *Talking Together: Public Deliberation and Political Participation in America* (Chicago: University of Chicago Press, 2009), p. 37.

17. According to the US Census Bureau, *Current Population Survey*, November 2008, 63.6 percent of adult US citizens voted in the presidential election that year. According to George Mason University political scientist Michael McDonald (http://elections.gmu.edu/Turnout_2008G.html), a count of the actual ballots cast yields a turnout rate of 62.2 percent, about 1.4 percentage points lower.

18. Markus Prior, "The Immensely Inflated News Audience: Assessing Bias in Self-Reported News Exposure," *Public Opinion Quarterly* 73, no. 1 (2009): 130–43.

19. There are 220 ADP campuses, but many students, faculty, staff, and members of community groups at or near these colleges are not involved with ADP activities. Still, I would assume (based on several site visits and participation in the national ADP conference) that at least 50 people per campus are involved.

20. Many of the employees work for a few large CDCs that have as many as 1,100 workers each. In such large organizations, most employees probably have little to do with deliberation, community organizing, civic education, or public work. However, the median staff size of a CDC is much smaller (just ten paid employees), and there are about 4,600 CDCs in all. Three democracy workers per CDC would

yield 13,800 in total. National Congress for Community Economic Development, *Reaching New Heights: Trends and Achievements of Community-Based Development Organizations*, 5th National Community Development Census (Washington, DC, 2005), www.ncced.org.

21. The competition generated 4,600 applications, a large sample of which I reviewed as the project evaluator. Applicants were required to write their own definitions of "citizen-centered work." I estimate that only about 40 percent of the applicants submitted definitions truly congruent with the deliberative and democratic values of the Case Foundation. (Some unsuccessful applicants thought that "citizen-centered" projects were ones that *served* all citizens equally or that promoted political and civic *rights*.) The 20 winning applicants each involved about 175 residents, on average, in their projects. But only 18 percent of the nonwinners reported in a later survey that they had done nothing toward their proposed projects. If we assume that each truly eligible applicant involved an average of 20 local peers, then they represented about 36,800 people.

22. CIRCLE, *Pathways into Leadership: A Study of YouthBuild Graduates* (Medford, MA: CIRCLE, 2012), www.civicyouth.org.

23. Rural Assistance Center, "FQHC Frequently Asked Questions," http://www.raconline.org/info_guides/clinics/fqhcfaq.php#board.

24. National Association of Community Health Centers, "United States Health Center Fact Sheet," 2009, www.nachc.org/state-healthcare-data-list.cfm.

25. US Dept. of Education, National Center for Education Statistics, "Schools and Staffing and Teacher Follow-up Surveys" (SASS:1999/00 TFS:2000/01), http://nces.ed.gov/surveys/sass/, analyzed by the author.

26. Gary J. Schmitt et al., *High Schools, Civics, and Citizenship: What Social Studies Teachers Think and Do* (Washington, DC: American Enterprise Institute, 2010), http://www.aei.org/paper/100145.

27. League of Women Voters, *Annual Report*, 2009, www.lwv.org.

28. Galston, personal communication, March 19, 2012.

29. Strengthening Our Nation's Democracy is a collection of political reform, community organizing, and deliberative democracy organizations that met in 2008 and 2009 and issued a common report; the Campaign for the Civic Mission of Schools is a coalition in support of civic education; the Deliberative Democracy Consortium is a coalition of groups that study or promote public discussion about issues; PACE—Philanthropy for Active Civic Engagement consists only of foundations that fund (or in some cases, conduct) work on civic renewal; the Democracy Imperative is a network of college-based centers and individual academics who strive to make universities institutions that support civic engagement; the Voices for National Service Steering Committee is one of several networks that support community service.

30. Network density as calculated by the author using SocNetV software.

31. Certain organizations play significant bridging roles, not as coalitions but as active members of multiple coalitions. The Kettering Foundation has four memberships

within this network; Everyday Democracy and CIRCLE have three. Several organizations belong to two coalitions.

32. Taylor Branch tracks the tense competition for members, funds, and attention between the SCLC and the NAACP in *Parting the Waters: America in the King Years* (New York: Simon & Schuster, 1988), pp. 222, 264, 578.

33. Steven M. Teles, *The Rise of the Conservative Legal Movement* (Princeton, NJ: Princeton University Press, 2010), pp. 20, 279.

34. Martín Carcasson and Leah Sprain, "Key Aspects of the Deliberative Democracy Movement," *Public Sector Digest*, Summer 2010, http://cpd.colostate.edu/keyaspects.pdf, p. 4.

35. For example, the Declaration of the No Labels campaign states, "We believe in the vital civil center," http://nolabels.org/about-us/declaration/.

36. For example, see Roberto Mangabeira Unger, *Democracy Realized: The Progressive Alternative* (London and New York: Verso, 1998).

37. E.g., William A. Schambra, "Local Solutions Are Still the Best Counter-Attack to Washington's Default Progressivism," Hudson Institute's *Conservative Home*, December 6, 2010, http://pcr.hudson.org.

38. Ben Smith, "Schism Brews in Coffee Party," *Politico*, March 24, 2011.

39. Eric Byler, "Response to Report on 'Coffee Party Schism' in *Politico*," March 25, 2011, http://www.coffeepartyusa.com/coffee-party-progressives.

40. Indeed, Americans have a preference for politeness and agreement and tend to shun heated debate. See Diana C. Mutz, *Hearing the Other Side: Deliberative versus Participatory Democracy* (Cambridge: Cambridge University Press, 2006).

41. Obama, Michigan graduation speech, May 1, 2010, http://www.huffingtonpost.com/2010/05/01/obama-michigan-graduation_n_559688.html.

42. Daniel M. Shea, *Nastiness, Name-calling & Negativity—The Allegheny College Survey of Civility and Compromise in American Politics* (Allegheny College, April 20, 2010), http://sitesmedia.s3.amazonaws.com/civility/files/2010/04/Allegheny-CollegeCivilityReport2010.pdf.

43. William H. Chafe, *Civilities and Civil Rights: Greensboro, North Carolina, and the Black Struggle for Freedom* (New York: Oxford University Press, 1981).

44. See Carmen Sirianni, *Investing in Democracy: Engaging Citizens in Collaborative Governance* (Washington, DC: Brookings Institution Press, 2009), p. 22.

45. Peter Levine, "Letter to President Obama: A Policy Approach for the Federal Government," in David Feith, ed., *Teaching America: The Case for Civic Education* (Lanham, MD: Rowman & Littlefield, 2011), pp. 211–12.

46. This is a theme of Carmen Sirianni and Lewis Friedland, *Civic Innovation in America: Community Empowerment, Pubic Policy, and the Movement for Civic Renewal* (Berkeley: University of California Press, 2001), p. 43.

47. See Peter Levine, "Education for Civil Society," in David Campbell, Meira Levinson, and Frederick M. Hess, eds., *Civics 2.0: Citizenship Education for a New Generation* (Cambridge, MA: Harvard Education Press, 2012), pp. 37–56.

48. Partnership for Public Service, "Where the Jobs Are 2009: Mission-Critical Opportunities for America," September 3, 2009, http://ourpublicservice.org/OPS/publications/viewcontentdetails.php?id=137.

49. See, e.g., Jennifer Steinhauer and Carl Hulse, "House G.O.P. Members Face Voter Anger Over Budget," *New York Times*, April 26, 2011.

50. Kevin Esterling, Archon Fung, and Taeku Lee, *The Difference That Deliberation Makes: Evaluating the "Our Budget, Our Economy" Public Deliberation* (Washington, DC: AmericaSPEAKS, 2010).

51. Beth Simone Noveck, "Wiki-Government: How Open-Source Technology Can Make Government Decision-Making More Expert and More Democratic," *Democracy: A Journal of Ideas* 7 (Winter 2008), http://www.democracyjournal.org/7/6570.php?page=1; and see www.peertopatent.org/.

52. Peter Levine, *Civic Engagement and Community Information: Five Strategies to Revive Civic Communication* (Aspen Institute and the Knight Foundation, 2011).

53. Kei Kawashima-Ginsberg and Emily Hoban Kirby, "Volunteering Among Youth of Immigrant Origin," CIRCLE Fact Sheet, July 2009, www.civicyouth.org.

54. The National Conference on Citizenship, the Florida Joint Center for Citizenship, and the Center for Democracy and Citizenship at Augsburg College in Minneapolis, *Tale of Two Cities: Civic Health in Miami and Minneapolis-St. Paul*, 2010, http://ncoc.net/ttcrelease.

55. Peter Levine, "Citizenship Isn't about Passing a Civics Test," CNN Opinion, May 6, 2013, http://www.cnn.com/2013/05/06/opinion/levine-citizenship/index.htm.

56. Port Huron Statement of the Students for a Democratic Society, 1962, courtesy of the Office of California State Senator Tom Hayden, http://www.h-net.org/~hst306/documents/huron.html.

A NOTE ON THE TITLE OF THIS BOOK

1. David Mathews, *Is There a Public for Public Schools* (Dayton, OH: Kettering Foundation Press, 1996).

2. Alice Walker, *The Ones We Have Been Waiting For* (New York: New Press, 2007), p. 3.

3. June Jordan, "Poem for South African Women," in *Directed by Desire: The Collected Poems of June Jordan* (Port Townsend, WA: Copper Canyon Press, 2007), pp. 278–89.

4. See John Edwards, "Ending Poverty: The Great Moral Issue of Our Time," *Yale Law and Policy Review* 25, no. 37 (2006–7): 348; and Jim Wallis, *God's Politics: Why the Right Gets It Wrong and the Left Doesn't Get It* (HarperCollins, 2006), p. 374.

Index

polites, 14

political parties, 21, 26, 74, 76, 115, 124, 180

polling, 117, 142

Pollitt, Christopher, 203n36

pollution, 43, 104, 108, 140

polycentric governance, 112

populism, 17, 76, 117–18, 179–80

Port Huron Statement, 61, 189

Portland, OR, 19, 139–40, 151

Portney, Kent, 196n39, 197n45

Positive Youth Development (PYD), 28–29, 30, 57–58, 130

positivism, 28–29

Potapchuk, Bill, 152, 213n6

poverty, 5, 10, 38, 65–66, 86–89, 97

pragmatism, 32, 75–78, 84, 112

Prairie Crossing, IL, 129

presidency, 65–66, 76, 106, 160, 165

press. *See* news; newspapers

primary elections, 11, 16, 153, 156

Prior, Markus, 220n18

problem-solving courts, 19, 70, 151, 198n63

professionalism, 22, 29, 66–70, 95–99, 202n25

Progressive Era, 72, 75–76, 147

propaganda, 115

psychology (discipline of), 45, 64, 67–68, 100, 197n47

Public Achievement, 138

Public Agenda Foundation, 54, 195–96, 204n47

Public Allies, 134, 153, 174–75

Public Citizen, 170

public interest, 21, 109, 116–19, 142, 146–47, 151

public journalism, 143

public work, 14, 42, 157

Puckett, John, 216n51

Pushpendra, 208n31

Putnam, Robert, 12, 54–55, 153, 164, 196n39

quiescence, 89

Quinn, Lois M., 215n29

race, 44, 59, 88, 91, 104, 122, 199n67

racism, 18, 36, 50, 59, 86, 154

radio, 141–46, 180

Ramirez, Virginia, 214n20

randomized experiments, 69, 79–80

Rao, Vijayendra, 37, 207n23

Ravitch, Diane, 195n28, 196n39

Rawls, John, 31–32, 77, 204n41

readers, 33, 164–65, 167, 172, 177

Reagan, Ronald, 77, 104, 112–13

realtors, 119

recession, 4, 15, 75, 86, 130

recruiting, 3, 14, 56, 92–93, 120–21, 124–27, 163

redistribution, 73, 86–87, 163, 208n30

Reese, T. David, 214n25

referenda, 17–18, 72, 117–18

regulation, 6, 83, 105–14, 118, 140, 163, 186

Reich, Robert B., 109

relational organizing, 55–58, 124–26, 129, 149, 151, 176

republic, 103, 106, 118

Republican Party, 92, 112, 154–55, 158–60, 184

restorative justice, 19–20, 151, 199n67

Reynolds v Simms, 210n23

Rhee, Michelle, 10–12

Rittel, Horst W.J., 193n2

River Network, 175

Rivers, June C., 195n24

Roberts, John, 71